Online Groomers

Profiling, Policing and Prevention

Julia Davidson
and
Petter Gottschalk

RHP

Russell House Publishing

Russell House Publishing
First published in 2010 by:
Russell House Publishing Ltd.
4 St George's House
Uplyme Road
Lyme Regis
Dorset DT7 3LS
Tel: 01297-443948
Fax: 01297-442722
e-mail: help@russellhouse.co.uk
www.russellhouse.co.uk

British Library Cataloguing-in-publication Data:
A catalogue record for this book is available from the British Library.

ISBN: 978-1-905541-56-0

Typeset by TW Typesetting, Plymouth, Devon

Printed in Great Britain by the MPG Books Group, Bodmin and King's Lynn

Russell House Publishing

Russell House Publishing aims to publish innovative and valuable materials to help managers, practitioners, trainers, educators and students.
Our full catalogue covers: social policy, working with young people, helping children and families, care of older people, social care, combating social exclusion, revitalising communities and working with offenders.

Full details can be found at www.russellhouse.co.uk and we are pleased to send out information to you by post. Our contact details are on this page.

We are always keen to receive feedback on publications and new ideas for future projects.

Contents

Preface

This important book provides numerous new insights and, in the process, provides a sound conceptual approach to understanding continuing developments in:

- The characteristics of the Internet.
- How they are explored and exploited by sexual offenders to groom their victims.
- Legislation against online grooming.
- The conviction, understanding and treatment of offenders.
- Preventing them from causing harm.

> *It is a useful tool as it pulls together such an enormous volume of diverse information into one place, and compares different ideas, and looks at how they may work in different settings. I certainly learned a few things from sources I had never even heard of.*
>
> Martin C. Calder

The first part of the book on **Profiling Online Groomers** outlines and discusses those characteristics of the Internet that are relevant to the process of online grooming and describes how offenders use the Internet to identify and communicate with potential child victims. It presents a staged model – a way of classifying offenders in terms of seriousness over the passage of time – for use in the assessment of online groomers, in order to record:

- The current stage of development of an Internet paedophile's offending behaviour.
- Previous (less serious) stages in the development of their Internet activities.
- In what ways they may undertake even more serious grooming and victimisation of children, if not stopped.

The second part of the book on **Policing Online Groomers** by all concerned agencies working together explains various approaches, and offers thoughtful analysis of:

- How legislation can be improved.
- The ways in which developments in knowledge management can help. (It has been suggested that some of the new thinking here could also usefully be applied in other contexts when considering evidence-based practice and decision making.)
- The potentially supportive roles of information technology.
- Police performance management.

The third part of the book on **Preventing Online Grooming Offences** again by all concerned agencies working together:

- Introduces concepts of online sex offending prevention.
- Describes recent initiatives to protect children online.
- Presents a new approach to educational awareness and Internet safety.

Who this book is for

Online grooming has – or at least should have – become a concern to anyone with any kind of role that includes responsibility for the care or safeguarding of children and young people. Therefore the book contains policy and practice information that is relevant to a wide range of practitioners, policy makers, managers, trainers, lecturers, researchers and students.

Its value to practitioners and managers will extend to:

- Police, especially those who are working with the Internet or in child protection.
- Anyone who is treating perpetrators.
- Anyone who works in formal or informal education with children or young people.
- Social workers in child protection and safeguarding.
- Information technology experts working on safer technology.

In academia, policy development and research it will be of assistance in:

- criminology and forensic psychology
- policing
- social work
- knowledge management
- internet and management information systems

It has potential use in Master's courses on these topics. Knowledge management students as well as law enforcement students at several levels might use this book in relevant university and college courses for their assignments and theses. This book will therefore be an acquisition of immediate and lasting value in university and college libraries, some public libraries and training institutions.

About the Authors

Dr Julia Davidson is Professor of Criminology and Sociology and is Director of Social Research at Kingston University. She is also Co-Director of the newly formed Centre for Abuse and Trauma Studies (with Professor Antonia Bifulco, Royal Holloway University of London). Professor Davidson has conducted a considerable amount of research in the criminal justice area and has a PhD in Social Policy from the London School of Economics and Political Science. She has extensive experience of applied policy and practice research and has directed work with young victims, serious violent and sexual offenders, criminal justice practitioners and sentencers. Professor Davidson's book *Child Sexual Abuse: Media Representations and Government Reactions* (Book series Editors: Professor David Downes and Professor Paul Rock, London School of Economics) has just been published (Routledge, 2008). Professor Davidson provides regular expert advice on criminal justice issues to the media and has worked extensively with the BBC and ITN News in the UK. j.davidson@kingston.ac.uk

Dr Petter Gottschalk is Professor of Information Systems and Knowledge Management in the Norwegian School of Management. He teaches Knowledge Management in Law Enforcement and Organized Crime in the Norwegian Police University College. Oxford University Press published the book *Knowledge Management in Policing and Law Enforcement* by Dr Dean and Dr Gottschalk in 2007. Professor Gottschalk's other books include *Entrepreneurship and Organized Crime – Entrepreneurs in Illegal Business* (Edward Elgar, 2009) and *Policing Organized Crime: Intelligence Strategy Implementation* (Taylor & Francis, 2010). Dr. Gottschalk has been managing director of several business enterprises including ABB Data Cables and the Norwegian Computing Centre. petter.gottschalk@bi.no

Introduction

Internet use has grown considerably in the last decade. Information technology now forms a core part of the formal education system in many countries, ensuring that each new generation of Internet users is more adept than the last.

Children, young people and the Internet

Research studies in the UK suggest that the majority of young people aged 9-19 access the Internet at least once a day. The Internet provides the opportunity to interact with friends on social networking sites such as Myspace and Bebo and enables young people to access information in a way that previous generations would not have thought possible. The medium also allows users to post detailed personal information, which may be accessed by any site visitor and provides a platform for peer communication hitherto unknown (Davidson and Martellozzo, 2008). There is, however, increasing evidence that the Internet is used by some adults to access children and young people in order to groom them for the purposes of sexual abuse. Myspace have recently expelled 29,000 suspected sex offenders and is being sued in the United States by parents who claim that their children were contacted by sex offenders on the site and consequently abused (BBC, 2007). The Internet also plays a role in facilitating the production and distribution of indecent illegal images of children, which may encourage and complement online grooming.

Child sex abusers and the Internet

Recent advances in computer technology have been aiding sex offenders, stalkers, child pornographers, child traffickers and others with the intent of exploiting children:

> Internet bulletin boards, chat rooms, private websites, and peer-to-peer networks are being used daily by paedophiles to meet unsuspecting children. Compounding the problem is the lack of direct governance by an international body, which will curb the illegal content and activity. Most countries already have laws protecting children, but what is needed is a concerted law enforcement and international legislation to combat child sex abuse.
>
> Kierkegaard, 2008: 41

Men who target young people online for sex are paedophiles (Kierkegaard, 2008; Wolak et al., 2008). According to Dunaigre (2001) the paedophile has become an emblematic figure, able to conjure up many of the fears, anxieties and apprehensions that are rocking our society today.

According to the World Health Organisation (WHO) paedophile acts are sexual behaviours that an adult (16 years or over) overwhelmingly of the male sex, acts out towards prepubescent children (13 years or under). The WHO also suggest that normally there must be a five-year age difference between the two, except in the case of paedophilic practices at the end of adolescence where what counts more is the difference in sexual maturity.

However, the definition of criminal behaviour varies among countries. For example paedophile acts in Norway are defined as sexual behaviour with a child of 16 years or under. There is no minimum age for the grooming person in Norwegian criminal law, but age difference and difference in sexual maturity are taken into account when determining criminal liability.

Wolak *et al.* (2009: 4) present two case examples of crimes by online sex offenders in the United States:

1. Police in a West Coast state found child pornography in the possession of a 22-year-old offender. The offender, who was from a North-eastern state, confessed to befriending a 13-year-old local boy online, travelling to the West Coast and meeting him for sex. Prior to the meeting, the offender and victim had corresponded online for about six months. The offender had sent the victim nude images via webcam and e-mail and they had called and texted each other hundreds of times. When they met for sex, the offender took graphic pictures of the encounter. The victim believed he was in love with the offender. He lived alone with his father and was struggling to fit in and come to terms with being gay. The offender possessed large quantities of child pornography that he had downloaded from the Internet. He was sentenced to 10 years in prison.
2. A 24-year-old man met a 14-year-old girl at a social networking site. He claimed to be 19. Their online conversation became romantic and sexual and the victim believed she was in love. They met several times for sex over a period of weeks. The offender took nude pictures of the victim and gave her alcohol and drugs. Her mother and stepfather found out and reported the crime to the police. The victim was lonely, had issues with drugs and alcohol and had problems at school and with her parents. She had posted provocative pictures of herself on her social networking site. She had met other men online and had sex with them. The offender was a suspect in another online enticement case. He was found guilty but had not been sentenced at time of the interview.

Online grooming

According to Davidson and Martellozzo (2008: 277) Internet sex offender behaviour can include:

- The construction of sites to be used for the exchange of information, experiences, and indecent images of children.
- The organisation of criminal activities that seek to use children for prostitution purposes and that produce indecent images of children at a professional level.
- The organisation of criminal activities that promote sexual tourism.

Child grooming is a process that commences with sex offenders choosing a target area that is likely to attract children. In the physical world, this could be venues visited by children such as schools, shopping centres or playgrounds. A process of grooming then commences when an offender takes an interest in a particular child and make them feel special with the intention of forming a bond.

The Internet has greatly facilitated this process in the virtual world. Offenders now seek out their victims by visiting Internet relay chat (IRC) rooms from their home or Internet cafés. Once a child victim is identified, the offender can invite them into a private area of the IRC to engage them in conversations covering intimate personal details including their sex life (Australian Institute of Criminology, 2008).

The structure of this book

This book consists of three parts. The **first part** is concerned with profiling online groomers by:

- Identifying characteristics of the Internet and related child abuse.
- Describing a stage model for online grooming.
- Presenting insights into online sex offending and offenders.

The **second part** is concerned with policing online groomers by describing:

- The legislative context of work with Internet sex offenders.
- Knowledge management in policing.
- Knowledge management in grooming investigations.
- Knowledge management technology.
- Police performance management.

The **third part** is concerned with preventing online grooming offences through approaches to educational awareness and Internet safety and other initiatives to protect children online.

1

Characteristics of the Internet and Child Abuse

The Internet is an international network of networks that connects people all over the world. Any computer can communicate with almost any other computer linked to the Internet. The Internet has created a universal technology platform on which to build all sorts of new products, services, communities and solutions. It is reshaping the way information technology is used by individuals and organisations. The Internet has provided an expedient mode of communication and access to a wealth of information (Dombrowski *et al.*, 2007).

In less than two decades, the Internet has moved from a strange communications medium to an obvious tool in our homes, schools, workplaces and travels. It enables us to search information, perform routine tasks and communicate with others. The technological aspects of the Internet are developing at the same high speed as the number of users globally. The Internet provides a social context for us to meet with others and to exchange information (Quayle *et al.*, 2006).

The World Wide Web is a system with universally accepted standards for storing, retrieving, formatting, changing and displaying information in a networked environment. Information is stored and displayed as electronic pages that can contain numbers, text, pictures, graphics, sound and video. These web pages can be linked electronically to other Web pages, independent of where they are located. Web pages can be viewed by any type of computer.

In a survey of young people in Norway between the ages 8 and 18 years old, 78 per cent of the respondents said that they are involved in chatting. The use of chatting for communication is more common than the use of e-mail in this age group. In the age group 17–18 years, all respondents said they do chatting. The percentage reporting that they have been plagued while chatting was nine per cent. Among chatters about one third has met people in reality that they first met while chatting (Medietilsynet, 2008).

The Internet is a valuable tool. However, it can also be detrimental to the wellbeing of children due to numerous online hazards:

> There is the potential for children to be abused via cyberspace through online sexual
> solicitation and access to pornography. Indeed, the Internet is replete with inappropriate

material, including pornography, chat rooms with adult themes and access to instant messaging wherein others could misrepresent themselves. Because children are actively utilising the Internet where unknown others can have access to them or where they can be exposed to inappropriate sexual materials, they require safeguarding and education in safe Internet use.

Dombrowski et al., 2007: 153

Online grooming might be compared to online learning and other forms of online activity. The purpose of such analogies is to identify both similarities and differences. Learning on the Internet, for example, is structured as a formal and non-anonymous activity. To some it is scary rather than safe, because students are asked to expose their (lack of) knowledge on the Internet and share it with others. Active and extrovert students enjoy this, while other students choose to be passive on-lookers.

Generally, going online enables individuals to play a personality role, which might be more or less similar to their real personality. There will always be a difference between your role in virtual reality and in the real world. We play roles as adults and parents, or children and students, both in the real world and in virtual realities. However, in the virtual world we may find it easier to live our dreams and fantasies. In the 'second life' type environments on the Internet, people tend to be unfaithful and to build their dream existence alone or with others.

What is then so special about being online? One answer to this question is that you can be in a different, informal and anonymous setting to live out dreams and fantasies.

Fourteen internet characteristics

We are all familiar with online services on the Internet. A typical example is online banking, where we complete our payments of bills at home. Most Norwegians have many years of personal experience using online services on the Internet. According to the United Nations (2008) Norway is ranked third in the world in terms of online services provided by the government. Sweden and Denmark are on the top of the list, and Norway is followed by the United States and the Netherlands. The United Kingdom is ranked tenth on the list.

A number of characteristics of the Internet for online services has been observed, which may shed light on methods offenders use to groom children in the next chapter:

1. Disconnected personal communication. While communication on the Internet might be personal in content, it is not perceived as interpersonal in meaning. A typical example is e-mail, where the sender might feel completely disconnected from the time and place the receiver reads the e-mail message. Even when chatting in real time, sender and receiver may perceive both involvement and disconnectedness at the same time. Some change their personality unconsciously when moving from face-to-face communication to e-mail communication (Weber, 2004). Internet grooming can be and often is different from 'real world' grooming in that offenders spend little time chatting and will come straight to the point, sometimes instantly, e.g. 'would you like to meet for sex'. This would suggest that

the Internet might act to remove inhibitions associated with face-to-face contact, which can be explained by the disconnected nature of personal communication on the Internet, thereby avoiding unpleasant emotional states (Quayle et al., 2006).

2. *Mediating technology.* The Internet is a mediating technology that interconnects parties that are independent or want to be (Afuah and Tucci, 2003). The interconnections can be business-to-business (B2B) business-to-consumer (B2C) government-to-business (G2B) person-to-person (P2P) or any other link between individuals and organisations. In the case of grooming, Internet serves as a mediating technology mainly for person-to-person (P2P) communication, but person-to-group (P2G) and group-to-person (G2P) do also occur.

3. *Universality.* Universality of the Internet refers to the Internet's ability to both enlarge and shrink the world. It enlarges the world because anyone anywhere in the world can potentially make his or her services, messages and requests available to anyone anywhere else in the world anytime. It shrinks the world in that distance is reduced on electronic highways (Afuah and Tucci, 2003). In the case of grooming, Internet enables each grooming individual to potentially contact anyone, anywhere and anytime. Contact is established without the groomer having to travel physically, all he needs to do is to travel electronically. The Internet combines global communications with an incredible range of resources (Calder, 2004).

4. *Network externalities.* A technology or product exhibits network externalities when it becomes more valuable to users as more people take advantage of it. A classic example is the first person in Norway who got himself a telephone. Until a second person got a telephone, there was nobody in Norway to talk to on the phone. The value of the telephone for each subscriber increases with the number of subscribers. Similarly, the value of the Internet increases with the number of Internet users. The more people that are connected to a network within the Internet, the more valuable the network is to each user (Afuah and Tucci, 2003). The more children that are connected to a network, the more valuable the network is to each groomer, since he is able to reach and get in contact with more potential victims. Since Internet access is found in more and more homes all over the world (Quayle et al., 2006) the number of potential victims rises accordingly.

5. *Distribution channel.* The Internet acts as a distribution channel for products that are information bits, such as software, music, video, news, tickets and money. There is a replacement effect if the Internet is used to serve the same deliveries, which were serviced by the old physical distribution channel. There is an extension effect if the Internet is used by more people and for new services (Afuah and Tucci, 2003). When grooming children, the offender may use the Internet not only for communications he can also use it to send gifts and other digital items that the child might be interested in. He can also send digital items that the child is not always interested in, such as pornographic pictures and videos to test reactions.

6. *Time moderator.* The Internet has an ability to shrink and enlarge time. It shrinks time for people who want information when information sources are closed. It enlarges time when related work can be done at different points in time (Afuah and Tucci, 2003). Both

dimensions of the Internet as a time moderator can be important in online victimisation of children. When a child is offline, the groomer can leave messages and gifts for the child to pick up next time the child logs on.

7. *Low cost standard*. Individuals could not exploit the properties of the Internet if it were technically and financially unavailable. Adoption has been easy for two reasons. First and foremost, the Internet and the web application are standards open to everyone and are very easy to use. Second, the cost of the Internet is a lot lower than that of earlier means of electronic communication (Afuah and Tucci, 2003). Given the low cost standard, access to the Internet is not limited to affluent or well-educated people. Both adults and children have access independent of social class in most countries. For a groomer, this enables access not only to a large number of children but also to a large variety of children.

8. *Electronic double*. It is not the real person who is present on the Internet. It is a digital copy of the person who is present. The digital information about the person creates an image of the person, which we call the electronic double. Everyone has his or her electronic double in government systems, for example, where my double causes taxes. If information about me is wrong, then my double will cause wrong taxes for me to pay. Even if I am honest and try to provide as much relevant information about myself as possible, my electronic double will be perceived as different from my real self. How a paedophile man is perceived by a child on the Internet is thus dependent both on the information the man provides and the image this information creates in the head of the child. Even if the man is completely honest in all communication with the child, the child may perceive the man as very different from reality and may be similar to someone the child already knows. Also the man may perceive the child and create an electronic double of the child in his head, which can be far away from reality.

9. *Electronic double manipulation*. The electronic double created on the Internet represents an image of the real person. The real person can change his or her electronic double and make it more or less similar to the real self. The most obvious change is age, where a grooming man may claim to be younger than he actually is. This requires consistency in all other information, so that the presented age matches other information about the person. Similarly, children may claim to be older than they actually are.

10. *Information asymmetry*. Information asymmetry is often reduced on the Internet. An information asymmetry exists when one party to a transaction has information that another party does not – information that is important to the transaction. The World Wide Web reduces such information asymmetries, as the other party can find the same information on the web (Afuah and Tucci, 2003). Neither the man nor the child has information monopoly in areas where information is available on the World Wide Web.

11. *Infinite virtual capacity*. Access to the Internet is perceived as unlimited; you do not have to wait on hold or in a long line. For example, virtual communities like chat rooms have infinite capacity for members who can talk anytime of the day for as long as they want (Afuah and Tucci, 2003).

12. *Independence in time and space.* While a traditional meeting requires that participants are present at the same place at the same time, meeting on the Internet is possible even if different participants are present at different places at different times. The online environment enables access to a wealth of information and communication across both distance and time (Kierkegaard, 2008). The independence in time and space is typically the case when using e-mail. When participating in a chat room, participants are required to respond within a short time frame, eliminating independence in time, but still keeping independence in space. On the mobile phone, SMS messages have the same characteristic of independence in time and space. The Internet promotes better social relationships as people will be freed from the constraints of time and place (Calder, 2004).

13. *Cyberspace.* Using the Internet is not just a supplement to or add-on to real life. It is also an enabler of an alternative life style in cyberspace with its own cyber culture. Cyberspace is an abstract space, rather than a physical space, where a culture has emerged from the use of computer networks for communication, entertainment and business. Cyber culture can for example be found in virtual communities, which is a group of people that primarily interact via communication media such as newsletters, telephone, e-mail or instant messages rather than face to face for social and other purposes (Whittaker, 2004). In terms of online grooming, both adults and children are sometimes members of virtual communities. Calder (2004) argues that there are many benefits that can be derived from the development of online relationships and online relationships that become sexual in cyberspace. Cyberspace can facilitate the formation of romantic relationships, improve the chances of finding an 'optimal' partner, stimulate relationships based on virtual attachments, and improve one's skills in interpersonal, yet virtual, communication.

14. *Dynamic social network.* The emergence of social network services has radically challenged our understanding of traditional, territorial social networks. An average Westerner's social network comprises about 150 individuals. Once a physical social network is established, this number of members tends to change little over time, and the members themselves do not change very much. In contrast, the Internet enables individuals to expand and reduce their social network and replace members in the network (CEOP, 2006). The Internet provides a social context for more and more people to meet more and more people (Quayle *et al.*, 2006). There is a dynamic social network rather than a stable social network on the Internet. When both offenders and potential victims dynamically change their social networks, the likelihood of contact increases.

The Internet is a special artefact system that has enormous technical and socially positive impact on modern society:

> *The online environment enables access to a wealth of information and communication across both distance and time. There is a vast amount of data available on virtually every subject, making it an effective learning tool.*

> Kierkegaard, 2008: 41

However, the Internet is also a double-edged sword with negative and positive consequences:

> It has a potential for misuse and has generated societal concerns. Today, the danger for children is even greater because the Internet provides anonymity to sex offenders.
>
> Kierkegaard, 2008: 41

Recent advances in computer technology have been aiding sexual offenders, stalkers, child pornographers, child traffickers, and others with the intent of exploiting children. While they have existed prior to the Internet, the advent of the new technology two decades ago has allowed for easier and faster distribution of pornographic materials and communication across national and international boundaries (Kierkegaard, 2008).

On the other hand, the Internet is not all negative concerning sexual communication:

> It can be used for healthy sexual expression. For example, the Internet offers the opportunity for the formulation of online or virtual communities where isolated or disenfranchised individuals e.g. gay males and lesbians can communicate with each other around sexual topics of shared interest; it offers educational potential; and it may allow for sexual experimentation in a safer forum, thus facilitating identity exploration and development.
>
> Calder, 2004: 3

The Internet allows paedophiles instant access to other online abusers worldwide, open discussion of their sexual desires, shared ideas about ways to lure victims, mutual support of their adult-child sex philosophies, instant access to potential child victims' worldwide, disguised identities for approaching children, even to the point of presenting as a member of teen groups. Furthermore, the Internet allows paedophiles ready access to chat rooms reserved for teenagers and children to find out how and who to target as potential victims, the Internet provides means to identify and track down home contact information, and the Internet enables adults to build long-term virtual relationships with potential victims, prior to attempting to engage the child in physical contact.

Relationships are built using social software. Through the Internet, people are discovering and inventing new ways to share knowledge and interests. People communicate on the Internet with each other in a human voice. These conversations using social software are collectively referred to as social media, a wide-ranging term than encompasses the practice and resulting output of all kinds of information created online by those who were previously consumers of that media:

> Philosophically, social media describes the way in which content (particularly news and opinion) has become democratised by the Internet and the role people now play not only in consuming information and conveying it to others, but also in creating and sharing content with them, be it textual, aural or visual.
>
> Cook, 2008: 7

For this reason, social media is interchangeably referred to as consumer- or user-generated content. Social media is often defined by the categories of software tools that people use to undertake this consuming, conveying, creating and sharing content with each other, including blogs, podcasts, wikis and social networking that have found their place on the Internet (Cook, 2008).

Blogs in terms of online personal journals is one of the examples mentioned by Cook (2008) and Mitchell et al. (2008) who phrased the following question: Are blogs putting youth at risk for online sexual solicitation or harassment? They conducted a telephone survey of 1,500 youth Internet users, ages 10–17, in the USA. They found that 16 per cent of youth Internet users reported blogging in the past year. Teenagers and girls were the most common bloggers, and bloggers were more likely than other youth to post personal information online.

However, Mitchell et al. (2008) found that bloggers were not more likely to interact with people they met online and did not know in person. Youth who interacted with people they met online, regardless of whether or not they blogged, had higher odds of receiving online sexual solicitations. Bloggers who did not interact with people they met online were at no increased risk for sexual solicitation. Moreover, posting personal information did not add to risk. The only difference found was related to harassment, since youthful bloggers were found to be at increased risk for online harassment, regardless of whether they also interacted with others online.

Virtual communities

Individuals join virtual communities, where they meet other persons who have the same interest. A virtual community provides an online meeting place where people with similar interests can communicate and find useful information. Communication between members may be via e-mail, bulletin boards, online chat, web based conferencing, or other computer-based media. As a business model, a virtual community can make money from membership fees, direct sales of goods and services, advertising, click-through, and sales commissions (Gottschalk, 2006).

Vidnes and Jacobsen (2008) surveyed 772 persons from 16 to 29 years of age. One of the key findings was that especially the youngest ones are active users of web cameras, and that young people who use web cameras have certain characteristics. They are more socially active on the Net than others, and more interested to get to know new people. 53 per cent of youngsters between 16 and 19 years use web cameras have come in contact with people on the Net that they later on have met outside the Net. Only 25 per cent of those who do not use web cameras report the same. This shows that web camera users to a greater extent than others expand their social network on and outside the Net. At the same time it is evident that web camera users are involved in activities to a far greater extent that are perceived as potentially dangerous.

However, most young web camera users communicate mainly with persons that they know already. When getting to know a new person, they seldom start by using their web cameras. Rather, they start by using Facebook or Nettby (Net village), which are characterised by openness in the sense that individuals present themselves by means of real pictures, name, interests and friends. These net societies function as a kind of cocktail party, where one can be introduced to another and move on, get contacts and expand networks (Vidnes and Jacobsen, 2008).

The study by Vidnes and Jacobsen emphasised the following findings (Thorgrimsen, 2008):

- 7 out of 10 youngsters between 16 and 19 years old have access to a web camera on their computer, 48 per cent of them use it at least once a month.
- Almost all youngsters are using MSN on a daily basis, but very few use their camera daily.
- First and foremost a camera is used with persons that one seldom meets.
- A Web camera is far less used than other communication tools such as net community and MSN.
- Young people are careful in providing identifiable information before feeling safe in new net relationships.
- The web camera also works as a control mechanism, as one cannot be sure who is on the line before the camera is turned on. Resistance to turn it on is interpreted to mean the other person has something to hide.

If young people want to get to know each other better, then they may move into more private tools such as MSN, which intensifies the communication. If the relationship is developed further, then the private arena of web cameras emerges. By choosing different tools for different relationships and for different phases in a relationship, Vidnes and Jacobsen (2008) thus found that young people are able to regulate the degree of intimacy in the relationship.

Myspace and other social networking sites like Myspace offer thriving communities where young people engage in countless hours of photo sharing. In addition to Myspace, other social networking and blogging sites such as Friendster.com, Facebook.com and MyYearbook.com allow users to post pictures, videos, and blogs, and they support email and instant messaging. Myspace and Facebook differ in that Myspace is open to anyone, and has loose age restrictions, while Facebook users are encouraged and often required to register using their real name (Kierkegaard, 2008).

The most prevalent examples of social network sites are Facebook, which started as a college site and is still dominated by college users, and Myspace, which has always been open to the public. Somewhere between 80 and 90 per cent of all college students have a profile on a social network site. All social network sites allow users to articulate their social network via links between their profile page and other profiles:

> *Profiles linked to each other in this manner are called* friends. *Profile owners also express an online persona through pictures, words and page composition, as well as through data fields where information ranging from favourite books and movies to sexual orientation and relationship status (single, in a relationship, etc.) is indicated.*

Tufekci, 2008: 546

On Myspace, people talk by creating profiles: a page on the service's website which can feature a picture, blurb about oneself, a Web log (basically, an online diary) and other information. The free service also features blogs, and instant messages. Users can create their profiles and ask others to exchange materials (Kierkegaard, 2008).

Kierkegaard (2008) argues that the anonymity, availability of extremely sensitive personal information and ease of contacting people make social networking sites a useful tool for online child sex offenders. While many of the sites have age restrictions, it is possible for offenders to misrepresent their age. To hide their IP addresses and locations, they piggyback on Wi-Fi connections or use proxy servers. Decentralised peer-to-peer networks prevent material from being tracked to a specific server, and encryption lets them keep online chats private from those policing the Web.

Social networking sites have been studied in different contexts. For example, Tufekci (2008) explored the rapid adoption of online social network sites by students on a US college campus. Using quantitative and qualitative data based on a diverse sample of college students, demographic and other characteristics of social networking site users and non-users were compared. A distinction was made between social grooming and presentation of self. In the study, non-users displayed an attitude towards social grooming (gossip, small-talk and generalised, non-functional people-curiosity) that ranged from incredulous to hostile. Contrary to expectations in the study, non-users did not report a smaller number of close friends compared with users, but they did keep in touch with fewer people. Users were also heavier users of the expressive Internet, which is the practice and performance of technologically mediated sociality.

Thus, while social grooming through language may well be an important human activity, there seems to be no reason to presuppose that everyone will be equally disposed to such activity. Interest in exchange and browsing social information about friends and acquaintances, and curiosity about people, is likely to be related to interest in how an application specifically facilitates such activity (Tufekci, 2008).

When we apply Tufekci's (2008) terminology to online grooming, online groomers will be heavier users of the expressive Internet than paedophilic non-users of social networking sites. As users of the expressive Internet, online groomers use the Internet as an instrument to express opinions and communicate information. *Expressive Internet* is the practice and performance of technologically mediated sociality. It is the use of the Internet to perform and realise interactions, self-presentations, public performance, social capital management, social monitoring, and the production, maintenance and furthering of social ties. The expressive Internet might be recognised as a social ecology involving other people, values, norms and social contexts.

Instrumental Internet, on the other hand, refers to information seeking, knowledge gathering and commercial transactions on the Internet, and non-social communication involved in such transactions. This is typically the Internet of online banking, shopping and checking the weather. Tufekci (2008) found no difference in the use of instrumental Internet for users versus non-users of social networking sites.

The expressive Internet has been expanding rapidly, a process often described in the popular press as the rise of social computing. These tools have been assimilated as a means of social interaction and social integration for increasing numbers of people and communities. People are increasingly using the expressive Internet in ways that complement or further their offline sociality (Tufekci, 2008).

The distinction between the two groups of users is a point also raised by some of the probation officers interviewed by Davidson and Martellozzo (2008). The probation officers were working with groomers in treatment programs. They spoke about offenders for whom the Internet played a significant role in their lives and who had many online relationships. Using the Internet to offend was almost a natural progression for these offenders as it played such a big part in other areas of their lives.

Because the sample of college students studied by Tufekci (2008) tended to have a high level of offline-online integration, students typically used their real names and engaged in high levels of self-disclosure, especially on Facebook. Facebook allows users to tag individuals on photographs uploaded to the site, which means identifying the person in the photograph and thereby linking the picture to that person's profile, and thus creating a searchable digital trail of a person's social activities. Since online groomers and their potential victims initially have no offline-online integration, we expect the behaviours of online paedophilic grooming to differ from campus social grooming.

According to the encyclopaedia Wikipedia (www.wikipedia.org) *online chat* can refer to any kind of communication over the Internet, but is primarily meant to refer to direct one-on-one chat or text-based group chat, formally also known as synchronous conferencing. Online chat uses tools such as instant messaging, Internet relay chat, talkers and other means. The expression, online chat, comes from the word chat, which means informal conversation.

The term *chatiquette* is a variation of netiquette (chat netiquette) and describes basic rules of online communication. To avoid misunderstandings and to simplify the communication between users in a chat, these conventions or guidelines have been created. An interesting issue is whether, how and why online groomers violate the chatiquette. Chatiquette varies from community to community, generally describing basic courtesy; it introduces a new user into the community and the associated network culture. As an example, it is considered rude to write only in UPPER CASE, because it looks as if the user is shouting (www.wikipedia.org).

Computer technology and the Internet enable paedophiles to locate and interact with other paedophiles more readily than before. The organisational aspects of a common gathering place and the resultant support child sex offenders are providing each other is probably their most significant advantage – and the most troublesome for a concerned public.

Child sex offenders are forming online communities and bonds using the Internet. They are openly uniting against legal authorities and discussing ways to influence public thinking and legislation on child exploitation. While paedophile web sites are being tracked down and removed from Internet servers in countries all over the world, they are popping up again at a higher pace in most parts of the world.

An example of a web site representing a virtual community for paedophiles is 'Boylove'. On the web site, The Boylove Manifesto could be found, which argued the case for intergenerational relationships:

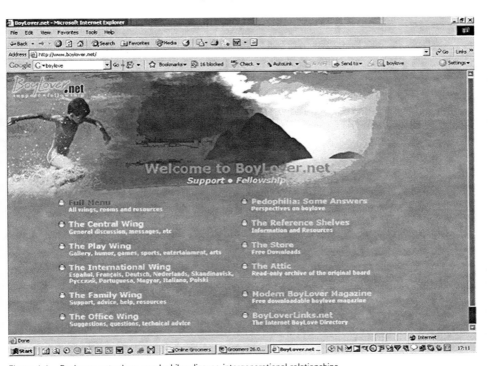

Figure 1.1   Boylovers.net where paedophiles discuss intergenerational relationships

As boylovers we distance ourselves from the current discussion about "child sexual abuse". Human sexuality plays the same part in a boylove relationship as it undoubtedly does in any relationship between human beings. A boylover desires a friendly and close relationship with a boy.

www.prevent-abuse-now.com

Similar text can be found on Boylovers.net (see Figure 1.1):

Over the years, paedophilia, or boylove as it is sometime known, has come under heavy criticism from those who are opposed to it in the media, government and general society. Often, this can be very one-sided and extremely vitriolic in nature.

Here at BoyLover.net, we believe that people deserve the chance to hear both sides of the argument. Doubtless, by now you will have read or heard many opinions against paedophilia. With this in mind, we have taken the opportunity to present different views so that people can make an informed decision regarding the subject.

Boylover.net seems important to mention here, as paedophile research in countries such as Norway, Sweden and the UK tend to focus on girls more than boys. As listed in the Norwegian court sentence, almost all cases are concerned with victimisation of girls. Lillywhite and Skidmore (2006) argue that the view that boys are not sexually exploited is very common among many professionals working with vulnerable young men. Do paedophiles interested in boys perform online grooming differently from paedophiles who are interested in girls? Different grooming behaviours may be employed with different genders.

Male children have been exploited in hidden locations such as public toilets, parks, bus and train stations, cruising areas, shopping areas and arcades. Because of the Internet, shifting sites for abuse are occurring. Young men are sexually exploited via the Internet in a range of ways. These include: a young man who was stripped, shaved and photographed by a friend of his so-called older 'boyfriend', a 15 year old client who was groomed over the Internet by a man in his thirties; and a young man whose photograph was placed on a website where men sell sex.

Giving mobiles is a common grooming technique when men are grooming boys:

> One young man we worked with was given ten mobile phones over a one-year period. Giving mobiles is now a common grooming technique experienced by the young men we work with. It means that a young man can be contacted at any time and place by a child sex offender.

> Lillywhite and Skidmore, 2006: 356

Do paedophiles who are grooming girls online employ different methods from paedophiles grooming boys online? This is an absolutely key question for the future study of online grooming and policing online groomers. The literature on contact offending seems clear that offenders' grooming behaviour is tailored to the victim's style or characteristics. It is hard to see any reason why it would be different online, but future research will be needed.

A *paedophile ring* is a group of persons working together across the Internet in different countries and jurisdictions to collect and distribute child pornography for their own gratification. This can also involve sharing expertise and experiences on avoiding detection and planning criminal activities against children. There is a strong perception that the Internet has become a major factor in the development of paedophile rings worldwide. For example, the Metropolitan High Tech Crime Unit in the UK has registered that large international abuser rings are commonplace. These rings share images, but how far they are contact abusing is another question and one that needs to be explored in future research.

Understanding online children

Children use the Internet a great deal, and this has been well documented in other research. More than 30 million in the USA alone used the Internet in 2000. It has been suggested that 1 in 4 children on the Internet have an unwanted exposure to sexually explicit pictures that were inappropriate for children to view. Approximately 1 in 5 receive a sexual solicitation or approach, 1 in 17 are threatened or harassed, and 1 in 33 receive an aggressive sexual solicitation from someone who asked to meet them somewhere, called them on the telephone, sent them regular mail, money or gifts (Davidson and Martellozzo, 2008).

The children interviewed in Davidson and Martellozzo's (2008) research were enthusiastic Internet users and enjoyed discussing the topic. Older children in the sample (12+) tended to use chat rooms and interactive games and chat facilities such as Myspace and MSN Messenger. Younger children (10–11) tended to play secure games on websites such as Disney's Toontown and were much less familiar with peer-to-peer networks. All of the children used the Internet for research and homework and were actively encouraged to do so at school.

Given that some of the younger children (10–11) had no experience of chat rooms and did not understand how they function, Davidson and Martellozzo (2008) argue that it may be better to target educational programs addressing Internet safety at the 12 plus age group, who are actively involved in chatting online, or to adapt such programs for younger children. Maybe older children retain such information more effectively and are more able to act upon it.

The majority of children (65 per cent) in Davidson and Martellozzo's (2008) study had access to at least one computer at home, 49 per cent had computers in their bedrooms. Other children did not have a computer at home, but had access to a computer at relatives' or friends' houses, 15 per cent used Internet cafés on a regular basis (more than once a week). The findings suggest that almost all of the children had access to the Internet outside school. 60 per cent accessed the Internet more than four times per week, this was particularly the case for the 12–14 age group. Of those children accessing the Internet, 76 per cent were largely unsupervised and spent long periods of time on their computer, particularly during school holidays and at weekends. Generally, the children had a great deal of knowledge about computing, and the majority of 12–14 year olds were extremely confident Internet users.

Children were questioned about their interactions in chat rooms, and 13 per cent reported occasions where they believed themselves or a friend/relative had been talking to an adult posing as a child. On several occasions this was clear as the person's Internet profile revealed their real age. 11 per cent of the children had been approached in a chat room regarding sex and had told their parents. They reported feeling uncomfortable and uncertain about to whom they were talking. The majority of children claimed they would always know if they were talking to a child as children use a unique computer slang online that adults would not be able to understand and would not use (Davidson and Martellozzo, 2008).

70 per cent of the children believed that girls were much more at risk of sexual abuse. The children seemed to use gender stereotypes in explaining why girls are more at risk. Girls were described as weaker and boys as stronger and more able to defend themselves. The children often noted that men seem to perpetrate this type of offence and would therefore target girls. Several children also noted that most cases covered by the media involve the sexual abuse of girls. Whilst it is the case that males perpetrate the vast majority of sexual abuse against female victims, Davidson and Martellozzo (2008) find it important to reinforce the point with children that boys are also at risk.

Perspectives on child sexual abuse

In the United States, an estimated one million children a year live in an environment of abuse or maltreatment (Conrad, 2006). Child abuse creates long-lived problems for those affected. Child abuse is defined as death, serious physical or emotional harm, sexual abuse or exploitation. Abuse is a non-accidental injury to a child, which, regardless of motive, is inflicted by an adult. It includes any injury, which is at variance with the history given, and maltreatment such as, but not limited to, malnutrition, sexual molestation, deprivation of necessities, emotional maltreatment or cruel punishment.

Children are particularly vulnerable to different kinds of victimisation because of developmental immaturity in key areas such as physical, cognitive and emotional capabilities. A range of different maltreatment types exist to which children are subjected that are defined either by perpetrator behaviour or by the resulting type of harm to the child (Higgins, 2004).

According to Higgins (2004) child maltreatment can be both a one-dimensional and a multidimensional construct. She argues that it may be more meaningful to talk about the degree of negative adult behaviour (high, medium, low) rather than about the type (e.g. sexual, physical). It is not maltreatment type *per se* but the extent of maltreatment that is important to understand. Victims of maltreatment are children who have experienced substantiated or indicated maltreatment or are found to be at risk of experiencing maltreatment.

In her book on child sexual abuse, Davidson (2008) argues that there is a need to define what is meant by childhood. Perceptions of childhood vary over time and across cultures. As sexual activity is associated with adulthood and maturity in western societies, the age at which a person can give consent to sexual relations implies the end of childhood.

The global encyclopaedia Wikipedia (wikipedia.org) describes child sexual abuse as a form of child abuse in which a child is abused for the sexual gratification of an adult or older adolescent. In addition to direct sexual contact, child sexual abuse also occurs when an adult indecently exposes their own genitalia to a child, asks or pressures a child to engage in sexual activities, displays pornography to a child, or uses a child to produce child pornography. Child sexual abuse is the engagement of a child in sexual activities for which the child is developmentally unprepared and cannot give informed consent. Child sexual abuse is characterised by deception, force or coercion. Child sexual abuse can include fondling, genital exposure, intimate kissing, forced masturbation oral, penile or digital penetration of the mouth, vagina, or anus. A central characteristic of any abuse is the dominant position of an adult that allows the adult to force or coerce a child into sexual activity.

Effects of child sexual abuse include depression, post-traumatic stress disorder, anxiety, propensity to re-victimisation in adulthood, and physical injury to the child. Children who experience the most serious types of abuse exhibit behaviour problems ranging from separation anxiety to post-traumatic stress disorder.

Most sexual abuse offenders are acquainted with their victims, and sexual abuse by a family member is called incest. However, in our perspective of Internet groomers, we focus on adults who did not know their victims before they met on the Internet.

Understanding sex offender behaviour

Little is known about online sex offenders, some have suggested that there is much to be learnt from existing sex offender literature (Beech and Elliot, 2009) as it is entirely possible that online sex offenders are simply sex offenders who now use the latest information technology to access victims and to make contact with other offenders. This section explores key findings form research literature in this area, drawing upon the author's own research with convicted child sexual abusers (Davidson, 2002).

A growing awareness regarding the high incidence of child sexual abuse and the harmful consequences to the victim during the 1980s and 1990s has resulted in a proliferation of writings and research on male abusers. However, little is really known about what distinguishes male abusers from non-abusers, what motivates them to offend and how frequently they offend. Research has relied upon male offenders self report (Kaplan, 1985; Abel and Becker, 1987) and the reliability of such work has been questioned given the extent of the denial and minimisation associated with child sexual abuse which throws doubt upon offender's own accounts.

Some have stressed the importance of confidentiality and immunity from prosecution in ensuring accurate findings (Kaplan, 1985) and in encouraging honesty, some researchers have been able and willing to make such guarantees (Abel and Becker, 1987, for example). Whilst it may be the case that better research will result from confidentiality, and this is usually a most important ethical consideration when undertaking research, the morality of concealing information regarding sexual offences committed against children can be questioned. Other variables are important in determining how forthcoming abusers are in interview. Abel *et al.* (1983) suggest that interviewer style and experience makes a difference, they found that subjects were much more willing to discuss their offending and offending history when re-interviewed by a more experienced interviewer.

The extent of recidivism amongst abusers is an extremely important issue allowing researchers to examine patterns of abuse. Recidivism should not however be confused with rates of reconviction. As discussed, self-report studies of abusers have demonstrated that a vast difference exists between the number of offences committed and the number of convictions received for those offences, simply because the majority remain undetected (Abel, 1983; Abel and Becker, 1987; Weinrott and Saylor, 1991).

Abel and Becker's (1987) self report recidivism study of 561 non-incarcerated sex offenders is probably the most comprehensive to date. Conducted in the United States, the study provides an overview of the characteristics of male abusers. The respondents were aged from 13–76 years, with a mean age of 31.5 years. The majority were employed and had formed a stable relationship with an adult partner(married or cohabiting). In keeping with other research, the ethnic origin and social class of the sample was representative of the general population. The majority had committed offences against female children.

The offenders reported a large number of offences, some 291,737 sexual acts were said to have been perpetrated against 195,407 victims, 153 child sexual abusers (non-familial offences against male children) admitted to 43,100 offences involving 22, 981 victims, constituting an average of 282 offences per offender and an average of 150 victims each (Barker and Morgan, 1993). The majority of respondents (53.6 per cent) also reported the onset of deviant sexual interest before their eighteenth birthday. In support of Abel and Becker's research, Weinrott and Saylor (1991) interviewed institutionalised child sexual abusers (and other sex offenders) and found that many undetected sexual offences were disclosed. Recent research conducted by Hernandez (2009) with 150 convicted, incarcerated online offenders (indecent image collectors) in an attempt to explore the link between image collection and contact abuse, suggests that by the end of the treatment programme 131 (85 per cent) of this group admitted that they had perpetrated a contact offence, the number of victims involved in this offending was 1,777, an average of 13.56 victims per offender (SD = 30.11). Polygraph testing was employed to validate the offenders self reports, but the validity of this method of validation has been questioned. Seto (2009) suggests, however, on the basis of his research with over 300 child pornography offenders that this group is unlikely to be convicted for contact sexual offences. 4 per cent of 301 child pornography offenders were convicted for sexual abuse contact offences over a 3.9 year period. This study is however based upon reconviction data and not offender self report.

Research incorporating reconviction rates does, however, show a distinct difference between child sexual abusers who have undergone treatment programmes and those who have not. Marshall (in Fordham, 1992) produced rates of re-offending for untreated abusers of between 15 and 20 per cent over a four year period. He states that this compares favourably to the rates for treated offenders. The rates are lower than those produced by Marshall and Barbaree's (1988) in their North American study, and this may be due to methodological or cultural differences. A sample of 126 treated and untreated child sexual abusers attending one clinic were followed over a period of between 12 and 117 months. The research subjects were divided into the following categories: men abusing non-familial girls; men abusing non-familial boys and incest abusers. The non-familial abusers were generally more likely to re-offend (or perhaps to be caught re-offending) than were the incest abusers. In all three categories the untreated abusers were much more likely to re-offend than were the treated offenders.

Even given the difficulties associated with the use of reconviction data the findings show a marked difference between those receiving treatment and those not receiving treatment. It should, however, be noted that no reference is made by the authors, to the number of offenders in the treatment group completing the treatment programme. Recidivism is also important in enabling researchers to isolate risk factors. This type of work aids criminal justice agencies in attempting to recognise those abusers most at risk of re-offending. Abel et al. (1988), in another important North American study, attempted to isolate risk factors in a sample of child sexual abusers. They found that those most likely to re-offend had assaulted both boys and girls and had committed offences against both familial and non-familial victims. Other similar studies such as Marshall and Barbaree's (1988) found no association between recidivism amongst child sexual abusers and social class or educational level. Marshall and Barbaree also state that no association could be found between the number of previous offences (or are they referring to convictions? This is unclear) and the risk of re-offending. This seems a questionable finding given that other recent research has clearly demonstrated that such a link exists and that those abusers with an established pattern of offending are by definition the most difficult group to treat and the most likely to fail in treatment programmes (Beckett *et al.*, 1994).

Age appears to be an important variable. Studies point to an age range from early adolescence upwards, with a mean average age between 30–35 (Nash and West, 1985). Little research has been conducted on the age of online offenders but it is likely that younger offenders will be increasingly adept at making use of new technologies in perpetrating abuse given educational emphasis on the topic from an early age. Hernandez (2009) in his study of indecent image collectors notes that the median age for the onset of contact sexual offending in the sample was 16 and the median age for the onset of online indecent image collection was 25, suggesting an escalation from contact abuse to collection. Further research is needed to validate this finding. Increasingly however, and in support of Abel *et al.*'s (1988) then controversial finding that the onset of deviant behaviour can occur prior to age 18, research has focused upon adolescent abusers and this reflects a boom during the 1990s in treatment programmes specifically aimed at such abusers (O'Callaghan and Print, 1994). Is such a focus justified? A prevalence survey conducted by Kelly *et al.* (1991) in England and Wales, in which a sample of 1,244 16–21 year olds were surveyed, concluded that 27 per cent of perpetrators were aged between 13 and 17 years. Whilst similar research conducted by the Northern Ireland Research Team (1991) reviewed 408 cases of child sexual abuse and found that in 36.1 per cent of cases the abuser was an adolescent.

Some research comparing adolescent sex offenders to other adolescent offenders has generally failed to find any significant differences between the two groups (Smith, 1988; Oliver, 1993). Fagin and Wexler (1988) for example, found that adolescent abusers were as likely to come from stable homes (defined as living with both natural parents) and had low reported rates of substance abuse. Becker and Kaplan (1988) found that adolescent abusers were less likely to have encountered the criminal justice system. Oliver's (1993) study comparing a group of adolescent abusers to a group of adolescent offenders committing property related crimes, found that the abusers were least likely to have a recognised mental health problem and showed fewer deviant characteristics (assessed by psychometric testing) than the non-abusing group. The only other difference between the two groups was that the abusers tended to score higher on measurements of inter-personal maturity. Other research has contradicted such findings in suggesting that such offenders tend to come from 'dysfunctional' families and may have experienced physical or sexual abuse (Kear-Colwell, 1996; Graves *et al.*, 1996; Smallbone and Dadds, 1998; Ward and Keenan, 1999).

Coulborn-Fuller's (1993) review of the literature on convicted female child sexual abusers provides a useful insight into the characteristics of such women. She describes the majority of female perpetrators as 'very dysfunctional' and states that their offences are frequently associated with a high incidence of mental disorder, substance misuse and parenting difficulties. Often, it would seem, where sexual abuse is perpetrated by women it is accompanied by neglect, physical and emotional abuse. A review of the literature suggests that a large proportion of offences perpetrated by women were done so with others in the context of the extended family. Here, children were sometimes used for pornography or prostitution; when 'lone abuse' was perpetrated it tended to be within a marriage or stable relationship. Several studies also reported cases of 'lone abuse' where a woman was living without a constant male partner and the eldest male child had taken over the male adult role and was also subject to sexual abuse on the part of their mother. Anecdotal evidence from police officer working on online abuse cases suggests similarly that women have assisted men in producing indecent images of children for example (Global Symposium Internet Abuse, 2009).

Coulburn-Fuller also created a category to describe adolescent female offenders, who tended to be 'inadequate' and have difficulty in building and maintaining peer relationships, selecting children as a substitute for peers. The other circumstances under which females abuse are described as 'ritual'. Here ritual abuse was practiced in groups, many of which were religious, including both women and men. The final group consisted of professional carers who were accused of sexual abuse by the children in their care.

A study conducted by Elliot (1993) explored the accounts of 127 adult respondents who were sexually abused by a woman as children. The respondents reported similarly negative effects to those of victims abused by men. The majority (78 per cent) who did report the sexual abuse at the time were not believed and could find little help. Whilst it would seem that men are more likely to sexually abuse children than women, the true extent of female sexual abuse is unknown and further research is needed. It is clear however, that a significant number of women do commit such offences and to characterise child sexual abuse as an exclusively male crime is to marginalise the few female offenders that do enter the criminal justice system and ensure that little substantial treatment provision is available to them.

Sex offenders' early lives, self-esteem and relationships

This section describes findings from one of the author's research with adult, convicted sex offenders (Davidson, 2002). Literature suggests that sex offenders are likely to have experienced some form of abuse in their early lives and have difficulty in maintaining adult relationships. The research sought to evaluate the effectiveness of a cognitive behavioural treatment programme for sex offenders who had committed offences against children. A combination of depth interviewing and psychometric or attitudinal testing was employed with a small group of male respondents over a period of three years (N = 21). A total of 97 interviews were undertaken. Documentary analysis of victim statements was also undertaken (where statements were available) and these were compared to offender accounts of offence circumstances over a period of time. The first part of the interview explored offenders' early lives and relationship experience.

Self-esteem

Research has suggested that child sexual abusers are more likely to have low self esteem and to be socially isolated, than are other offenders (Marshall, 1996; Marshall and Mazzucco, 1995).

The concept of self-esteem proved a difficult one to address in the context of an interview. Much existing research has relied upon psychometric testing (Pithers, 1999; Wolf,1984) but the validity of such testing may also be questioned on the grounds that respondents may provide what is perceived to be an acceptable response.[1] A psychometric test was used in an attempt to validate the interview findings. The Great Ormond Street Self Image profile was developed by Monck *et al.* (1992) and seeks to establish how respondents rate their feelings of self worth. The findings from this test indicated that the group's self-esteem had increased over the duration of the programme. The group mean scores showed a gradual increase over time, with a slump at interview two, six months into the treatment programme. These findings are largely consistent with the interview findings which identified a similar low point. The standard deviation scores were extremely high, casting doubt upon the validity of the mean scores, and this was possibly attributable to several extreme values and the small sample size. The test findings appear positive but their validity must be questioned on the basis of the problems discussed.

The difficulty here was in establishing how far the depression and low self-esteem, which respondents described at the outset of the research, was an enduring feature of their lives and how far this might be attributable to their circumstances. The research group were drawn from a convicted population. Each one had recently experienced the trauma of arrest and subsequent conviction for an offence for which society has little tolerance and understanding. The question remains: did respondents have enduring low self-esteem or did their current circumstances produce depressed and lonely individuals? In order to address this issue the accounts of early childhood provided by the respondents were explored. There was evidence to suggest that respondents did suffer low self-esteem as children; this was particularly apparent in accounts of school experience and bullying. Although the majority of respondents were articulate, literate adults who were able to express themselves well during interview, many underachieved academically and disliked school.

Extracts from offender interviews illustrate these points:

Q. Why were you truanting?
Well, the usual thing, bullying. There was a gang of around six, they would wait for me after school, they would pick on me if I was in the way. They would often beat me up, I used to have cuts and bruises.
Q. Did you tell your parents?
They knew, but they didn't pay much attention, Dad said I should just get on with it and stand up to them.
Q. How did you feel about the bullying?
I didn't want to go to school, no one cared so I didn't go, I got behind with things and I couldn't catch up. I just felt stupid. Now I feel like I really missed out.

(Respondent, G1.7) Davidson, 2002

---

[1] Referred to as 'faking good' (Anastasi and Urbina, 1997) in the Methodology Chapter.

This respondent described the way in which he was bullied at school:

I was bullied, usually by younger kids. I never fought back.

(Respondent G1.9) Davidson, 2002

This respondent was asked to describe what kind of child he was:

I don't know (long pause) unhappy I suppose.
Q. *What made you unhappy?*
If anyone walked into a classroom I knew that they would blame me, I knew that they would blame me for something. If anyone spoke to me I would blush. I was shy, my mother said that if a smaller kid shit on me I would stand there and take it.
Q. *Do you think that's true?*
Yes, that's the kind of kid I was.

(Respondent G1.1) Davidson, 2002

Social isolation and loneliness

The extent of social isolation experienced during childhood was also significant. Many reported that they were lonely, isolated children. The findings from interview one, and indeed subsequent interviews, would appear to support the contention that low self-esteem is an enduring problem for this group of offenders, which is doubtless exacerbated by arrest, subsequent conviction and public labelling as a 'sex offender'. The findings from Beckett *et al.*'s research (1994) would appear to support this. Their sample of abusers were characterised as *'emotionally isolated individuals lacking self-confidence'*.

Social isolation proved easier to explore and respondents were asked a series of questions regarding their daily lives and the nature and frequency of social contact. The literature characterises sex offenders as social isolates, with few social contacts. As discussed, the difficulty of decompartmentalising concepts became clear as the research progressed, and where social isolation was a significant element of respondents lives this often accompanied feelings of low self-worth. The extent of isolation experienced was addressed via exploration of the nature and frequency of respondents' contacts. The data from interview one indicated that some of the respondents had a relatively large number of social contacts and busy lives.

The research also sought to explore the concept of 'loneliness', which is taken to be qualitatively different to social isolation. An individual might have social contacts but remain lonely. Peplau and Perlman (1982) have suggested that individuals with many social contacts might feel isolated and lonely, where those relationships lack depth and meaning. They point to the importance of having significant others to whom we can turn in difficult times and who offer support. In order to accommodate this concept respondents were asked if they felt there was anyone in whom they could confide their problems. Only two of the respondents throughout the research felt that they had such a significant other. Some of the respondents were socially isolated at interview one, and the extent of such isolation became worse for many as friends and family discovered the nature of their offending. The majority of the respondents appeared to be lonely individuals who had no significant others with whom to share their problems. It proved difficult throughout the research to establish how far the self-esteem of offenders had altered from one interview to the next. At interview two the majority of respondents were extremely depressed and many felt ostracised by family and friends who had recently learned of their conviction. It could be said that respondents did appear to have extremely low self-esteem and were socially isolated at this point in the research.

By interview three (1.5 years into the research) some respondents appeared to have rebuilt their lives and developed new social contacts and this appeared to have impacted positively upon their self-esteem, whilst some remained isolated, not wishing to socialise with others. Respondents had certainly been encouraged to join social clubs by their probation officers. This remained true at interviews four and five, although here respondents generally felt more confident and able to get on in life. The majority of respondents continued to state throughout the research that they felt unable to confide in anyone beside the group and their probation officer regarding their sexual and other problems. This might indicate that respondents continued to experience loneliness. An attempt to explore other aspects of the lives of those respondents who appeared to be socially isolated throughout the research was made (a core of 15 respondents fell into this category).

Table 1.1   Social isolation compared to other key characteristics

	Physically abused by father	Poor relationship with both parents	Socially isolated as a child	Difficulty in forming adult relationships
Socially isolated throughout research (N = 15)	12	13	14	14

This exercise proved interesting, however, it is difficult to draw any conclusions given the limitations of the data. It is worth noting that fourteen of fifteen of those remaining socially isolated throughout the research, experienced isolation in childhood. Such isolation had been an enduring feature of their lives. It is clear, in the light of these findings, how the Internet may have provided such individuals not only with new opportunities to offend, but also with a means of communicating to overcome social isolation.

As discussed, it is extremely difficult to explore ambiguous concepts such as self-esteem and social isolation, and to attribute any increase in levels of confidence to the treatment programme is problematic. Respondents may have become more confident and, in some cases, less socially isolated as a consequence of the passage of time.

If abusers are characteristically social isolates with low self-esteem, and evidence from respondents' childhoods presented here does suggest that this may be so, perhaps it is unrealistic for a comparatively short treatment programme to impact significantly upon abusers confidence and social circumstances. The only treatment programme in Beckett et al.'s (1994) study to significantly impact upon abuser self-esteem was that run by the Gracewell Clinic in Birmingham (which has since closed). This residential programme offered 462 hours of intensive therapy to attendees on a daily basis. The length of the programme, the residential nature and the intensity of the programme are identified as key ingredients for success in this area.

Adult relationships

At interview one, 18 of the 21 respondents claimed to have been, or were currently involved in a sexual relationship with an adult woman, 12 had been married or co-habiting at some point in their lives, two remained in a long term relationship following their conviction.

Table 1.2   Adult relationships – respondents self report (qualitative count)

	N
Experienced long term heterosexual relationship	18
Experienced problematic adult sexual relations	16
Relationship breakdown a consequence of conviction	17 (interview 3)
Difficulty in forming adult relationships	16
Less likely to offend whilst in an adult sexual relationship	5

Respondents discussed their adult relationships freely at interview one, and they frequently described ongoing problems and feelings of rejection. In some cases the offending had clearly contributed to a breakdown in their relationship. This and other research has shown that: male abusers have difficulty in relating to adult women (Hammer and Glueck, 1957) and expect isolation and rejection in their sexual adult relationships (Smallbone and Dadds, 1998).

Many respondents continued to experience relationship problems, which were reported at subsequent interviews. Several respondents had split up with partners as a consequence of their offending and their continuing sexual attraction to children. Several actively avoided any intimate adult contact for fear of rejection. Respondents were, however, noticeably more able to discuss and analyse previous relationships. Several respondents appeared more honest regarding the role they played in the destruction of previous relationships. Some respondents openly admitted the extent of their violent behaviour in past relationships. Although respondents' circumstances remained largely unchanged, they had a much greater understanding of the problems.

Respondents' early lives

Respondents gave detailed accounts of their childhood experience during the research. There were few inconsistencies over time in the accounts provided by offenders. This would suggest that respondents believed their accounts to be truthful, although the validity of such accounts must always be questioned on the basis of the accuracy of respondent recall. The pain experienced in recounting childhood memories was apparent, many respondents became emotional and cried openly during interview one and subsequent interviews.

At interview one and later interviews, accounts of early childhood revealed a significant amount of emotional and physical abuse on the part of parents and carers. Many respondents recounted difficult, unhappy childhoods, describing relations with both parents as often characterised by abusive behaviour. Where fathers were present in the respondents' young lives they tended to be either emotionally or physically detached (sometimes for long periods of time) from the family unit. Here fathers were violent, uninterested or both. Relations with mothers were often strained, leaving respondents feeling unloved. Research conducted during the 1980s found that the parents or carers of a sample of juvenile sex offenders were typically distant and inaccessible, leaving the abusers feeling unloved and uncared for as children (Smith and Israel, 1987). Similarly Bagley (1992) found high levels of parental instability in his sample of convicted child sexual abusers. Kear-Colwell (1996: 262) asserts that 'most sex offenders come from seriously maladaptive social and family backgrounds and are significantly damaged individuals'.

Some of the respondents frequently experienced bullying on the part of their peers and abuse on the part of their parents:

> Q. Did you feel wanted as a child?
> I don't know, that's what I'm trying to find out. Mother said I was her favourite but I was always the one who got hit. My Father wasn't around much but he remembers me being hit. It was only ever one slap, but she was very strong and athletic, so there was quite a lot of force. But you know just bang and finished with. I use to be puzzled why I got it, I think because I was too slow doing things.
> Q. You weren't fast enough for her?
> No. You know, doing household chores.
> Q. How often did she hit you?
> It's difficult to say really . . . probably most days. It was always round the face, that still rankles with me, I feel really angry when I see that.
>
> (Respondent G1.1) Davidson, 2002

As the research progressed it became more apparent that this respondent had experienced quite severe, systematic physical abuse on the part of his mother. He felt more able to discuss this in later interviews. He was frequently moved to tears when recounting childhood experiences. There is very little qualitative research addressing the family histories of child sexual abusers, although many writers have pointed to the importance of childhood experience in the development of a sexual attraction to children. Some have described the negative influence of living with a dysfunctional family (Graves et al., 1996; Smallbone and Dadds, 1998). Others have described the negative effect of frequent, inconsistent and severe punishment on the part of parents, as contributing to the development of emotionally immature individuals, who may sexually abuse children (Rada, 1978). This research lends weight to such work and the early life histories of the respondents reveals a high level of both physical and emotional abuse.

A large amount of research into the family backgrounds of juvenile sex offenders has been undertaken by psychologists. Findings indicate that: parents or carers tended to be distant or inaccessible (Smith and Israel, 1987) and families displayed high levels of mental illness and instability (Bagley, 1992), a large proportion of parents had suffered considerable physical or sexual abuse as children. Lankester and Meyer (1986) report that 64 per cent of parents of their sample of 153 juvenile sex offenders had such experiences. It is possible that these insecure attachments extended to school and relationships with peers also, although there is little research evidence to suggest that this is the case.

In this research several respondents reported physically abusive behaviour on the part of their mothers. It is also interesting to note here that some research has suggested that high levels of physical and sexual abuse can be found in the family histories of child sexual abusers' parents (Lankester and Meyer, 1986). Respondents also experienced difficult relations with peers. Many were isolated, lonely children with few friends, who were systematically bullied and ridiculed by other children. The evidence from interviews suggested that respondents experienced problematic relations with others from early childhood to adulthood. It is difficult to validate this finding with reference to other research, given that there has been no thorough attempt to document the life histories of abusers, although Yalom (1975) has suggested, on the basis of his experience as a practitioner, that the origin of relationship problems from this group may lie in experiences of early family life. Research undertaken by Smallbone and Dadds (1998: 569) which is based upon small sample of convicted male child sexual abusers, does suggest that poor, abusive relations with parents or carers serve to create problems experienced in adult relationships. The suggestion here is that abusers expect their adult partners to behave in a similar way to their childhood carers, the expectation being that partners will be 'unloving, unresponsive, inconsistent and rejecting'. These findings have been supported by other research (Ward and Keenan, 1999).

In order to explore the claim that an emotionally deprived childhood might be linked to an inability to form successful adult relationships, an attempt was made to explore how far those respondents experiencing problematic relations with parents or carers claimed to have experienced problematic relations in adulthood. No real inference can be drawn regarding a positive association between these two issues, given the small number of respondents in the group and the qualitative nature of the data.

Of the 15 respondents claiming to have experienced problematic relations with both parents, 13 appeared to have experienced difficult adult relations and 14 had experienced difficulty in building successful adult relationships. This finding would seem to support the work of Smallbone

Table 1.3   Respondents' early relationships with parents and adult relationships

	Experienced difficult adult sexual relations	Experienced difficulty in forming adult relations
Respondents experiencing poor relationships with both parents (N = 15)	13	14

and Dadds (1998) and Ward and Keenan (1999) but should be treated with caution given the methodological limitations discussed.

At interview one, less than half of the respondents claimed to have been sexually abused as children. The treatment programme leaders, following Wolf (1984) expected that attendees would have experienced sexual abuse at some point during their childhood. As the research progressed, two respondents claimed to have 'recalled' being sexually abused as children. To work on the basis that all attendees will have experienced some form of sexual abuse in treatment programmes as children, is clearly problematic when a proportion claimed not to have.

In summary the existing literature suggests that: child sexual abusers tend to be male, although women do perpetrate sexual offences against children and have been largely ignored by the literature; the mean age of those abusers studied is between 30 and 35, although recent research is increasingly addressing adolescent abuse and this may lend support to the view that the onset of deviant sexual behaviour occurs in adolescence (Abel *et al.*, 1988), no association has previously appeared to exist between the sexual abuse of children and social class, ethnic origin or geographical region; victims tend to be female although reticence amongst male victims in disclosing abuse may have affected this finding. Recent research suggests, however, that online indecent image collectors tend to be overwhelmingly male and white, whilst victims are predominantly female and white (Baartz, 2009). Wolak *et al.* (2003; 2005) in their research on Internet abuse amongst young people suggest that 99 per cent of the offender sample was male. Quayle notes that:

> The analysis of the COPINE archive in 2003 indicated that the majority of images available were of white Caucasian and Asian children, with very few African or African-American children (Taylor and Quayle, 2005). Indeed, in 2003, websites started to appear advertising specialist sites that included interracial pictures.

> Quayle, 2009: 13

Research suggests that offenders are likely to experience some form of abuse in childhood and have difficulty in building and maintaining adult relationships. It would seem that new information technologies have afforded some sex offenders the opportunity to maintain anonymity and it is probable that online relationships are more manageable and easily maintained than offline relationships. Beech (2009) suggests that online sexual relationships can become particularly significant for individuals who have difficulty in building actual sexual relationships:

> Along with its ability to provide a level of perceived pseudo-sexual intimacy with children, the Internet also would appear to provide a social outlet for individuals who have difficulties initiating, and maintaining relationships with other adults.

> Beech, 2009: 8

What do we know about online offenders' use of the Internet and the role the Internet plays in their fantasy and offending behaviour? Laulik *et al.* suggest that online sex offenders lack assertiveness and empathy in relationships, and demonstrate low levels of self-esteem (Laulik,

Allam, and Sheridan, 2007), whilst Middleton *et al.* (2006) note that such offenders are in-adequate, have low self-esteem, and show little victim empathy (Middleton *et al.*, 2006). Preliminary findings from ongoing doctoral research employing documentary analysis of online offender case files and conducted with a Police High Technology Crime Unit in the UK (Martellozzo, 2009) suggest that:

1. The majority of sex offenders in the study began to satisfy their fantasies of abusing children by simply exploring cyberspace. In doing so they quickly discovered sites that would satisfy their imagination to the point of actively engaging in erotic dialogues with children and other offenders and downloading pornography.

2. The majority of groomers sent undercover police officers some type of adult pornography or child abuse images during the grooming process. Almost two-thirds of the subjects exposed themselves to the undercover officer via photograph or web-cam. However, some suspects used images as a grooming tool and most stated that they used them principally for sexual gratification.

3. Existing literature demonstrates that sex offenders have a tendency to deny responsibility for their offending and to attribute blame to either the victim or to circumstances (Gudjonsson, 1988). Martellozzo's (2009) research with online offenders demonstrates that they tended to minimise their intention to sexually abuse a child. Several subjects claimed the communication was just 'fantasy' and that they thought they were talking to an adult. However a significant proportion of subjects who met the undercover police officers thinking they were meeting a 12-year-old girl. Of these subjects only one declared his intention to abuse the child. The others were in denial even when found in possession of condoms and other child abuse items. Respondents had a tendency to deny their interest in children and blame either their personal circumstance, boredom or the easy access provided by the Internet.

4. Finally Martellozzo's research demonstrated that the majority of the sex offenders viewed the Internet as a tool that can offer security and anonymity to the point that the risk of committing offences is minimised. Offenders did not blame the Internet but saw it as a safe environment where all forms of behaviour are acceptable, including child abuse.

Martellozzo, 2009

2

Stage Model for Online Grooming Offenders

'I am Stian 15' said the Norwegian man on the Internet and made young girls take off their clothes in front of their web cameras at home. He had sex with two girls and made sixty girls aged 10–16 strip in front of their cameras. In 2008, the man (33) was sentenced to four years in prison in Norway. The same year, pictures of child abuse in Asia by a Canadian were found on a PC in Norway. Norwegian police informed Interpol in Lyon in France. While raping boys younger than 10, the Canadian had taken, and later distributed, pictures of himself and the boys (NRK, 2008).

Online victimisation has been a serious problem for many years. Children and young people are active users of online technologies and have in many instances more expertise and experience in the use of information technology than their parents, teachers or other adults. However, as a consequence of the possibilities that lie within the services offered online, like social network services, their own behaviour and the behaviour of people with a sexual interest in children in terms of harmful conduct, they are vulnerable and may become victims of sexual abuse. How many children are targeted or become victims in the online environment and the dynamics of children's own behaviour and that of the perpetrators is only to a certain extent known (European Commission, 2008).

Risks for, and negative impacts on, children online can result from being exposed to *illegal content, harmful conduct* and *harmful content* (European Commission, 2008):

- *Illegal content* is defined by national law. Illegal content is primarily dealt with by law enforcement agencies, prosecuting offenders and bringing them to trial. The main type of illegal content, which falls under our scope, is child abuse material.
- *Harmful conduct* includes conduct preparatory to committing a sexual offence against a child by contacting them online (grooming) and harassment happening in the online environment (cyber-bullying). The preparatory acts for committing sexual offences are not, as such, yet considered as an offence in most European countries, but grooming is a criminal offence in the UK and in an increasing number of other countries.
- *Harmful content* is content, which parents, caretakers, teachers and other adults responsible for children consider to be harmful for them. The conception of what is harmful also varies across countries and cultures. A variety of means exist to deal with harmful content, such as enforcement of legal provisions where they exist.

This chapter represents a knowledge enhancement effort in law enforcement. According to the European Commission (2008) knowledge enhancement projects are important projects within the general field of safer Internet and online technologies in electronic government. The aim of such projects is to strengthen the knowledge base relevant to police work, law enforcement work and government work in general. Specifically, our project aims to enhance the knowledge of online-related sexual abuse and victimisation, in particular online grooming. Grooming is the process by which a person befriends a child with the intention of committing sexual abuse.

Stages of growth models

Stages of growth models have been used widely in both organisational research and management research. According to King and Teo (1997) these models describe a wide variety of phenomena – the organisational life cycle, product life cycle, biological growth, etc. These models assume that predictable patterns (conceptualised in terms of stages) exist in the growth of organisations, the sales levels of products and the growth of living organisms. These stages:

- are sequential in nature
- occur as a hierarchical progression that is not easily reversed
- evolve a broad range of organisational activities and structures

Benchmark variables are often used to indicate characteristics in each stage of growth. A one-dimensional continuum is established for each benchmark variable. The measurement of benchmark variables can be carried out using Guttman scales (Frankfort-Nachmias and Nachmias, 2002). Guttman scaling is a cumulative scaling technique based on ordering theory that suggests a linear relationship between the elements of a domain and the items on a test.

Various multistage models have been proposed for organisational evolution over time. For example, Nolan (1979) introduced a model with six stages for information technology maturity in organisations, which later was expanded to nine stages. Earl (2000) suggested a stage of growth model for evolving the e-business, consisting of the following six stages: external communication, internal communication, e-commerce, e-business, e-enterprise, and transform-ation, while Rao and Metts (2003) describe a stage model for electronic commerce development in small and medium sized enterprises. In the area of knowledge management, Housel and Bell (2001) developed a five level model. In the area of knowledge management systems, Dean and Gottschalk (2007) present a four-stage model applied to knowledge management in law enforcement. Gottschalk and Tolloczko (2007) developed a maturity model for mapping crime in law enforcement, while Gottschalk and Solli-Sæther (2006) developed a maturity model for IT outsourcing relationships, and Gottschalk (2009) presented maturity levels for interoperability in digital government. Each of these models identifies certain characteristics that typify firms in different stages of growth. Among these multistage models, models with four stages seem to have been proposed and tested most frequently.

A recent example is a stages of growth model for corrupt organisations, where the four-stage model proposed by Pfarrer et al. (2008) is concerned with organisational actions that potentially increase the speed and likelihood that an organisation will restore its legitimacy with stakeholders following a transgression. The four stages are labelled discovery, explanation, penance, and rehabilitation respectively.

The concept of stages of growth has been widely employed for many years. Already two decades ago, Kazanjian and Drazin (1989) found that a number of multistage models have been proposed, which assume that predictable patterns exist in the growth of organisations, and that these patterns unfold as discrete time periods best thought of as stages. These models have different distinguishing characteristics. Stages can be driven by the search for new growth opportunities or as a response to internal crises. Some models suggest that organisations progress through stages while others argue that there may be multiple paths through the stages.

Kazanjian (1988) applied dominant problems to stages of growth. Dominant problems imply that there is a pattern of primary concerns that firms face for each theorised stage. In criminal organisations, for example, dominant problems can shift from lack of skills to lack of resources to lack of strategy associated with different stages of growth, as suggested by Gottschalk (2008) in his stage model for organised crime.

Kazanjian and Drazin (1989) argue that either implicitly or explicitly, stages of growth models share a common underlying logic. Organisations undergo transformations in their design characteristics, which enable them to face the new tasks or problems that growth elicits. The problems, tasks or environments may differ from model to model, but almost all suggest that stages emerge in a well-defined sequence, so that the solution of one set of problems or tasks leads to the emergence of a new set of problems and tasks, that the organisation must address.

Online grooming offence

In the UK, the sexual offences act clarifies the position with regard to sexual abuse of children, outlining several distinct offence categories (Davidson, 2008):

- rape and other sexual offences against children under 13 years
- child sex offences (which includes the new offence of 'meeting a child following sexual grooming')
- abuse of position of trust
- familial child sex offences
- production and collection of indecent photographs of children
- abuse of children through prostitution and pornography

Meeting a child following sexual grooming applies to the Internet, other technologies such as mobile phones and to the real world as well. Grooming involves a process of socialisation during which an offender seeks to interact with a child (and sometimes the child's family) possibly sharing their hobbies, interests and computer slang in an attempt to gain trust in order to prepare them for sexual abuse. The process may also involve an attempt to persuade a child that sexual relations between adults and children are acceptable.

Sex offenders use the Internet to target and groom children for the purposes of sexual abuse, to produce and/or download indecent illegal images of children for distribution, and to communicate with other sex offenders. Internet sex offender behaviour includes (Davidson, 2007):

- construction of sites to be used for the exchange of offender and victim information
- experiences and indecent images of children
- organisation of criminal activities that seek to use children for prostitution purposes
- production of indecent images of children at a professional level
- organisation of criminal activities that promote sexual tourism

The demand for indecent images through, for example, the use of file-sharing technologies, has expanded so much that law enforcement agencies are finding it difficult to identify and track down all child victims and the perpetrators involved. Possible motivations of online child sex abusers are many. It is suggested that sex offenders perceive the Internet as a means of generating an immediate solution to their fantasies. Factors including presumed anonymity, interactivity and ready accessibility might encourage offenders to go online. The unique structure of the Internet may play a major role in facilitating online child abuse. Offenders' Internet use is not limited to abuse; the Internet often plays a significant role in other areas of their lives.

Typologies of Internet child sex offenders have been developed to guide the work of police officers. One typology does include those offenders targeting and grooming children online, a group largely excluded from other typologies. For example, nine categories of offenders might be identified (Krone, 2004):

- **The browser** is an offender who accidentally comes across indecent images and saves them.
- **The dreamer** applies fantasy to digital image.
- **The networker** is an offender engaging in exchange with others.
- **The collector** looks for indecent images in open search to update his collection.
- **The member** belongs to an online, hidden paedophile network.
- **The connector** targets children via peer-to-peer technology and chat rooms.
- **The abuser** enjoys images of their own abuse.
- **The producer** records sexual abuse of children.
- **The distributor** is an offender who distributes indecent images for financial gain or as part of their collecting behaviour.

Child pornography represents indecent images. However, what is 'indecent' differs among legislations, and it is often left to the courts to decide. In some countries a jury has to decide. The jury is shown the images and asked to consider whether they believe they were indecent images of children. Traditionally, definitions of child pornography emphasise the sexual nature of the representation and, as such, seek to distinguish child pornography from innocent images of children (Gillespie, 2005).

The definition of grooming in the UK legislation is such that (Davidson, 2008):

- The offence only applies to adults over 18.
- There must be a meeting with the victim.
- The communication can take place anywhere in the world.
- The offender must either meet the child or travel to the prearranged meeting.
- The meeting or at least part of the travel must take place within the jurisdiction.
- The person must have an intention to commit any offence under the sexual offences act or any act which would be an offence in the jurisdiction. This may be evident from the previous communications or other circumstances: for example, an offender travels in possession of ropes, condoms or lubricants.
- The child under 16 and the adult does not reasonably believe that the child is over 16. However, if this is not the case, for example, the child's place has been taken by an undercover police officer, an attempt could be charged.

In sentencing under the sexual grooming category, judges are advised to consider the following aggravating case circumstances (Davidson, 2008):

- the seriousness of the intended offence (which will affect both the offender's culpability and the degree of risk to which the victim has been exposed)
- the degree to which the offence was planned
- the sophistication of the grooming
- the determination of the offender
- how close the offender came to success
- the reason why the offender did not succeed, that is, was it a change of mind or did someone or something prevent the offender from continuing
- any physical or psychological injury suffered by the victim

Stages of online offenders

While most stages of growth models are concerned with the organisational level, this research is concerned with the individual level. In the following, we propose a stage of growth model for online grooming offenders. Our model represents a stage hypothesis for offenders. The idea of stages of growth is that it might be assumed that the offender starts at stage 1 and over time develops into higher and more serious stages. This assumes that an offender found to be at stage 4, was at a lower stage some years ago.

The model suggests escalation to more serious contact offending over time. This model suggests a possible link between the possession and collection of indecent child images and the propensity for contact abuse. Given the lack of empirical evidence in this area, the development of any stage of growth model must be tentative. The work of Hernandez (2009) suggests a link, whilst Seto's (2009) research is less conclusive. There is, however, some evidence of escalation from relatively minor offences, including indecent exposure, to serious contact offences in the general sex offender literature (Finkelhor, 1984) which is pertinent here. The stage of growth model presents a possible behavioural movement or escalation from the use of indecent images of children towards contact abuse. It is not suggested that all Internet sex offenders will follow this route and categories are not mutually exclusive, however the model offers one possible offending route or 'pathway' (Ward and Siegert, 2006).

In this model the offender begins at stage 1 as a user or consumer of online indecent images. These images are used to fuel fantasy. The role of deviant sexual fantasy in fuelling offending is well documented in the sex offender literature and has formed a cornerstone of sex offender treatment programmes in the US and the UK. Over time the offending behaviour escalates into higher and more serious stages facilitated by the Internet and possibly in conjunction with other online abusers.

The stages in the stage model for online grooming offenders are as follows (Figure 2.1):

Stage 1: Online Consumer. This person may start as a browser, who accidentally comes across indecent images and saves them. This is also a person who seeks indecent images and saves them. After a while, such images are purchased via credit card. Indecent images are used to satisfy private fantasies. Digital images are consumed for personal use. As a consumer, the paedophile is mainly concerned with combining image impression and personal fantasy to achieve personal satisfaction. Indecent images are used to satisfy personal fantasies and such offenders will have an existing sexual attraction to children. Consumption of indecent images of children on the Internet is the main activity of the abuser. In some cases, the person has experienced prior contact abuse. Some offenders may stop at Level 1, while others may progress to Level 2.

According to Davidson (2007), sex offenders use the Internet to access indecent images of children, to select victims for abuse and to communicate with other sex offenders. This activity has expanded so much that law enforcement agencies have difficulties tracking down child victims and perpetrators involved.

According to Kierkegaard (2008) about thirty thousand Internet users are viewing pornography every second. The Internet is aiding sex offenders, stalkers, child pornographers, child traffickers and others with the intent of exploiting children. Child pornography is defined in Norwegian criminal law as the sexual presentation of real children in images (Skybak, 2004).

The online consumer at Stage 1 is similar to Krone's (2004) *browser*, who uses indecent images to satisfy private fantasies (Wortley and Smallbone, 2006).

Stage 2: Online Communicator. This person searches indecent images through open browsers and may engage in some networking. Also, this person looks for indecent images in open areas of the Internet such as chat rooms and peer-to-peer networks and may engage in some networking. As a communicator, the person might communicate with other paedophiles and potential victims. For example, the person may both exchange and trade in indecent images with men who share the same interest. Here we find collection of certain images (same victim time and same level of seriousness).

According to Kierkegaard (2008) Internet bulletin boards, chat rooms, private websites, and peer-to-peer networks are being used daily by paedophiles to meet unsuspecting children. Teenagers are especially vulnerable because they are often trusting, naive, curious, adventuresome, and eager for attention and affection.

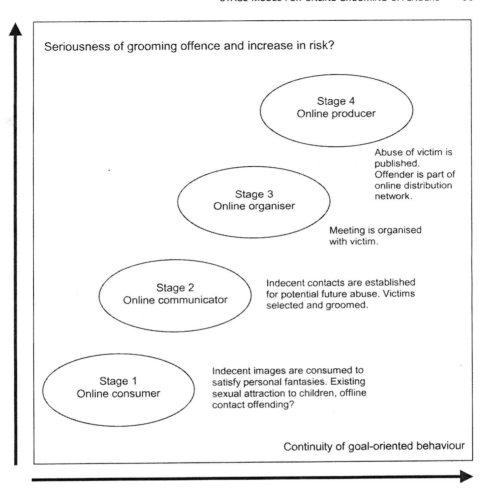

Figure 2.1   Stages of online grooming

Online sex offences and online contacts leading to offline sex offences against children in Sweden were studied by Bra (2007). In a school survey of a representative Swedish sample aged 15, 31 per cent reported online sexual contact from someone they 'know or believe is an adult' over the past 12 months (46 per cent of girls, 16 per cent of boys).

The online communicator at Stage 2 is similar to Krone's (2004) *trawler*, who searches for indecent images through open browsers and may engage in some networking. It is also similar to Krone's (2004) *non-secure collector*, who looks for indecent images in open areas of the Internet such as chat rooms (Wortley and Smallbone, 2006). It is entirely possible that the online communicator has already committed offline contact offences.

Stage 3: Online Organiser. This person uses peer-to-peer technology, interactive Internet games and chat rooms to organise meetings. The person is grooming online for the purposes of abuse. If not, the person remains an indecent image user at a lower stage. If a meeting is organised, personal sexual abuse of the child or children is the goal. Here we find online also, that abuse is ongoing with family children or other children known to the offender.

According to Wolak *et al.* (2008) most Internet-initiated sex crimes involve adult men who use the Internet to meet and seduce underage adolescents into sexual encounters. The offenders use Internet communications such as instant messages, e-mail and chat rooms to organise meetings and develop intimate relationships with victims.

'Stian 15' is one of the few offenders caught in Norway in recent years. Twenty-two per cent of all Norwegian children between nine and 16 years (about 70,000 children) have met someone on the Internet. Most of these meetings were with persons of their own age and occurred without any problems. However, in some cases the children meet adults who claimed to be children on the Internet. Only ten per cent of those children who have gone to such meetings report that they experienced anything unpleasant in terms of words or physical abuse. It is mostly girls of 15–16 years who have unpleasant experiences. Most of those children who have unpleasant experiences in terms of physical or psychological abuse at such meetings with adults, report that they are dissatisfied with friends, school or their own family. Most of them have parents born in a country other than Norway. A total of 6,000 children aged nine to 16 years had unpleasant experiences at meetings following Internet contact in 2006 in Norway (Justis, 2007).

The online organiser at Stage 3 is similar to Krone's (2004) *groomer*, who target, and groom, children via peer-to-peer technology, interactive Internet games and chat rooms. These offenders may send indecent images to children as part of the grooming process and become what Krone (2004) labels *physical abusers*, who have an interest in indecent images as part of their fantasy cycle. These offenders may photograph their abusive behaviour for their own use (Wortley and Smallbone, 2006).

Stage 4: Online Producer. This person records the sexual abuse of children for the purposes of distribution to networks and to satisfy their own fantasy. Also, the person may distribute indecent images and contact details either for financial gain or as part of an exchange relationship. The person may expand into a more business-focused role by use of children for prostitution and by promoting sexual tourism as part of a larger personal fantasy scheme.

Twenty-five male members of an Internet criminal organisation called 'Fun Club' were arrested, mainly fathers who photographed or filmed with web cameras as they abused their daughters, aged between two and 14 years. One father had contacted Sergio Marzola, an Italian producer of child pornography, and offered 250 Euros for his daughter to be filmed dressed in paedophile lingerie, 500 Euros to film her naked and 750 Euros for him to rape one of them (Croy, 2006). Sergio Marzola is an example of an offender at Stage 4 being an online producer. He had his own photo studios where he abused children whom he first contacted on the Internet. In his photo studio in Ukraine, many poor children were abused. Before he was arrested, he managed thirty Internet sites intended for the exchange of child pornography.

A 51-year-old man was sentenced to 60 years in prison in the US. He had videotaped himself sexually abusing three children under six. A laptop computer was seized and was found to contain over 16,000 images and over 1,000 video files depicting children – many of whom were between the ages of two and ten years – being sexually assaulted. The suspect admitted to sexually assaulting the children. He pleaded guilty to manufacturing child sexual abuse images in a Federal court and was sentenced to 60 years in US Federal prison, without parole, the highest possible sentence under Federal law (IWF, 2007).

The online producer at Stage 4 is similar to Krone's (2004) secure collector who belongs to an online hidden paedophile network. These offenders are highly organised, likely to be collectors and employ sophisticated security to conceal their offending (Wortley and Smallbone, 2006).

A typical offender at Stage 2 (online communicator) potentially developing into higher stages (online organiser and online producer) is described by O'Connell (2003) as follows, where 'the child' is an adult:

'The 'child' is befriended by another chat room user who claims to be slightly older than the child and to have similar likes and dislikes. These similarities are discerned throughout the course of a conversation about music, sports, computers etc. These topics can be discussed during one on-line conversation or the process may span a number of on-line encounters, which can occur over a number of days, weeks or even months. The duration of the 'friendship-forming' stage can vary quite a bit but the effect is the creation of a shared virtual friendship. Typically, the 'virtual friend' presents him or herself as slightly older in age than 'the child' and therefore often assumes the role of advisor, confidant or teacher who guides a child toward increasing his or her self-knowledge and self-confidence. Naturally 'the child' feels comfortable confiding with this 'virtual friend', because the 'virtual friend' understands and often proclaims a 'deep love' for 'the child'. When the virtual friend begins to ask 'the child' about issues relating to sexuality, sexual development or sexual experiences, the child may not interpret these questions as a deviation from mutuality. It is important to recognise the psychological dynamics underpinning the shift in the tone of a conversation into these realms, which serves a number of functions for an alleged paedophile. It seems reasonable to suggest that this kind of conversation is sexually titillating for an adult with a sexual interest in children. Furthermore, the conversation serves to prime the child for the sexual suggestions which typically follow these introductory remarks. In addition, the disclosures 'the child' makes in response to such requests for intimate insights into the 'child's' developing sexuality serves to lure the child into an emotionally abusive arena, which they may feel complicit in creating. It seems reasonable to suggest that similar to off-line paedophile grooming practices, the typical net result is that a child feels unable to inform a responsible person about the on-line activities because of a mixture of shame and guilt. The adult with a sexual interest in children may engage in these activities for any number of reasons and may choose to disengage at any number of points. The adult may simply engage in these activities out of curiosity, to hone his grooming skills, or for masturbatory

purposes. Alternatively, the adult with a sexual interest in children may wish to meet the young child in the real world and the encounters may escalate to an off-line meeting. The incidence and outcomes of these meetings have been well documented by the press over the course of the last year. Therefore, it seems reasonable to suggest that there is a need to educate children to be able to detect these shifts in conversation. These activities are very similar to off-line grooming practices except the child often has far fewer cues with which to discern the identity of the person with whom they are conversing.'

O'Connell, 2003

However, O'Connell's (2003) sample was small, and police officers dealing with hundreds of 'hits' every week tend to have a somewhat different story to tell. For example, police officers working as under cover children in High Tech Crime Units in the UK have suggested that Internet grooming can be and often is different from 'real world' grooming in that offenders spend little time chatting and will come straight to the point, sometimes instantly, for example 'would you like to meet for sex'. This would suggest that the Internet might act to remove inhibitions associated with face-to-face contact (Davidson, 2007).

Potentially dangerous contacts through the Internet with strangers are intriguing to many children. Even the appearance of a meeting suggestion is often not treated as something that could cause anxiety. Sometimes it even inspires imagination. It is more alarming to children when the Internet interlocutor wants to learn specific personal details such as name, surname and address. Most children know that they are not supposed to provide such information. The exception is if the person they are talking to has a web cam. This is often the proof they need that the person is who they say they are (MMI, 2007).

This finding from Norway by MMI (2007) was included in a pan-European qualitative study Eurobarometer (2007) covering 29 European countries, where children of 9–10 and 12–14 years old were interviewed in-depth about their use of online technologies. In the interviews, the children were told a story of a young person of their age who, after putting their profile online on the Internet and gradually giving personal details, had established a relationship with someone unknown.

The participants were asked to react to this story. One Danish boy responded (Eurobarometer, 2007: 47).

I met him at a station and then it was an old, nasty, 44 year old man. Then I walked away! I have never told my parents about it! They would get angry. It might have consequences. I might have my mobile phone taken from me.

In almost all groups, in a large majority of the European countries, the study collected a number of personal anecdotes like this one. These anecdotes attested to real, potentially dangerous contacts. It therefore seems that some children adopt more risky behaviour than they say and think they do. In particular, young people aged 12 to 14 can show themselves to be very confident – both in their own insight in unmasking false identities and interlocutors who are especially 'friendly' towards them. They are reluctant to warn their parents.

Offender-related perspectives on online victimisation of children include:

- understanding the ways in which sexual abuse is caused with the help of online technologies
- understanding how offenders use online technologies to find and target children
- the changing nature of grooming behaviour
- the link between consumption of child abuse material and contact sexual abuse
- the changing profiles of online child abusers

European Commission, 2008

It is very difficult to identify key stages in the grooming process as the case files we have seen on these men demonstrate very different approaches and style. However, it could be that we just have not seen enough of these men (no women yet) to be sure about their behaviour, and that is why we think our proposed stage hypothesis is so important.

According to Seto and Eke (2005), the likelihood that child pornography offenders will later commit a contact sexual offence is unknown. In their study, a sample of 201 adult male child pornography offenders were identified. 56 per cent of the sample had a prior criminal record, 24 per cent had prior contact sexual offences, and 15 per cent had prior child pornography offences.

It is important to stress here that stages of growth models are very different from life cycle models. While stage models define and describe accumulated progression and escalation by online groomers, life cycle models represent a cycle of birth, growth, decline, and eventually death of paedophiles.

In future research there is a need to validate the stage model both theoretically and empirically. Furthermore, there is a need for benchmark variables that will have different content for different stages. In the current paper, the stages are lacking both theoretical background and practical situations. While stage 4 may seem understandable and viable, the remaining stages are in need of further conceptual work. Core questions in future research will be whether consumer, communicator, organiser, and producer are valid, practicable, and accountable.

In future research, pros (strengths) and cons (weaknesses) to the suggested model have to be taken into account. We need to provide a more critical analysis of a stage model such as the one suggested. It is not at all intuitively obvious to all readers that the progression over time is from consumer, via communicator and organiser, to producer. Why not communicator, consumer, organiser, and producer; or producer via organiser and communicator to consumer? Thus, the conceptual research presented in here is lacking empirical evidence. Only a questionnaire based on Guttman scaling rather than Likert scaling can verify the suggested sequence or alternatively identify another sequence.

The important contribution of this chapter, however, is the introduction of the stage hypothesis to our understanding of online grooming behaviour. Rather than thinking of online grooming behaviours in terms of alternative strategies, we suggest an evolutionary approach where the future is building on the past, rather than the future being a divergent path from the past. Rather than thinking that what was done in the past is wrong, the past actions are the only available foundation for future actions. If past actions are not on the path to success, direction is changed without history being reversed when online groomers are developing their strategy.

Police investigations

While the expansion of the Internet and the proliferation of information technology has created new opportunities for those who engage in illegal activities (Taylor and Quayle, 2003) the area of digital forensics has grown rapidly as well (Ferraro and Casey, 2005). This has helped in the discovery of new ways of criminal activities. According to Davidson (2007) sex offenders use the Internet to access indecent images of children, to select victims for abuse and to communicate with other sex offenders. This activity has expanded so much that law enforcement agencies have difficulty tracking down child victims and perpetrators unless they have the capability of professional digital forensics and intelligence (Smith, 2008).

Rapid growth of the Internet and advances in technology mean enormous benefits to society and children should be able to enjoy the benefits that the Internet offers safely. However, it is necessary to recognise that with the spread of the Internet comes the growth in the possibility of the system being abused by sex offenders; making contact with children with intent to groom the youngsters through chat rooms and social Internet sites (Davidson, 2007).

Dealing with illegal content, on the one hand, and harmful content, on the other, may require using different methods, strategies and tools. However, some tools can be used for all categories. For instance, awareness raising can be used in respect to illegal content and harmful conduct (crime prevention) as well as for harmful content (European Commission, 2008).

Successful cyber crime investigations require computer skills and modern systems in policing. Furthermore, modern information systems in policing with access to all relevant electronic information sources require a modern electronic government. Digital government infrastructure must be in place to support the breadth and depth of all government activities, including computer forensics in cyber crime investigations by law enforcement agencies.

Online victimisation of children is a global issue in need of international law enforcement solutions. This is particularly true for illegal content. Material depicting child sexual abuse may be produced in one country, hosted in a second, and accessed and downloaded all over the world. Commercial payment systems operating worldwide may be used to fund sale and purchase of the images (European Commission, 2008).

Digital forensics is the art and science of applying computer science to aid the legal process. It is more than the technological, systematic inspection of electronic systems and their contents for evidence or supportive evidence of a criminal act. Digital forensics requires specialised expertise and tools. As a term, digital forensics refers to the study of technology, the way criminals use it, and the way to extract and examine digital evidence (Ferraro and Casey, 2005).

Digital forensics is an approach to identifying evidence from computers that can be used in trials. A typical forensics investigation consists of two main phases, exploration and evidence, respectively. During the exploration phase, investigators attempt to identify the nature of the problem and what exactly happened or is expected to happen at the crime scene. The evidence phase takes place after the exploration has been concluded. It consists of accumulating all documentation which will work in court.

From a data viewpoint, this two-phase procedure can be broken down into six stages: preparation, incident response, data collection, data analysis, presentation of findings, and incident closure. Some of these stages may be so complex in certain circumstances that they are divided into sub-stages. The most time-consuming tasks in digital forensics investigation are searching, extracting, and analysing. Therefore, there is a need for a forensics model that allows formalisation of the digital forensics process, innovative data mining techniques for the forensics process, and a dedicated infrastructure for digital forensics.

Mitchell et al. (2005) explored the extent and effectiveness of proactive investigations in which investigators pose as minors on the Internet to catch potential sex offenders. Results suggest that proactive investigations represented a significant proportion (25 per cent) of all arrests for Internet sex crimes against minors. The online person as assumed by investigators paralleled the ages and genders of real young people victimised in sex crimes that started as online encounters.

Paedophile progression

Contrary to common wisdom, Wolak et al. (2008) argue that most Internet sex offenders are not adults who target young children by posing as another youth, luring children to meeting, and then abducting or forcibly raping them. Rather, most online offenders are adults who target teens and seduce victims into sexual relationships. This is supported in the Norwegian findings, where mainly fifteen and sixteen year-old-girls have unpleasant experiences in terms of physical or psychological abuse at such meetings with adults (Justis, 2007).

While this chapter presents a stage model where it is assumed that many paedophiles move from one stage to the next over time, several researchers have developed typologies which implicitly seem to indicate an underlying stage hypothesis. An example is O'Connell (2004a) who developed a typology of child cyber exploitation and online grooming practices. Her typology really represents stages: friendship-forming stage, relationship forming stage, risk assessment stage, exclusivity stage, and sexual stage.

Only future research can validate the stage hypothesis presented in this paper. Empirical studies are needed to evaluate developmental behaviour by offenders over time.

A stage model for offender behaviour in victimisation of children was presented in this section. By identifying development and escalation in individual abuse, social and law enforcement authorities may gain new insights into contingent approaches. Future empirical research is needed to validate and potentially revise the suggested model.

3

Insights into Online Sex Offending and Offenders

This chapter further explores perpetrators' online behaviour. It is clear that the Internet is more than just a medium of communication. It constitutes a new virtual reality, or a cyber world, with its own rules and its own language. It provides a supportive context within which the child sexual abuser is no longer a lonely figure, but forms part of a larger community that shares the same interests. The Internet gives new meaning to the term 'paedophile ring', as the potential for offenders to organise to abuse children is so considerable. It might be argued that peer-to-peer file sharing facilitates the most extreme, aggressive and reprehensible types of behaviour that the Internet will allow.

In Japan, child prostitution and child pornography are matters of growing concern and the Law for Punishing Acts Related to Child Prostitution and Child Pornography was enacted in 1999. In 2003 alone 7,304 juveniles were victimised, of which 1,731 were obvious cases of child prostitution, about 12 per cent of which involved the use of telephone clubs, and 46 per cent were related to online services. Telephone clubs have their shops in amusement quarters. Men are invited into a cell with a telephone and receive phone calls from girls outside at a rate of a few thousand yen per hour. To urge girls to make these calls, telephone clubs distribute small gifts with their phone number to girls on the street. According to Higuchi (2008) many girls making calls to telephone clubs out of curiosity have subsequently become victims of sexual offences.

In Japan, most online dating services are fee-charging websites paid by cellular phone. Individuals exchange their own profile through the sites and search for a partner who suits their taste. According to Higuchi (2008) many victims have suffered in the same way as through telephone clubs. The number of victimised girls taken from online dating services is on the increase in Japan, where 18 per cent of the girls in high school have used online dating services and 47 per cent of these girls met a partner whom they got to know through the Internet services.

Paedophiles explore new Internet arenas all the time to target young victims. A new example emerged in Norway in 2009. It was a game site for children with the web address jippii.no as shown in Figure 3.1 The moderator of jippii.no told Ruud (2009) that adult men search for young sex partners on this site. Men show up on the game page and expose themselves naked in front of their web cameras. They try to get young girls to undress in front of their cameras.

Figure 3.1   Paedophiles in Norway expose themselves naked on this site for children games

Understanding online grooming

The Internet represents an attractive medium for grooming and soliciting youth for sexual encounters:

> It provides access to countless children in a relatively anonymous environment. An online predator can masquerade as a young person with similar background, age and interests. Further, the cyber predator can join with the young person in the disinhibition process and encourage discussion of sexual fantasies at too early an age. The purpose of this dialogue might be to play out sexual deviant fantasies. However, the purpose might also be to desensitise the young person to child-adult sexual activity, with the ultimate goal of perpetrating offline.
>
> Dombrowski et al., 2007: 155

Unwanted sexual solicitations are defined as requests to engage in sexual activities or sexual talk or give personal sexual information that are unwanted or, whether wanted or not, made by an adult. Online harassment episodes are defined as threats or other offensive behaviour (not sexual solicitation) sent online to the youth or posted online about the youth for others to see (Mitchell et al., 2008).

The criminal paedophiles are using the Internet to solicit sexually explicit images of young people. Internet bulletin boards, chat rooms, private websites and peer-to-peer networks are being used daily by paedophiles to meet unsuspecting children:

> The misuse of the Internet for pornography, cyber bullying, grooming and paedophilia has become a major issue of international concern. Because of the freedom and the anonymous environment offered by the Internet, child molesters and pornographers are increasingly using the Internet to further their criminal activity.

Kierkegaard, 2008: 41

The tactic of grooming, where paedophile criminals contact children and gain their trust for the purpose of meeting them and engaging in sexual behaviour, consists of a wide spectrum of approaches. The Internet enables paedophiles to entice multiple victims at once. Aside from chat rooms, grooming is facilitated through mobiles, email exchange, blogs and other types of social networking sites where offenders can create their own social contents and make it accessible to potential victims (Kierkegaard, 2008).

According to Quayle et al. there is increasing evidence that people use the Internet to avoid negative emotional states, such as boredom, anxiety, or depression:

> This may be of increasing relevance for sex offenders. While the primary function of accessing the Internet for sex offenders is to obtain material that aids sexual arousal, the Internet functions to help people address some of the more immediate feelings of distress or dissatisfaction in their lives. For those with a sexual interest in children, once online, offenders can download child pornography and masturbate to such images, providing a highly rewarding or reinforcing context for further avoidance. The intensity of such behaviour often has properties that offenders call 'addictive', with high levels of activity associated with the avoidance of unpleasant emotional states.

Quayle et al., 2006: 1

An online groomer is someone who has initiated online contact with a child with the intention of establishing a sexual relationship involving cyber sex or physical sex. A groomer is a kind of traveller, in that he uses the Internet to gain access to a child whom he coerces into meeting him for sexual purposes. Quayle et al. phrased the question 'Who are these people?' in relation to child pornography:

> We have no idea of the numbers of people who offend on the Internet. We can examine conviction rates, but these reflect only the countries where possession and distribution of child pornography is both illegal and where there are either the resources or inclination to act upon detection.

Quayle et al., 2008: 27

It has been estimated that there are between 50,000 and 100,000 paedophiles involved in organised pornography rings around the world, and that one-third of these operate from the

United States. In the US, law enforcement made 3,000 arrests in one year for Internet sex crimes against minors. These crimes were categorised into three mutually exclusive types:

- Internet crimes against identified victims (39 per cent)
- Internet solicitations to undercover law enforcement (25 per cent)
- possession, distribution or trading of child pornography with no identified victim (36 per cent)

Two-thirds of offenders who committed any of the types of Internet sex crimes against minors possessed child pornography (Quayle *et al.*, 2008).

There are a number of grooming practices on the Internet. Victim selection methods vary, and the groomer may go through the following grooming phases (O'Connell, 2004b):

1. *Friendship-forming phase* involves the paedophile getting to know the child. The length of time spent at this phase varies from one paedophile to another and the number of times this stage of the relationship is re-enacted depends upon the level of contact the paedophile maintains with a child.
2. *Relationship-forming phase* is an extension of the friendship-forming phase, and during this phase the adult may engage with the child in discussing, for example, school and/or home life. Not all adults engage in this phase but generally those who are going to maintain contact with a child will endeavour to create an illusion of being the child's best friend.
3. *Risk assessment phase* refers to the part of the conversation when a paedophile will ask the child about, for example, the location of the computer the child is using and the number of other people who use the computer. By gathering this kind of information it seems reasonable to suppose that the paedophile is trying to assess the likelihood of his activities being detected by, for example, the child's parents, guardians, or older siblings.
4. *Exclusivity phase* typically follows risk assessment phase where the content of the conversation changes so that the child is invited to reveal personal problems in the context of a private conversation. The interactions take on the characteristics of a strong sense of mutuality, where secrets are shared.
5. *Sexual phase* is introduced after the adult has positioned the conversation so that a deep sense of shared trust seems to have been established. It is during this phase that most distinctive differences in conversational patterns occur. For those adults who intend to maintain a relationship with a child and for whom it seems to be important to maintain the child's perception of a sense of trust and love having been created between child and adult, the sexual phase will be entered gently. The relational framing orchestrated by the adult is for the child to perceive the adult as a mentor and possible future lover.

Dombrowski *et al.* (2007) argue that the full extent of technology used by sex offenders remains largely unknown. There are a wide range of Internet technologies that are reasonably accessible to online sex offenders. Website portals and internetworked synchronous chat are two examples of technological resources that sex offenders have access to and employ in online grooming.

Like many criminals, paedophiles try to decriminalise or normalise their crimes. They say they are misunderstood. Paedophiles are trying to eliminate the world 'paedophile' and replace it with the more positive term 'boy lover', 'girl lover' or 'child lover'. Rather than use the word 'victims', paedophiles refer to 'young friends', which is what they call the children that they are either grooming for sexual abuse or actually molesting. Suggesting that they are 'friends' with the child places the abusive relationship on an even footing, establishing equality between the sexual abuser and the child that does not exist.

Paedophiles want to have sex with children, but that is illegal, so they seek to promote a child's right to have sex with them. One point of most paedophile agendas is a belief that there are children who want to have sex with adults.

Profiling online groomers

Offender profiling is a well-known task within police science (Tong, 2007; Walker, 2005) and there is even profiling software available (Rich and Shively, 2004). In forensic science techniques, police apply DNA profiling and other sophisticated methods in criminal and offender profiling. Criminal profiling is concerned with the process of inferring distinctive personality characteristics for committing criminal acts (Turvey, 1999). This process has also been referred to — among many other less common terms — as behavioural profiling, crime-scene profiling, criminal-personality profiling, offender profiling, and psychological profiling. The history of profiling reveals terms like psychological profiling, criminal profiling, criminal personality profiling, criminal investigative analysis, and behavioural evidence analysis. Some of these terms are used almost interchangeably to describe a similar process of coming up with a profile of a likely perpetrator of a crime. The FBI used to apply the term psychological profiling but now call what they do in the profiling arena criminal investigative analysis.

As well as terminological differences, there are also definitional differences in regard to what exactly does the term profiling mean. A selection of definitions of profiling is offered below by several writers at the time to depict the concept of profiling (Dean and Gottschalk, 2007):

- *Psychological profile* is an educated attempt to provide investigative agencies with specific information as to the type of individual who committed a certain crime.
- *Profile analysis* is the identification of the major personality and behavioural characteristics of an individual based upon an analysis of the crimes he or she has committed.
- *Criminal personality* profiling is the process of analysing various aspects of violent crime to derive a set of hypotheses about the characteristics of an unknown assailant.
- *Offender profiling* is an approach to police investigations whereby an attempt is made to deduce a description of an unknown offender based on evaluating minute details of the crime scene, the victim, and other available evidence. Offender profiling is commonly associated with inferring characteristics of an offender from the actions at a crime scene.
- *Offender profile* is based on the premise that the proper identification of crime scene evidence can indicate the personality type of the individual who committed the offence.

The profiling field contains about as many approaches to profiling as there are definitions. However, the task of sorting out approaches becomes a little easier if viewed from the perspective of the nature of the framework or orientation that underpins a particular approach. In broad terms, the profiling field can be divided into two quite distinct orientations based on whether or not a particular approach is based on a more clinical or statistical methodological framework. A brief review of the types of approaches that fit under each of these frameworks or orientations is presented below (Dean and Gottschalk, 2007).

Clinical orientation to profiling

This methodological framework includes profiling approaches that are deemed to be based on a clinical perspective in the construction of a profile. However, this does not mean that each approach has to be practiced by clinicians in the sense of a medical practitioner or similarly allied professional, like a therapist or mental health worker. Rather, the emphasis is that the approach is clinically based in terms of the perspective drawn upon involves a psychological and/or psychiatric knowledge base.

Approaches that rely on a clinical orientation can be subdivided into two distinct groups of profilers. Those that are more investigative-driven and those that are therapy-driven as indicated below:

- *Investigative-driven approaches.* This sub-group of profilers can be grouped as having a general clinical orientation which is more experientially focused and tends to rely on investigative intuition and experience to reconstruct an offender profile from a detailed analysis of the crime scenes. Typically, such profilers are detectives and police investigators like FBI special agents. More recently, the method called Behavioural Evidence Analysis (BEA) fits comfortably within this orientation. BEA does not so much present a new approach but rather is a more sophisticated process of much of the FBI's work without being tied to and therefore hamstrung by the original and simplistic organised/disorganised crime scene typology in the earlier work of the FBI.
- *Therapy-driven approaches.* This sub-group, because of their professional training, takes a more therapeutic insight-oriented approach to profiling. Such profilers are typically forensic psychologists and psychiatrists.

Statistical orientation to profiling

This type of methodological framework is statistically based and hence includes profiling approaches that are deemed to be based on this type of perspective in the construction of a profile. Again, this does not mean that each approach has to be practiced by statisticians or only practitioners who are well versed in the rigors of statistical analysis like psychologists or forensic scientists.

The framework emphasises that an approach is statistically based if it uses various statistical techniques to test hypotheses, model theories, and/or develop databases based on offender populations to augment its knowledge base. For example, the *Investigative Psychology (IP)* approach fits within this statistically based framework. The IP approach uses police records and other data sources to build an empirical database from which to develop theories and test hypotheses.

Approaches that rely on a statistical orientation can be subdivided into two distinct groups of profilers. Those that are more 'database-driven' and those that are 'theory-driven' as indicated below:

- *Database-driven approaches.* One group of researchers use descriptive statistics from police records, interviews, victim and witness statements etc. to develop crime-specific *databases* of likely offender characteristics. The work on Geographic Profiling can be related to this group since, like databases, it is an information management strategy that relies on collecting geographical data on a crime series.
- *Theory-driven approaches.* The other group of researchers is guided more by theories and hence makes specific use of inferential statistics to analyse crime.

The extrapolation of characteristics of criminals from information about their crimes, as an aid to police investigation, is the essence of criminal profiling. Canter and Heritage (1990) proposed that for such extrapolations to be more than educated guesses they must be based upon knowledge of (1) coherent consistencies in criminal behaviour and (2) the relationship those behavioural consistencies have to aspects of an offender available to the police in an investigation. Coherent consistencies are concerned with the behaviour of offenders during a crime having some comprehensible coherence to them.

Criminal profiling is a subcategory of criminal investigative analysis; a term that accounts for several of the services that may be performed by forensic behavioural specialists. These services are said to include: indirect personality assessment, equivocal death analysis, trial strategy, and criminal profiling. The profiling community is made up of professionals and non-professionals from a variety of related and unrelated backgrounds (Turvey, 1999).

Dean and Gottschalk (2007) argue that profiling and cross check approaches in police investigations are examples of law enforcement work that can benefit from technologies such as artificial intelligence, knowledge-based systems and case-based reasoning (Becerra-Fernandez *et al.*, 2004). Artificial intelligence (AI) is an area of computer science that endeavours to build machines exhibiting human-like cognitive capabilities.

Assessing internet sex offenders

Sullivan and Beech (2004) applied the following assessment tools when assessing Internet sex offenders: actuarial assessment approaches, psychometric evaluation, clinical assessment, offence analysis, victim existence assessment, and fantasy deviance evaluation.

Actuarial assessment seeks to identify a risk categorisation for an individual offender based upon the characteristics they have in common with re-offending sex offenders. Often based upon study groups of convicted sex offenders, these assessment tools attempt to identify the common characteristics of sex offenders.

Psychometric assessment seeks to examine the key aspects of a perpetrator's personality, which research has shown contributes to sexual offending. This is achieved through an examination of their stated attitudes and responses to self-reported questionnaires.

Clinical assessment seeks to determine the nature of any risk posed by the offender and highlight the treatment needs specific to that individual. The cognitive behavioural approach to sex offender treatment is generally regarded as the most effective.

Offence assessment lets the offender give his account of the offence. If the assessment is undertaken in a group, as is the more common approach, other participants and professional involved will then examine the account identifying justifications, distortions and the manner in which the victim is portrayed.

Victim existence assessment is particularly relevant to the Internet sex offender. Many Internet sex offenders will deny they have sexually abused anyone by looking at images which have been created and uploaded by others. Paedophiles' perception of victim existence, awareness and empathy is assessed here.

Fantasy deviance assessment seeks to identify desires to sexually offend. If an individual repeatedly masturbates to images of children, the adult is sexually aroused by children. However, it is not only sex offenders who fantasise about deviant sex.

In addition, there is *polygraph* and *screening*. Often referred to as a lie detector, the polygraph has just begun to feature in the assessment of sex offenders in the UK. There are a number of computer based assessment programmes in terms of screening, that are based on the assumption that when presented with a series of images, men spend longer looking at images they find sexually attractive (Sullivan and Beech, 2004).

An obvious target for assessment with sexual offenders is their sexual interest and the degree to which there may be a deviant pattern underlying their behaviour. Hammond (2004) argues that a psychiatric classification of such offending, particularly paedophilia, may be useful here in that the symptomatic features are clearly stated.

Interviews with online grooming sexual offenders

The process of finding interviewees and setting up interviews is central to the outcomes of empirical research. There are four key areas around recruitment of interviewees:

- initially finding a knowledgeable informant
- getting a range of views
- testing emerging themes with new interviewees
- choosing interviewees to extend results

Once an interview has been arranged, issues to be covered with this specific interviewee have to be considered. The list of questions is initially generated in negotiation with the relevant academic and non-academic literature, alongside research thoughts about what areas might be important to cover in the interview (Rapley, 2004).

When Hanoa (2008) interviewed inmates in Norwegian prisons about violence and threats among inmates, she recruited interviewees who had personal experiences in the area. Her study took an exploratory and qualitative approach. An appropriate method was therefore to interview inmates and let them provide insight into their experiences and perceptions of why and how threats occur. She interviewed 13 inmates in four different prisons.

Hanoa (2008) approached potential interviewees through prison management. She wrote a letter to each prison explaining what her research was about and what the desired characteristics of interviewees would be. Management in each prison communicated her request to relevant inmates. Hence, she relied on the knowledge of prison management concerning inmates' exposure to internal violence. She got a total of 19 answers from inmates. However, one prisoner was released before the scheduled interview, one was moved to another prison and four withdrew from the interview for various reasons.

Another example of interviewing inmates in Norwegian prisons is the study by Brantsæter (2001: 235), who met men convicted of sexual abuse of children:

Interviewer: Perhaps you should tell about your own case, what it was about.
Inmate: It was sexual activities with children, from four years and up to thirteen.
Interviewer: Were there many?
Inmate: Yes, quite a few.
Interviewer: Both boys and girls?
Inmate: Yes.
Interviewer: Where did you meet the children?
Inmate: Family gatherings and some external.
Interviewer: How old were you the first time?
Inmate: Thirteen − fourteen years.
Interviewer: What kind of thoughts did you have in your head before it happened?
Inmate: It just happened.

The Correctional Service of Norway Staff Academy (www.krus.no/en) is a centre of expertise for correctional services in Norway. The job is to provide specialised training for all 3,400 employees of correctional services, carry out research and provide information on the services. The Norwegian Correctional Services (www.kriminalomsorgen.no) are responsible for carrying out remands in custody and penal sanctions in a way that takes into consideration the security of all citizens and attempts to prevent recidivism by enabling the offenders, through their own initiatives, to change their criminal behaviour. The correctional services make remand places available to the police and execute penal sentences that have been imposed.

O'Brien and Webster (2007) constructed an Internet behaviour and attitude questionnaire. The questionnaire intended to measure the attitudes and behaviour of convicted men whose offences were related to child pornography in terms of abusive images. An initial measure was constructed through the generation of items with reference to emerging research literature on these offenders. The first phase involved piloting this first version of the measure with 40 Internet sexual offenders incarcerated in Her Majesty's Prison Service, while the second phase involved 123 Internet sexual offenders filling in the revised questionnaire.

Following factor analysis, a two-factor solution, 'distorted thinking' and 'self-management', emerged from the attitudinal items in the study. A total of 16 items measured distorted thinking (O'Brien and Webster, 2007) and here are some item examples:

- The child was often smiling in the child pornography I have looked at and so I believe that the child is not being harmed.
- I feel I have committed a victimless crime given that I have not created any contact victims in these Internet offences.
- The sexual pictures on the Internet were there anyway, so I was not harming anyone by looking at them.
- I think my life is better when I'm able to view child pornography from the Internet.
- Looking at sexual pictures of children on the Internet does not mean I have committed a sexual offence.
- Child pornography is similar to art.

A total of 18 items measured self-management (O'Brien and Webster, 2007) and here are some examples:

- Using the Internet makes me feel important.
- I prefer the idea of casual sex to sex in a relationship.
- I have few friends outside of the Internet.
- As an adult my sexual relationships with other adults have been very dissatisfying.
- I like to look at child pornography pictures when I masturbate.
- Looking at child pornography on the Internet makes me feel good.

In terms of behaviour items, O'Brien and Webster (2007) measured offenders' use of the following for a purpose relating to child pornography: Usenet news, Internet relay chat, File transfer protocol, Multi-user dungeon, video-conferencing software and hardware, chat rooms, web sites, specific image sharing software, bulletin boards, and newsgroups. The following items also measured the offender's behaviour:

- I made efforts to contact others in order to share or discuss child pornography.
- I made efforts to cover my child pornography activity.
- I created a new personality to aid my child pornography activity.
- At times I accessed child pornography when children were in close proximity.
- I downloaded child pornography video clips.
- Adult pornography also aroused me.

In Oslo, Norway, there is an institute for clinical sexology and therapy, where sex offenders participate in group therapy. Lauvanger (1997) studied a sample of participants from these sessions. The sample consisted of 18 men aged from 30 to 63. The most frequently found personality description in the study was concerned with symptoms of fear and negative thoughts.

From a treatment perspective, it was found that an offender would need several years of therapy to learn about his own needs, behaviours and reactions.

In Sweden, Andersson (2002) interviewed 20 men convicted of sexual abuse of 38 children. The group of convicted child molesters were interviewed in-depth and tested with a number of psychological measurements including a projective test. The men's personal stories were followed from childhood through adolescence and adulthood up until the committed perpetrations were revealed. Each period of their lives was identified, analysed and interpreted from the attachment theory point of view, the phase theory as well as the theory of mind concept. Various aspects of each interview were also related to relevant test results.

As boys, the majority of men in Andersson's (2002) study were exposed to emotional neglect and sometimes to sexual abuse. There was often a general lack of behavioural borders, sometimes including sexual limits. There was a non-order norm about what was permitted or prohibited, and behaviours and actions were not given a reasonable meaning. The study indicated that many sexual perpetrators have to develop a capacity for self-reflection before they can acquire an insight into their own functioning and that of others.

In the USA, Mercado et al. (2008) surveyed offenders. A survey was sent to all (N = 1,601) sex offenders listed on the New Jersey Sex Offender Internet Registry, which includes only higher risk (Tier II and Tier III) sex offenders. Offenders were provided with a description of the study and were invited to offer their perceptions on certain topics.

Similarly in the UK, Craissati et al. (2008) surveyed offenders. Over an 8-month period, 241 offenders were assessed. The sample comprised convicted adult male contact sex offenders, 162 with child victims (child molesters) and 79 with adult victims (rapists) resident within the London Probation area.

Key challenges in empirical study of convicted groomers include:

- extent of any barriers professionals have experienced in gaining clinical and/or research interviews with these men
- online groomers' general presentation and extent of openness to discuss their offending behaviour at interview
- the location of convicted groomers in the country
- to achieve access to convicted groomers for interviews in prisons, there is often a need for letters of recommendation for relevant criminal justice services, prison governors and prison officials. Evidence of cooperation is needed from prison management, so that interviews are possible. We as researchers assume this will happen, but do not provide evidence

Interviews serve the research need to find answers and carry out classification. For example, general classification of paedophilia is possible into two main categories (Dunaigre, 2001):

- Situational paedophilia: Some adults sexually assault children without necessarily feeling any real sexual attraction towards them. These are often isolated, impulsive acts committed by individuals with pathological personalities.

- Preferential paedophilia: This is the conventional form of paedophilia that involves sexual deviance regarding prepubescent children, acted out in various forms. It can be described using criteria such as sexual preference, exclusive or non-exclusive type, type of sexual offence, strategies used, ways of perpetration, character traits, and weak or strong social competences.

To access inmates who are convicted for online grooming, they first have to be identified. In the case of Norwegian prisons, inmates have to be convicted for sections in the criminal law as presented earlier in this book.

4

Internet Sex Offenders – UK Context

This chapter presents the UK context of Internet sex offenders. Legislation, risk assessment, management and treatment are discussed. The UK context is expanded into seeking global solutions.

Sex offenders use of the Internet

It is clear that sex offenders use the Internet to access indecent images of children, to select victims for abuse and to communicate with other sex offenders. Gillan (2003) has suggested that the demand for indecent images through, for example, the use of file-sharing technology, has expanded so much that law enforcement agencies are encountering increasing difficulties in tracking down the child victims and the perpetrators involved (this was confirmed during interviews with police practitioners).

Internet sex offender behaviour can include:

- The construction of sites to be used for the exchange of information, experiences and indecent images of children.
- The organisation of criminal activities that seek to use children for prostitution purposes and that produce indecent images of children at a professional level.
- The organisation of criminal activities that promote sexual tourism.

Indecent images of children are frequently shared by sex offenders using the Internet and the industry in such images is becoming increasingly large and lucrative (Wyre, 2003). Taylor, Holland and Quayle (2001) suggest that some online sex offenders are 'collectors' of indecent images of children who routinely swap images with other collectors. It is also suggested that some of these images are photographs taken by people known to the children such as members of their family (Interview, Metropolitan Police HTCU: Interview Quayle, 2006) although at present there is little empirical evidence to support this claim and more research is needed.

Quayle and Taylor (2003) also comment on the possible motivations of online child sex abusers. It is suggested that sex offenders perceive the Internet as a means of generating an immediate solution to their fantasies. Factors including presumed anonymity, disinhibition and ready accessibility undoubtedly encourage offenders to go online. Quayle and Taylor (2003) also acknowledge, however, that the unique structure of the Internet may play a major role in facilitating online child abuse. One practitioner respondent working with Internet sex offenders has suggested that offenders' Internet use is not limited to abuse and that the Internet often plays a significant role in other areas of their lives (Interview. Probation Officer Facilitator 2, National Probation Service).

The UK legislative context of online child sexual abuse

The concept of 'grooming' is now recognised in UK legislation. This new offence category was also included in the Sexual Offences Act 2003 in England and Wales (this section of the Act also applies to Northern Ireland)[2]: section 15 makes *'meeting a child following sexual grooming'* an offence, this applies to the Internet, other technologies such as mobile phones and to the 'real world'. The Protection of Children and Prevention of Sexual Offences (Scotland) Act 2005 includes *'meeting a child following certain preliminary contact'* (s1). Where a person arranges to meet a child who is under 16, having communicated with them on at least one previous occasion (in person, via the Internet or via other technologies) with the intention of performing sexual activity on the child.[3]

'Grooming' involves a process of socialisation during which an offender seeks to interact with a child (a young person under 16 in Scotland, England and Wales) possibly sharing their hobbies and interests in an attempt to gain trust in order to prepare them for sexual abuse. The process may also involve an attempt to normalise sexual relations between adults and children.

Several countries have followed the UK lead in legislating against 'grooming' behaviour. Sexual grooming has also recently been added to the Crimes Amendment Act 2005 in New Zealand. In the United States it is an offence to electronically transmit information about a child aged 16 or under, for the purpose of committing a sexual offence (US Code Title 18, Part 1, Chapter 117, AS 2425). The Australian Criminal Code (s218A) makes similar restrictions as does the Canadian Criminal Code (s172.1). The legislation in Scotland, England and Wales differs in that the sexual grooming offence applies both to the Internet and to the 'real world'; legislation in other countries addresses only electronic grooming via the Internet and mobile phones. In reality it would be extremely difficult to police and evidence grooming behaviour in the 'real world', it is therefore unsurprising that few cases have been brought to court on this basis under the Protection of Children and Prevention of Sexual Offences (Scotland) Act 2005 and the Sexual Offences Act 2003 (England and Wales).

The concept of sexual grooming has in reality been drawn from the sex offender literature where it is well documented (Finkelhor, 1984) into legislation and is now filtering into policy, crime detection and prevention initiatives. For example, the Child Exploitation and Online Protection Centre (CEOP), a recently launched (April, 2006) UK Government and communications

---

[2] The Sexual Offences Act 2003 (England and Wales) is currently under review in Northern Ireland. Some concerns have been raised regarding a lack of clarity around the age of consent and informed consent. Currently the age of consent is 17 in Northern Ireland (it was raised from 16 to 17 under the Children and Young Persons Act 1950). NI Office, July 2006.

[3] Six cases of 'grooming' have been brought under the new legislation in England and Wales since 2004 (Metropolitan Police, 2006. Interview 3).

industry funded organisation which includes representatives from the police and other criminal justice agencies. CEOP draws upon expertise from Internet service providers (such as AOL and Microsoft) and children's charities such as the NSPCC, in attempting to confront online abuse (http://www.ceop.gov.uk). This new centre aims to raise awareness amongst children and parents about the potential dangers of the Internet and to create a database of known offenders. Police officers visit chat rooms posing as children in order to detect any grooming behaviour. False websites will be set up to attract sex offenders seeking to groom children. These policing tactics are not new, the National High Technology Crime Unit Scotland and the Metropolitan Police High Technology Crime Unit, for example, have placed undercover officers in teen and other chat rooms likely to attract children since the introduction of the Protection of Children and Prevention of Sexual Offences (Scotland) Act 2005 and the Sexual Offences Act 2003 (as have other HTCUs). These officers have learnt to interact as children do online through the use of text language in order to prompt and encourage conversation with child abusers seeking to groom a child. Several recent convictions have been secured on this basis and an increasing number of online groomers are being arrested under the legislation. The police employ similar tactics in other countries such as Italy (Vulpiani, 2001: Strano, 2004) where legislation allows.

The international trade in indecent images of children

The legislation in England and Wales (the Sexual Offences Act 2003 (England and Wales) s.45–46)[4] and Scotland (the Protection of Children and Prevention of Sexual Offences (Scotland) Act 2005, s.16) attempts to curb the production, distribution and possession of indecent images of children on the Internet. The age of the child is raised from 16 to under 18 in both acts with certain provisions.[5] The purpose of the legislation is to protect children from abuse in the creation of such images in order to curb the circulation.

In the United States the law is similar (Child Online Protection Act 2000) (COPA) indecent images of children do not have to be overtly sexual; the possession of suggestive images of children may be prosecuted under the legislation. It is also an offence to simply access images without saving them on a computer. There has been considerable debate in the United States regarding the introduction of COPA: the act has been returned to the Supreme Court several times on the basis of representations made by the American Civil Liberties Union (ACLU) regarding its restrictiveness. The ACLU have argued consistently and fairly effectively that the act infringes upon civil liberties and that it is possible to accidentally encounter such images online. The ACLU also object to the inclusion of the possession of suggestive images, although presumably offence circumstances would be taken into account here. The ACLU has undoubtedly formed a powerful lobby in the United States. No such objections have been voiced in the UK in such an organised manner, it could be argued that groups such as the Internet Watch

---

[4] The Sexual Offences Act 2003 does not create any new offences in this category but raises the age from 16 to under 18 by making amendments to the Criminal Justice Act 1991 and the Protection of Children Act 1978.

[5] The provisions allow a defence to the charge if: the picture is of a 16 or 17 year old; the 16/17 year old 'consents'; the picture/s of 16/17 year olds are not distributed; the perpetrator and the 16/17 year old are in long term relationship/married/co-habiting. S. 8H 2005.

Foundation and key individuals such as John Carr, have campaigned more successfully in the UK for the rights of child victims of Internet abuse. In the United States under COPA the making available of material that is harmful to children for commercial purposes on the Web is also illegal unless child access has been restricted. It was argued by the ACLU that more effective, less restrictive mechanisms exist to protect children and that educating children and their parents about internet awareness would be a more effective approach (Supreme Court Transcripts, *Ashcroft v ACLU* 2/3/04).

The scale of the problem is considerable. The National Society for the Prevention of Cruelty to Children estimate that approximately 20,000 indecent images of children are placed on the Internet each week (NSPCC, 2005). Many of these child victims are amongst the most vulnerable, from poor countries and are repeat victims. The police and CEOP are attempting to identify victims from the images produced on the Internet but the process is slow and time consuming and yields little identification (Davidson, 2007). In the UK the Internet Watch Foundation have reported a rise in the number of websites containing indecent images of children from 3,438 in 2004 to 6,000 in 2006. The websites are hosted outside of the UK, and are therefore extremely difficult to police and control.

There is no doubt that such abuse has a damaging and negative impact upon child victims. It has been claimed that in many instances children are abused and the abuse recorded by members of their own family or people known to them (Klaine, Davis and Hicks, 2001). Many indecent images depict the sexual abuse of children who are victimised both in the creation of the image and in the distribution of the image. It could be argued that a child is re-victimised each time their image is accessed and images on the Internet can form a permanent record of abuse.

Online sexual abuse: moves to protect children

A considerable amount of work has been done internationally to protect children online. The G8 countries have agreed a strategy to protect children from sexual abuse on the Internet. Key aims include: the development of an international database of offenders and victims to aid victim identification; offender monitoring and the targeting of those profiting from the sale of indecent images of children. Work has also been done with Internet service providers and organisations such the Association For Payment Clearing Services in the UK, and other credit card companies in different countries, in attempting to trace individuals using credit cards to access illegal sites containing indecent images of children. An attempt to put mechanisms into place to prevent online payment for illegal sites hosted outside the UK has also been made.

Organisations like the Virtual Global Taskforce (VGT) and the Internet Watch Foundation (IWF) are making some headway in their attempts to protect children online. VGT is an organisation that comprises several international law enforcement agencies from Australia, Canada, the United States, the United Kingdom and Interpol. Through the provision of advice and support to children VGT, aims to protect children online and has recently set up a bogus website to attract online groomers. The Internet Watch Foundation (IWF) is one of the main government watchdogs in this area. Although based in the UK, the IWF is a part of the EU's *Safer Internet Plus Programme*. This programme has four main aims: to fight illegal Internet content; to tackle harmful Internet content; to promote a safer Internet environment and to raise awareness about Internet dangers (Robbins and Darlington, 2003). The IWF seeks to raise awareness about Internet dangers and provides a confidential reporting facility. The IWF also provides an international information service to law enforcement agencies and government bodies. Importantly the IWF also works with the Internet industry to educate organisations about the trade in indecent images of children and online grooming. The IWF has been operational for 10 years.

It would, however, appear that there is much work to be done in educating Internet service providers. Recent research (2005) undertaken by the IWF suggests that 72 per cent (of a sample of 1,000 IT senior professionals) were unaware of the implications of amendments to the Sexual Offences Act 2003 upon their industry and only 56 per sent had heard of the IWF. Internet service providers have, however, taken some action to address child safety online: British Telecom's Operation Clean Sweep resulted in the closure of all of its chat rooms following concerns over sex offenders' use of the service to target children. Other providers such as MSN and Yahoo[6] have taken some action to protect children in chat rooms. A Scottish company (Net ID) has just launched the world's first virtual ID card which aims to protect children and young people online. The card aims to remove the anonymity of the internet thus preventing paedophiles posing as children in chat rooms to gain their trust (Lunchtime Scotland Today, 2/8/06).

Many police forces both in the EU and the United States are working to trace Internet sex offenders and their victims. In the UK, National and local High Technology Crime Units currently investigate the grooming of children on the Internet and indecent online images of children. Successful prosecutions have been brought under the acts in Scotland, England and Wales, both for 'grooming' online and for the possession of indecent Internet images on the Internet following Operation Ore. This operation was launched following information provided to the UK police by the FBI in the United States regarding peer-to-peer technology in sharing indecent images of children. The National Crime Squad (which targets serious and violent crime) has made 2,200 convictions since 2002 under Operation Ore.

Measures to protect children also include school-based programmes aiming to educate about the dangers posed by sex offenders in cyberspace. Such programmes are now routinely delivered to secondary school children and their parents in the UK and other countries such as New Zealand and Canada (Davidson and Martellozzo, 2004).

Despite moves on the part of law enforcement agencies, governments, the IT industry and organisations such as VGT and IWF to control online abuse, John Carr of the National Childrens Home in the UK suggests in a recent report (2006) that such efforts are largely failing as the number of indecent images of children on the Internet continues to increase and the images

---

[6] Yahoo were forced into action in 2005 by a New York State Attorney General's Office investigation which found that users were creating chat rooms explicitly for the purpose of grooming children for abuse. Yahoo then agreed to put in place procedures to ensure that the creation of such chat rooms would not continue.

become ever more disturbing, involving a greater degree of violence and increasingly younger children. It is suggested that governments are failing to make the growing trade in indecent images of children a high enough political priority and that, as the title of the report '*Out of Sight, Out of Mind*' (2006), suggests the hidden nature of the offending and lack of public awareness makes this possible. Indeed, other recent research conducted in the UK suggests that child victimisation and protection issues are not a high priority for the criminal justice agencies involved in the investigative process (Davidson *et al.*, 2006). Carr advocates a global initiative, and identifies key areas where action should be taken. Carr is correct in suggesting that the key issue is one of effective leadership, and that a 'global leadership mechanism' (Carr, 2006: 1) should be developed. This mechanism, it is suggested, should take the form of a new NGO or a network that draws upon existing NGOs. This central body would act to scrutinise and advise governments, law enforcement agencies and the industry. It would also provide a hitherto absent degree of IT industry public accountability. This is undeniably an essential move as at present attempts to protect children online are ad-hoc and some international police forces have only just begun to recognise the scale of the problem. The difficulty will be in setting up a central mechanism that is really able to scrutinise international approaches to the problem and that will have the power to intervene effectively where there is inaction or indifference.

Categorising offenders: the basis of risk assessment

There is a scarcity of any good empirical research in this area both internationally and in the UK. As discussed, risk assessment techniques employed by the police and other agencies in England, Scotland and Wales presently focus upon the use of a risk assessment tool called RISK MATRIX 2000 and the advice of the Sentencing Advisory Panel (2000) on classifying categories of Internet offender, convicted for possession of indecent images of children. The Sentencing Advisory Panel (SAP) system does not, however, extend to offenders grooming children nor to those using extreme pornography depicting the abuse of adults. The system has been criticised by police practitioners for being too limited and not accurately assessing risk with Internet sex offenders (Davidson, 2007). One police officer interviewed by the author described a recent case where a sex offender was assessed as low risk using RM2000 when his offences involved the filming of abuse he had perpetrated, and subsequently posting the indecent images on the Internet. Clearly there is much work to be done in adapting RM2000, but it is also clear that practitioners are simply using the scale as a baseline indicator (Davidson, 2007).

The SAP advice is based upon a system developed by Taylor, Holland and Quayle (2001) on behalf of the COPINE. The typology developed by Taylor *et al.* lists 10 categories of offence that increase in seriousness from Level 1 to 9. Level 1 offences include images often freely available on the Internet depicting children in their underwear or swimsuits, whilst levels 9 and 10 include grossly obscene and sadistic images of children. It is recognised that offenders may possess images that cross several categories, but that 'overt sexual intent and content' (Taylor *et al.*, 2001: 6) are key issues which the police and practitioners working with Internet offenders presumably should address in assessing risk. Other factors which may impact upon risk assessment are identified as:

1. The size of a collection of images and the manner in which it is organised; this is taken to be indicative of the extent to which an offender is using such material offline.
2. New and private material is taken to be indicative of access to sex offender communities and possibly producers.
3. The child's age. It is argued that the younger the child the greater the imbalance of power between perpetrator and victim.

In terms of judging seriousness and risk when sentencing, the Court of Appeal accepted the advice of the Sentencing Advisory Panel (SAP, 2002) in sentencing Internet sex offenders using indecent images of children following *R v Oliver, Hartrey and Baldwin*.[7]

The possession of indecent images of children offence can be tried either way under the Sexual Offences Act 2003 in England and Wales and carries a maximum penalty of five years custody for possession and up to 10 years custody for production and distribution. Aggravating circumstances include: distribution; evidence of a systematic collection; use of drugs or alcohol; collection stored so that others may view it accidentally; intimidation or coercion; financial gain. Mitigating factors include: a small number of images held for personal use and images viewed but not stored.[8]

As discussed the levels of seriousness are based loosely on Taylor *et al.*'s 2001 typology. Although this provides a valuable structure in which to locate different categories of Internet sex offenders use of indecent child images, there is no empirical evidence to suggest that the most serious Level 4 and 5 Internet offenders constitute the greatest risk to children in terms of contact offending. Indeed, police practitioners have suggested that the system clouds the risk issue. An offender may, for example, possess images at Level 1 but have regular access to children within his family circle, whilst an offender may possess images at Level 3 but have no such contact and restrict his behaviour to the Internet (Davidson, 2007).

A police officer commenting on the author's research identified very different types of behaviour amongst Internet offenders. It is apparent that some such offenders are not simply 'collectors' of images:

> *I suspect that many Internet sex offenders are really just sex offenders who now have access to the Internet with the advantages it affords in terms of access and anonymity and are not just 'collectors' at all. I recall a recent case for example involving an offender who claims the Internet led him to offend. He had a senior job in the IT industry (very wealthy), and he used the Internet to target and groom a family with children. He started by using indecent*

---

[7] R V. Oliver, Hartrey and Baldwin (2003) 2 Cr App R28: (2003) Crim LR 127. Here the two determining factors of seriousness were taken to be the nature of the material and the degree of the offender's engagement with the material. In considering the custody threshold the fact that the material upon which the convictions were based constituted a small part of the collection and that the potential for others to access and view the collection was great. The defendants all received a custodial sentence.

[8] The sentencing guidelines may be viewed at http://www.sentencing-guidelines.gov.uk/docs/advice-sexual-offences.pdf (SAP, 2004: 99).

images of young children but then arranged to meet the family and over a considerable period of time helped with babysitting etc. and became trusted (typical grooming behaviour). He eventually raped their young child.

Davidson, 2007: 10

Whilst there is some research evidence to suggest that offenders collecting indecent images of children limit their offending behaviour to non-contact abuse (Quayle and Taylor, 2003), a number of recent convictions under the Sexual Offences Act 2003 (England and Wales) suggest otherwise and respondents in this research have expressed concern about the danger of making assumptions regarding the offending behaviour of such offenders on the basis of little empirical evidence. It is clear from some recently prosecuted cases that sex offenders are using the Internet to contact other sex offenders; groom children for abuse and are collecting indecent Internet images of children (Davidson and Martellozzo, 2006).

Internet offenders grooming children constitute a higher risk than those whose offending is limited to possessing indecent images of children. Practitioners must effectively explore the real possibility that 'Level 1' Internet offenders are engaged in contact abuse. Although such offenders may be the exception to the rule (and this has not really been empirically established), any attempt to neatly categorise and risk assess Internet sex offenders must take into account the diversity of this offending group and the potential for contact abuse.

Research into this issue has been conducted by Seto and Eke (2005a, 2005b) in Canada. The criminal records of 204 male offenders using indecent images of children[9] were analysed. The researchers suggest that offenders using indecent images of children, and who had committed a previous or concurrent contact sexual offence were the most likely to re-offend over a 2.5 year period (2005a). This has implications for risk assessment practice with this group. Seto and Eke (2005b), on the basis of their follow up study with 198 of the original sample of 204 male offenders, claim that criminal history is an important indicator of risk of re-offending in offenders using indecent images of children but that age at first charge or conviction did not seem to be a good predictive indicator of further offending. It is also suggested that risk of contact offending posed by this offender group is lower that that posed by other sex offenders. This finding should, however, be treated with caution. The authors acknowledge that given the limitations of the study in terms of sample size and that there may be differences between Internet offenders using indecent images and offenders accessing such images via a different media.

Other unpublished research by Seto, Cantor and Blanchard (2005c, permission to cite provided), with a large sample (N = 685, 100 of whom were convicted for use of indecent child images), of sex offenders who had offended against children aged under 15, does, however, suggest that the use of indecent images of children is a strong indicator of paedophilia. The work of Seto *et al.* is important in that it sheds light upon the nature of such offending behaviour.

---

[9] Not all of whom were Internet offenders

Further large-scale research on Internet sexual abuse is ongoing, which will play an important role in informing risk assessment approaches. Adding to the risk debate, Seto suggests that:

- *greater paedophilic sexual arousal appears to be equated with greater risk of committing a contact offence*
- *low non-sexual criminal history lowers the risk of contact abuse in indecent image users*

Interview cited in Davidson, 2007

Little work has been undertaken in attempting to address risk with those who target and groom children online other than that undertaken by Strano (2004) in Rome and ongoing doctoral research with the Metropolitan Police in London (Martellozzo, 2009 unpublished) and O'Connell (2003), who spent some time in children's chat rooms posing as a child in order to engage would-be online groomers. O'Connell identifies several different stages in the online grooming process during which an offender will seek to identify and target a potential victim, develop an online relationship with them, explore vulnerability and availability and ultimately arrange to meet. The process described by O'Connell is very similar to the grooming process in the 'real world', however, respondents from the police in this research, have suggested that online grooming behaviour rarely follows this pattern and that offenders are making direct and swift approaches to children and young people regarding the possibility of sex (Interviews, Metropolitan Police HTCU and PU). Quayle has identified a number of possible types of Internet groomer:

> *It's much more difficult to categorise offenders in terms of risk here as little is known about this group and few cases have been brought under the new legislation. They probably fall into several categories:*
> - *those who enjoy talking online and interacting with children but don't meet with them*
> - *those interested in child cybersex but who don't meet*
> - *those targeting and grooming children to meet for sex*

Interview, cited in Davidson, 2007

Exploration of online grooming behaviour should be a research priority as police are encountering an increasing number of such offenders in peer-to-peer networks and chat rooms (Interview, Metropolitan Police HTCU) and relatively little is known about how these offenders might be effectively risk managed.

A typology of Internet child sex offenders has been developed by Krone (2004), this has been adapted for use by Wortley and Smallbone (2006) to guide the work of police officers in the United States. Whilst some of the categories are questionable, the typology does include those offenders targeting and grooming children online, a group largely excluded from other typologies. Nine categories of offender are identified: *Browser's* (Wortley and Smallbone, 2006: 15–17) are offenders who accidentally come across indecent images and save them. In reality, such images are either purchased via credit card or are swapped by collectors. The second category are *private fantasisers* who create digital images for their own private use; third, *trawlers* who search for indecent images through open browsers and may engage in some networking; fourth, *non-secure collectors* who look for indecent images in open areas of the Internet such as chat rooms, and they will probably be networking; fifth, *secure collectors* are offenders who belong to an online hidden, paedophile network. These offenders are highly organised, likely to be collectors and employ sophisticated security to conceal their offending; sixth, *groomers* are offenders targeting and grooming children via peer-to-peer technology, interactive Internet games and chat rooms and these offenders may send indecent images to children as a part of the grooming process; seventh, *physical abusers* are contact abusers who have an interest in indecent images as a part of their fantasy cycle. These offenders may photograph their abusive behaviour for their own use; eighth, *producers* are offenders who record the sexual abuse of children for the purposes of distribution to networks and to satisfy their own fantasy. The final category includes *distributors* who are offenders distributing indecent images either for financial gain or as part of their collecting behaviour.

These categories should not be seen as mutually exclusive and further research is needed to explore the nature of Internet offending, but this typology is useful in isolating different types of

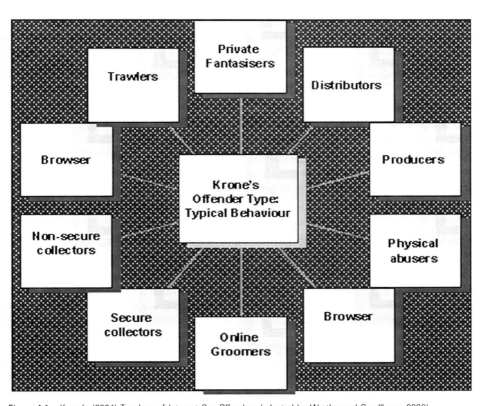

Figure 4.1   Krone's (2004) Typology of Internet Sex Offenders (adapted by Wortley and Smallbone, 2006)

Internet offending behaviour, including online grooming, and it would be possible to begin to identify the risk associated with different types of behaviour on the basis of some of these categories, both in terms of type of Internet abuse and the boundary with contact abuse.

The assessment of risk in work with Internet sex offenders

Risk assessment and management of sex offenders occurs at several levels. There is clearly a need for criminal justice organisations to attempt to control and manage this group of offenders via MAPPA arrangements but police, social work and probation practitioners have the difficult task of attempting to make assessments at an individual and treatment group level. Whilst organisations such as the National Probation Service in the UK provide general guidance on risk[10] management, no formal specific advice or techniques appear to have been developed regarding Internet sex offenders.[11]

Some practitioner training (criminal justice social workers) in risk assessment with Internet sex offenders in Scotland has begun and probation officers in England and Wales are currently undergoing training in the delivery of a new cognitive behavioural treatment programme. However, research conducted by Quayle and Taylor with social workers and probation officers suggested that practitioners did not understand 'the function of the Internet for adults with a sexual interest in children' (Quayle and Taylor, 2002: 32) and did not routinely screen sex offenders for Internet use, an issue that is of concern and that was also raised by a representative from the High Technology Crime Unit of the Metropolitan Police.[12] Quayle and Taylor comment in this work that there are currently no specific assessment tools to aid practitioners in managing Internet sex offenders (this has been confirmed by representatives from the Family Protection, Scotland and the National Probation Service in England and Wales, 2006). Practitioners in Quayle and Taylor's study were relying upon the standard assessment interview to make judgments about risk. Quayle and Taylor go on to suggest a series of useful questions that practitioners might employ during the assessment interview but these do not appear to have been taken up in practice (Interview, Quayle. 2006).

Such an approach may be useful in raising awareness amongst practitioners about key areas upon which to focus during supervision sessions with Internet sex offenders. However if practitioners have no confidence in assessment tools that are imposed upon them, they will probably not be used accurately or effectively in managing and assessing risk. Research undertaken with practitioners by the Scottish Executive in 2002 into the use of risk assessment tools in Scotland, suggested that some found standard risk assessment tools such as Risk Matrix 2000 (RM2000) to be complex and too academic. If such tools are to be effectively integrated into practice and perceived as useful by practitioners, their views based upon professional and

---

[10] The Home Office *Risk Management Framework* identifies four rather obvious steps for practitioners: 1. identify risks; 2. assess risks; 3. address risk responses; 4. risk review and report. (Home Office, 2004:10).

[11] Although it is clear that key developments are taking place in this area in Scotland, England and Wales and that further guidance and training will be offered to practitioners.

[12] This unit is responsible for policing online child sexual abuse, including the possession, production and distribution of indecent images of children and online grooming.

clinical judgment and experience with different groups of offenders should be actively sought during the developmental phase of any risk assessment work.[13]

The National Probation Service Sex Offender Strategy (2004) makes reference to provision in the Criminal Justice Act 2003 regarding Internet offending. It is clear from the document that risk assessment is considered key at various stages of the criminal justice process, but risk assessment tools for use with Internet sex offenders are currently under development and advice offered to probation practitioners acknowledges the difficulty of applying RM2000 to work with this group of offenders. Practitioners have been advised to omit the aggravating factor of 'non-contact' offence and to continue to apply dynamic risk factors to assess risk on an individual basis (*Probation Circular*, 85/2005).

Practitioner risk assessment of Internet sex offenders is of paramount importance at pre-sentence report/pre-court stage in informing sentencing decisions and suitability for treatment. It is equally important during the sentence (in informing release decisions for custodial sentences and risk issues in the community) and post release. Police practitioners have commented upon the lack of inter-agency knowledge sharing and collaboration at the pre-sentence report stage and beyond, and it has been suggested that much greater collaboration is needed between police officers and social workers/probation officers in continually assessing risk with all categories of Internet sex offender (Davidson, 2007).

Respondents in the author's research (Davidson, 2007) identified some key risk assessment issues in working with Internet sex offenders. At the pre-sentence report stage it was suggested that practitioners should be using RM2000 (with the suggested changes) but also should be talking to the police about the exact nature of the offence and the evidence, as the evidence gained from the case can be usefully employed to confront denial. It was suggested that practitioners do not need to know a great deal about the technical aspects of Internet use, but should be asking the right screening questions regarding offenders' computer use (nature and frequency of use for example) and that they do need some basic IT knowledge in order to do this effectively. The probation officers and facilitators participating in this research suggested that the inclusion of screening questions about computer/Internet use should be incorporated into work with all sex offenders at PSR stage. It was also recognised that risk is a dynamic concept and that practitioners should be checking this throughout supervision.

Risk assessment should be an ongoing process that is built into practice and that is carefully informed by existing research and best practice with this particular offender group. The consequence of not addressing risk appropriately and effectively with this group of offenders could be high and any mistakes potentially damaging to the reputation of the agencies concerned.

Respondents in the author's research (Davidson, 2007) were asked to comment upon the factors that should be taken into account by practitioners in assessing risk and managing Internet sex offenders. Many very important issues were raised by respondents which are divided into

---

[13] The work of the RMA in inviting practitioner comment and input into the development of risk assessment techniques is an example of good practice in this area.

1. Practitioners should be seeking to establish if sex offenders are using the Internet, how often they access the Internet and for what purpose. A number of screening questions should be asked routinely.
   It's important for practitioners to explore the nature of Internet behaviour at the outset of supervision/treatment and I don't think that practitioners do this on a regular basis at present. It is also really essential to explore the boundary between online and offline abuse. Is there one? Or is the person collecting as part of a fantasy cycle and then putting fantasy into action? That's the danger that practitioners should be aware of and looking for.
   Interview. Quayle, 2006

2. Practitioners compiling SERs/PSRs need some specialist IT knowledge if they are to effectively challenge and explore offenders' claims.

3. Evidence from the offender's case should be used to assess risk, help determine treatment and confront denial.

4. A greater degree of collaboration between Criminal Justice Social Work Services (Scotland) the National Probation Service (England and Wales) and the police in assessing and managing the risk posed by Internet sex offenders throughout the sentencing process and beyond is essential as is some specialist IT knowledge.
   If I were a probation officer charged with producing a pre-sentence report assessing dangerousness, I'd be routinely checking the details of the police case to determine the exact nature of the offending before forming any opinion concerning risk.
   Interview. Metropolitan Police HTCU

Figure 4.2   Assessing risk at social enquiry report/pre-sentence report stage

two general risk areas. The first area includes situational risk, the risk of contact abuse and the way in which agencies collaborate in risk assessment. The second includes questions to pose in risk assessing offenders using indecent images of children.

Respondents raised many important points regarding effective risk assessment and management of Internet sex offenders. Both situational and individual risk factors should be taken into account at the pre-court stage and into the sentence and that effective assessment can only occur in the context of inter-agency collaboration.

Multi-agency public protection arrangements in the UK

In the UK Internet sex offenders will be subject to the restrictions placed upon other sex offenders in terms of Multi-Agency Public Protection Arrangements (MAPPA).[14] Arrangements require criminal justice, housing, health, local authority and social work services to put into place arrangements for establishing and monitoring risk with sex offenders. Cautioned and convicted sex offenders must sign the sex offenders register which was introduced in the Sex Offenders Act 1997 and amended by the Criminal Justice Court Services Act 2000 in Scotland, England and Wales.[15]

In Scotland MAPPA arrangements have recently come into force (September 2006). The arrangements will address several areas of good practice: ongoing risk assessment; the

---

[14] Established by the Management of Offenders (Scotland) Act 2005 in Scotland and by the Criminal Justice and Court Services Act 2000 and re-enacted and strengthened by the Criminal Justice Act 2003 in England and Wales.

[15] The Metropolitan Police estimate that approximately 4,000 new sex offenders are added to the register in Scotland, England and Wales each year (Interview 3. Metropolitan Police Clubs and Vice Unit).

1. Offenders access to the internet and level of technical IT knowledge. Has the offender gained any IT qualifications for example?

   Did they try to conceal their offending and what lengths did they go to? Some go to extraordinary lengths in getting IT education to enable them to hide their offending more effectively.

   Interview. Chair, National Police Sex Offender Working Group, Scotland

2. Is the offender operating as part of an Internet network?

3. Explore any history of previous allegations (not just convictions) but also, importantly, the nature of the allegations.

4. Explore any history of contact sexual offending.

5. Did the offender attempt to conceal their offending and what lengths did they go to in order to achieve this?

6. The extent of denial Graf (2006) suggests that Internet offenders demonstrating extreme denial should be categorised as high risk.

7. Does the offender have immediate or other access to children?

8. What does the offender do in his free time? Are there any unaccounted for frequent gaps in time?

   How do they spend their days? Are there any unaccounted for frequent gaps? It's a question of digging here. And this is what MAPPA Officers and probation officers should be doing. Dropping in on offenders on the register without appointment: looking at their living environments, asking questions about what they have been doing. Viewing their computing equipment. I regularly visit the offenders I'm in touch with unannounced; I visited one man on the register and saw lots of pairs of children's underpants around his house- he has been reconvicted – unannounced visits are important.

   Interview. Metropolitan Police PU

Figure 4.3   Situational risk factors

---

1. Explore the way in which images are sourced. Is the offender a serious collector or an amateur? Where do the images come from? Are they home produced or professionally produced?

2. Is the offender involved in the production and distribution of images also?

3. Is there a great deal of swapping of images?

4. What is the nature of the collection in terms of its seriousness and the degree of violence involved?

5. Is the collection highly organised?

6. Is the collection highly focused on a type of victim?

7. Does the nature of the collection suggest a pre-occupation.Is it highly organised and has it taken a long time to amass? Does the offender use it on a regular basis? How often is it used?

   Really looking here for obsessive behaviour, how much of their time is focused on the obsession and the nature of the obsession. As a screening question I would be asking about computer use and about how they spend a typical day. I really want to know initially how much time they are spending on their computer and if they have a computer at home (although could be using an Internet café- I know of one such case – but the more obsessive would be working at home/somewhere quiet).

   Interview. Quayle, 2006

8. Do the images form a part of the offender's fantasy abuse cycle? This may be indicative of obsessive behaviour.

Figure 4.4   Questions to ask in assessing risk: indecent images of children

development of risk management plans that focus upon public protection and performance evaluation. There are four core functions: identifying MAPPA offenders; sharing relevant information across agencies involved in the assessment of risk; assessing and managing risk of serious harm.[16]

In England and Wales violent and sex offenders are divided into three distinct categories under MAPPA arrangements: Category One includes all registered sex offenders; Category Two includes violent and other sex offenders on licence to the National probation Service and Category Three includes offenders with previous convictions whose behaviour suggests that they pose a continuing risk. Offenders are also categorised by seriousness at Levels 1 to 3 (Level 1 offenders pose low to medium risk; Level 2 offenders pose high risk and Level 3 offenders pose the highest risk). Under MAPPA arrangements in England and Wales Level 1 offenders are overseen by one agency, usually the police or the probation service, whilst Level 2 offenders are subject to multi-agency oversight (the Multi-Agency Risk Conference structure (MARC)) and Level 3 offenders (known as the critical few) may be subject to intensive measures beyond the MARC structure, such as monitoring on a daily basis by a private care firm or police surveillance.

In Scotland, risk assessment of dangerous offenders is a key issue that is monitored by a central body (the Risk Management Authority) and is becoming an integral element of practice. This is an unusual approach and other countries may follow the Scottish lead. Proposed legislation will shortly afford the police the power to routinely enter the homes and check the computers of any sex offender on the register for the purposes of risk assessment (Police, Public Order and Criminal Justice (Scotland) Bill, 2006).

A statutory obligation is now placed upon criminal justice agencies working with violent and sexual offenders in Scotland subject to an Order of Lifelong Restriction (OLR)[17] to prepare and act upon a risk management plan. The plan should include an assessment of risk and describe how the perceived risk will be monitored and how the offender will be managed by all relevant agencies. The OLR formed part of the recommendations by the MacLean Committee on serious violent and sexual offenders (2000) and has been made available to the High Court since June 2006 for offenders appearing on indictment for an offence without a mandatory life sentence of imprisonment. The statutory provisions for the OLR are set out in section 210F of the Criminal Procedure (Scotland) Act 1995 (as inserted by Section 1 of the Criminal Justice (Scotland) Act 2003). The MacLean Committee also recommended establishing an independent body to ensure that statutory, voluntary and private sector agencies worked together systematically to address the risk posed by serious offenders. The proposal led to the establishment of the Risk Management Authority (RMA). It is the role of the RMA to approve and monitor the risk management plans of prepared by agencies for those offenders serving an OLR. The Authority's remit also includes: Setting standards and accrediting risk assessors and the methods to be used

---

[16] S10 and 11 of the Management of Offenders Act (Scotland) 2005 introduce a statutory function for the police, local authorities and the SPS which includes the establishment of joint working arrangements to assess and manage risk with sexual and violent offenders. ACPOS, ADSW and the SPS will work with the Justice Department.

[17] It is the responsibility of the 'lead' agency to prepare the plan.

in the assessment of those offenders for whom the court is considering an OLR; the development of policy and conduct of research in the fields of risk assessment and management and the provision of guidance and training for criminal justice agencies and practitioners. RMA publications include: the *RMA Standards and Guidelines for Risk Assessment* (2006) and a directory of risk assessment tools (RMA 2006).

Effective management of offenders: respondents' views

Respondents in the author's research (Davidson 2007) were asked to reflect upon how Internet sex offenders might be effectively managed and controlled as a group and how far MAPPA arrangements (Scotland, England and Wales) might address this. All respondents supported the principle of multi-agency working and MAPPA arrangements but some questioned the adequacy of the system in assessing and managing risk with sex offenders (including those convicted of Internet related offences). One police respondent questioned how far agencies are currently committed to enforcing MAPPA arrangements: 'It's (MAPPA) certainly a step in the right direction, but is this really a priority for the agencies involved? It's not really and resourcing is an issue'.

Respondents identified some useful steps that might be taken in ensuring more effective management of Internet sex offenders:

---

1. Unlimited access to registered sex offenders' home computers (aided in Scotland by the Police, Public Order and Criminal Justice (Scotland) Bill, 2006).

2. MAPPA officers should be regularly making unannounced visits to sex offenders in order to view home environments and computers.

Regular and effective collaboration between police officers from specialist sex offender units and social workers/probation officers regarding risk assessment and management at social enquiry/pre-sentence report stage and throughout the sentence.

Figure 4.5   The effective management of Internet sex offenders

These proposals carry a considerable resource implication. It may, however, soon be possible to monitor sex offender computer use electronically and remotely This may initially prove costly, but such a move may provide a more cost effective alternative in the long term. In the UK the Home Office is currently exploring the possibility of introducing software in England and Wales that has been developed in the United States.

It is clear that MAPPA arrangements provide a useful framework for the management of Internet sex offenders in the UK. Davidson (2007) has however suggested that a more proactive approach should be taken by agencies in monitoring Internet sex offenders particularly via regular access to home computers in order to assess risk and that a greater degree of collaboration between agencies would aid this process.

Theoretical context of treatment in the UK

Quayle *et al*. (2004) have developed a cognitive behavioural treatment (CBT) module for Internet sex offenders along with the NSPCC and Greater Manchester Probation Service. The module sought to build upon the accredited probation sex offender programme (SOTP) in guiding practitioners' work with Internet sex offenders. Elements of the module will be used in the new accredited Home Office probation programme for Internet sex offenders, which has been developed by Middleton (2006). There appear to be few treatment programmes dedicated to Internet sex offenders other than small scale, ad-hoc projects largely developed by practitioners. In Switzerland, for example, 40 Internet sex offenders have undergone a tailored CBT programme (Interview, Graf, 2006) and some work is underway in the Netherlands at the Amsterdam Clinic.

There is work in the UK to address risk assessment and treatment for Internet sex offenders who possess, produce and distribute indecent images of children,[18] most notably that undertaken by O'Brien and Webster (2005, unpublished) on behalf of the UK Prison Service Offending Behaviour Programmes Unit, and developmental work conducted by Middleton *et al*. (2005) on behalf of the National Probation Service, and these developments are discussed below.

Middleton *et al*. (2005) conducted research exploring the applicability of the Ward and Siegert Pathways Model of Sexual Offending to a sample of 72 Internet sex offenders, who had been convicted for possession and distribution of indecent images of children (no Internet 'groomers' were included in the sample). The sample was drawn from the 15 Probation Service Regions in England and Wales. RM2000 was used to risk assess 67 per cent (N = 49) of the sample and 17 per cent had been categorised as high risk. Drawing on existing theoretical explanation for sexual offending, the Pathways Model identifies four key areas to be addressed in treatment programmes for internet sex offenders: intimacy and social skills deficit; distorted sexual scripts; anti-social cognitions and emotional dysregulation (Ward and Siegert, 2002).

The aim of Middleton *et al*.'s research was to explore implications for assessment and treatment. The Internet offenders tended to fall within the 'intimacy deficits' and 'emotional dysregulation' pathways. The 'intimacy deficits' pathway contains offenders who offend at irregular intervals particularly when isolated or lonely; these offenders usually have normal sexual scripts. The 'emotional dysregulation' group contains offenders who have difficulty in regulating their emotions but have normal sexual scripts. Middleton *et al*. did not find high levels of cognitive distortions amongst their sample, but this finding has been contradicted by the work of O'Brien and Webster (2005) and Quayle and Taylor (2003) (2002) who identified four characteristics of cognitive distortions in Internet sex offenders: justification of possession of indecent images as 'only' images and non-contact abuse;[19] 'normalisation' as many others are engaged in this behaviour; 'objectification' through the collection of images, which is possible as there is no direct

---

[18] None of this research has focused upon those who groom children online, possibly as there are currently few such offenders in the system and cases are difficult and time consuming to evidence.

[19] A similar concept to that of 'denial 'in sex offender populations (Davidson, 2006) and one worth exploring with those using the Internet.

contact with the victim and 'justification' through participation and collusion via an online network of abusers some of whom have similar psychological problems to other sex offenders

Middleton *et al.* conclude that Internet sex offenders are a diverse group. This is confirmed by O'Brien's and Webster's (2005) work. The implications for assessment and treatment are that risk assessment tools and treatment should take account of these differences and the CBT approach adopted by both the probation and prison service with sex offenders in the UK at present may not be entirely relevant. This contention is however contradicted by the work of O'Brien and Webster (2005) whose research was conducted with Internet sex offenders. O'Brien and Webster sought to design and validate a risk assessment measure to guide the work of practitioners. The *Internet Behaviour and Attitudes Questionnaire* (O'Brien and Webster, 2007) draws upon Quayle and Taylor (2002; 2003) interview guidelines for practitioners in work with Internet sex offenders. Other items on the scale were developed following a literature review and interviews with the Metropolitan Police. The IBAQ contains a series of 42 behaviour items that require a 'yes/no' response and 34 attitude items. The questions explore the nature of the offender's Internet behaviour in relation to indecent images of children and general attitudes towards Internet abuse. Many of these statements seek to explore denial and minimisation regarding the seriousness and extent of the behaviour. These concepts are well established in treatment work with sex offenders and evidenced in the general sex offender literature (Finkelhor, 1984; Gudjonsson, 1991; Davidson, 2005).

O'Brien and Webster's research was divided into two phases: 40 sexual offenders with a history of using indecent images participated in phase one (pilot) and 123 sexual offenders convicted of Internet child pornography participated in the second phase. All respondents were serving custodial or probation sentences. The internal consistency of the measure used with phase two respondents increased following changes made as a consequence of data produced at phase one. The IBAQ may shortly be used in the new cognitive behavioural treatment (CBT) development by Middleton (2006). The authors do however caution that the scale does not yet have the capability to accurately measure risk. It is suggested, however, on a more optimistic note, that elements of the CBT treatment model currently in use for sex offenders may have some relevance for Internet sex offenders, but in the absence of any conclusive empirical evidence this conclusion must be tentative.

A number of key areas to be addressed in treatment programmes designed for Internet sex offenders using indecent child images are suggested by the literature as listed in Figure 4.6.

Treatment approaches in work with Internet sex offenders

Treatment approaches with sex offenders whose offending is Internet related tend to be based on the cognitive behavioural treatment (CBT) model. However the structure and delivery of such programmes differs. In England and Wales there has been a recent attempt to centrally develop and organise a CBT programme for Internet sex offenders that is now in use by the National Probation Service (July 2006) and will possibly be introduced to prisons. The Internet Sex Offender Treatment Programme (i-SOTP) runs alongside the existing sex offender treatment programme.

• intimacy and social skills deficit
• distorted sexual scripts
• anti-social cognitions
• emotional dysregulation
	• cognitive distortions:
	    justification of possession (only an image)
	    normalisation (many others do this)
	    objectification of victim/victims
	    collusion (with wider network)

Ward and Siegert, 2002; Quayle and Taylor, 2003; O'Brien and Webster, 2005; Middleton, 2006

Figure 4.6   Key treatment areas guiding work with Internet sex offenders using indecent child images

Another CBT treatment programme is currently operational at a local level at the Forensic Department, University Hospital, Basel, Switzerland. This inpatient and outpatient clinic for sex offenders includes those remanded in custody, on probation, post release from prison and some self referring (approximately 15–20 per cent of all Internet offenders are self referring). So far, 40 men have attended the programme and therapy lasts for one year (weekly sessions of 1.5 hours) and is based upon relapse prevention models adapted for use with Internet sex offenders. The majority of offenders have been charged with possession of child internet pornography. The programme has been running for four years and the CBT model used is based upon the work of Marshall, Laws and Barbaree (1990), which has been adapted for use with sex offenders using indecent Internet images of children.

The remainder of this chapter describes the Internet sex offender treatment approach in England and Wales. The section draws upon the author's research (Davidson, 2007) and also draws upon relevant probation circulars.

The National Probation Service in England and Wales has launched a cognitive behavioural treatment programme (the Internet Sex Offender Treatment Programme, i-SOTP) designed specifically for those men convicted of Internet related sexual abuse crimes against children (although it is possible that adults convicted for the possession of extreme pornography under the proposed legislation may at some point join the programme).

The National Probation Service programme began to roll out on a regional basis from July 2006. Probation practitioners were concerned that there would be an insufficient number of

• 6 modules and 35 sessions
• Internet sex offender behaviour characterised by:
  Lack of victim awareness (more so than empathy) compulsivity, collecting behaviour, emotional avoidance and investment in online pseudo relationships.
<div align="right">Probation Circular 92, 2005: 2</div>
• Areas covered in the programme include:
  1. motivations and values
  2. skills development in relationships and emotions
  3. relapse prevention
<div align="right">Middleton et al, 2006</div>

Figure 4.7   Internet Sex Offender Treatment Programme (i-SOTP) key features

Internet sex offenders to run rolling programmes, but an increasing number of offenders are under probation supervision. The programme has been developed alongside the standard programme (Sex Offender Treatment Programme) and is specifically designed for Internet sex offenders accessing indecent images of children.

The difficulty is that given the lack of research in this relatively new area and the small, non-random samples of such offenders (drawn from the convicted sex offender population) who have participated in recent work, the assumptions regarding Internet sex offender behaviour upon which the programme is based must be tentative.

The i-SOTP programme was accredited by the Correctional Services Accreditation Panel in December 2005 and 90 plus probation staff (intervention staff/facilitators) have been trained in its use. Intervention staff run the accredited offender management programmes and often have specialist experience/knowledge in the sex offender area. The CBT programme is restricted to offenders categorised as 'low deviance' in terms of RM2000 (MAPPA Level 1).

Although the programme has been designed for those convicted of indecent image related offending, the content and structure of the programme should allow for the allocation of different types of Internet sex offender to different and appropriate treatment streams. For example, the effective management of online groomers may require more one-to-one supervision, along with elements of the original SOTP and i-SOTP.

Risk assessment and management should be an integral element of the new CBT programme; probation offender managers and facilitators must currently produce approved risk plans. Standard training materials for trainers are currently under development, as is a standardised Internet sex offender test battery which will be used by the Prison Service and the National Probation Service (across all 42 probation areas). These will be developed by early 2010 along with a new standardised test battery for Internet sex offenders using indecent images of children, and will also be used to aid risk assessment. Evaluative research will be conducted to assess these developments and to explore how offenders might be assigned to different pathways (following Ward and Siegert, 2004).

Much treatment practice with Internet sex offenders is new and innovative; the effectiveness of different approaches will not be apparent until the work has progressed sufficiently to allow for the collection of data and evaluation.

Conclusion and recommendations: moving forward

Criminal justice agencies in the UK and internationally are attempting to build upon existing good practice in terms of assessment and treatment for sex offenders and to adapt this practice for use with sex offenders whose offences are Internet related. Although practitioners are dedicated and much of the work is innovative, it is essential that good quality research underpins practice. There is a scarcity of such research regarding the behaviour of different types of Internet sex offender (Quayle and Taylor's (2003) and Krone's (2004) work are the exception). Research has focused upon those who produce and collect indecent images of children, whilst very little is known about those who groom children online and the boundary between online abuse and contact abuse. The police have suggested that a greater number of such cases are now being prosecuted under the legislation in the UK. It is therefore of concern that so little is known about this potentially high risk group.

There is an urgent need for research to explore: the behaviour of online groomers who target children; the link/boundary between non-contact online sexual abuse of children and Internet offenders' propensity for contact abuse. Any attempt to further develop risk assessment tools such as RM2000 should be undertaken with reference to such work, as should further developments in treatment practice.

Whilst criminal justice agencies in the UK are making good progress in developing treatment practice with Internet sex offenders (as are other countries) there is a need for more effective inter-agency communication and collaboration in approaching risk assessment and management with this group. Specifically, criminal social workers in Scotland and Probation Officers in England and Wales should work more directly with specialist police units in assessing risk with Internet sex offenders at the pre-court stage and throughout sentence.

Agencies should give high priority to the monitoring of internet sex offenders in the community under MAPPA arrangements:

1. All registered sex offenders should be screened regarding possible Internet use. Basic IT training may be necessary for some practitioners.
2. All registered sex offenders' home computers should be regularly monitored. Failing this, monitoring of high risk Internet sex offenders home computers should be targeted.
3. MAPPA officers should make regular, unscheduled visits to Internet sex offenders to check their living environments for evidence of offending.
4. Ongoing offender questioning regarding the nature of computer use is important in seeking to establish how offenders spend their time.

Research has suggested (Davidson, 2007) that a number of factors should be taken into account by practitioners in assessing risk with Internet sex offenders producing or possessing indecent images of children,[20] some of which draw upon the advice of the SAP and Quayle and Taylor's (2003) typology:

1. the way in which images are sourced
2. offender involvement in the production and distribution of images
3. the nature of the collection in terms of its seriousness and the degree of violence involved
4. the degree of collection organisation
5. the extent to which the collection suggests a pre-occupation and the frequency of offender use
6. the extent to which the images form a part of the offender's fantasy abuse cycle

---

[20] These categories may be applicable to risk assessment with offenders possessing 'extreme pornography' depicting the abuse of adults, but research is yet to be conduted in this area.

There are many examples of international innovative assessment and treatment practice with Internet sex offenders. Much of this work is ad-hoc and information is not readily available. Good research should form the basis of risk assessment, offender management and treatment practice with Internet sex offenders. There is an urgent need for agencies to share practice and research information in work with internet sex offenders. Such a research/information repository could be facilitated by an organisation such as the National Organisation for the Treatment of Abusers at national level and the International Association for the Treatment of Sexual Offenders at international level.

5

Legislative Context of Work with Internet Sex Offenders

This chapter will describe and critically evaluate legislation recently introduced in Norway designed to protect children and young people from Internet abuse. One of the key problems in policing the global crime is the variation in legislation between countries. Several other countries are beginning to follow the UK lead in legislating against grooming behaviour. For example, sexual grooming was added to the legislation in Norway in 2007 and we will use Norwegian legislation as the case study in this chapter.

The case of Norwegian law

'On The Road to A Safer Norway' is one of the slogans used by the Minister of Justice (Justisdepartementet, 2007). While 22 per cent of all Norwegian children between the age of nine and 16 (about 70,000 children) have met someone on the Internet, almost all meetings occurred between children of about the same age without any problems. However, cases of online grooming leading to sexual abuse of children by men do occur. A recent example was a 33-year-old school assistant who wrote on a web page on the Internet 'I am Stian 15'. He had contact with several girls who undressed in front of their web cameras. He met two of the girls in a hotel room for sexual intercourse. The man was sentenced to four years imprisonment (Oftedal, 2008).

In cases where a child has met an adult after contact on the Internet in Norway, less than 10 per cent of the children report that the meeting was unpleasant in terms of words or physical assault. Girls aged 15 to 16 most frequently experience unpleasant behaviour when meeting an adult after Internet contact. Most of those experiencing physical or psychological offence at such meetings say that they are dissatisfied with friends, school and/or their own family. Most of them have parents that were born in another European country (Justisdepartementet, 2007).

A number of studies concerned with online victimisation of children have recently been completed in Norway. All of them tend to focus solely on the child as a victim. Save the Children Norway has published two studies (Hegg, 2008; Nicolaisen, 2008) while the Ministry of Justice has published one study (Faremo, 2007) and a social research institute has published one study

(Suseg *et al.*, 2008). There were no studies yet on the process of online grooming in terms of understanding the behaviour of men who target young people online.

Relevant sections in the General Civil Penal Code ('straffeloven') concerned with sexual offenders in Norway are (Nicolaisen, 2008):

- **Section 195.** *Any person who engages in sexual activity with a child who is under 14 years of age shall be liable to imprisonment for a term not exceeding 10 years. If the said activity was sexual intercourse the penalty shall be imprisonment for not less than 2 years.*
  Imprisonment for a term not exceeding 21 years may be imposed if
  (a) the act is committed by two or more persons jointly
  (b) the act is committed in a particularly painful or offensive manner
  (c) the act is committed against a child under 10 years of age and there have been repeated assaults
  (d) the offender has previously been convicted and sentenced pursuant to this provision or section 192, or
  (e) as a result of the act the aggrieved person dies or sustains serious injury to body or health. Sexually transmitted diseases and generally infectious diseases, cf. section 1–3, No. 3, cf. No. 1, of the Act relating to control of communicable diseases, shall always be deemed to be considerable injury to body or health pursuant to this section.
  Criminal liability shall not be excluded by any mistake made as regards age.
  A penalty pursuant to this provision may be remitted or imposed below the minimum prescribed in the second sentence of the first paragraph if those who have engaged in the sexual activity, are about equal as regards age and development.
- **Section 196.** *Any person who engages in sexual activity with a child who is under 16 years of age shall be liable to imprisonment for a term not exceeding 5 years.*
  Imprisonment for a term not exceeding 15 years may be imposed if
  (a) The act is committed by two or more persons jointly,
  (b) The act is committed in a particularly painful or offensive manner,
  (c) The offender has previously been convicted and sentenced pursuant to this provision or section 192 or 195, or
  (d) As a result of the act the aggrieved person dies or sustains considerable injury to body or health. Sexually transmitted diseases and generally infectious diseases, cf. section 1–3, No. 3, cf. No. 1, of the Act relating to control of communicable diseases, shall always be deemed to be considerable injury to body or health pursuant to this section.
  Criminal liability shall not be excluded by any mistake made as regards age, unless there is no element of negligence in this respect.
  A penalty pursuant to this provision may be remitted if those, who have engaged in the sexual activity, are about equal as regards age and development.
- **Section 200.** *Any person who commits a sexual act with a child less than 16 years of age shall be liable to imprisonment for a term not exceeding three years. Any person who misleads*

a child under 16 years of age to behave in a sexually offensive or otherwise indecent manner as referred to in section 201 shall be liable to imprisonment for a term not exceeding three years. In cases referred to in the second paragraph the offender may be sentenced to imprisonment for a term not exceeding six years if the act has been committed under especially aggravating circumstances. In deciding whether especially aggravating circumstances subsist, particular importance shall be attached to how long the relationship has endured, whether the act is a misuse of a blood relationship, care relationship, position, or relationship of dependence or close trust, and whether the act has been committed in a particularly painful or offensive manner.

Section 196, third and fourth paragraphs, shall apply correspondingly.

- **Section 201**. *Any person who by word or deed behaves in a sexually offensive or otherwise indecent manner*

  (a) [. . .]

  (b) [. . .]

  (c) In the presence of or towards children under 16 years of age, shall be liable to fines or to imprisonment for a term not exceeding one year.

- **Section 201a**. *With fines or imprisonment of not more than 1 year is any person liable, who has agreed a meeting with a child who is under 16 years of age, and who with intention of committing an act as mentioned in sections 195, 196 or 200 second section has arrived at the meeting place or a place where the meeting place can be observed.*

  Criminal liability shall not be excluded by any mistake made as regards age, unless there is no element of negligence in this respect.

  Criminal liability according to this section can be excluded if those who meet are about of the same age and maturity.

Section 201a is the new grooming section in Norwegian criminal law. This section was included in The General Civil Penal Code in April 2007. The grooming section is different from other sections about sexual activity in that it does not concern a completed offence, but *the intention of committing an act*. However, the perpetrator must actually appear for a meeting (sometimes a police trap) an intention to meet is not enough, possibly it should be, but it is difficult to prove beyond doubt. Therefore, the legal phrase is: ' . . . has arrived at the meeting place or a place where the meeting place can be observed'. It is the potential scene of the crime, which is the meeting place where the offence is intended to take place, that the offender has arrived at, or the offender can observe the potential crime scene from where he is located.

The crime description is such that it is technologically neutral. It is therefore not important how the adult and the child came in contact or agreed to meet. The important thing is that there is an agreement to meet physically. Agreement is to be understood in a wide sense. There is no requirement that there is an explicit agreement to meet. It is sufficient that the offender had a reasonable expectation to meet the child at a specific location within a specific time frame. It is irrelevant who initiated the meeting.

Where an adult communicates with a child and agrees to meet with the intention of committing a sexual offence, the adult can be sentenced for the grooming crime. It is the intention, the goal and the purpose of the appointment that is a crime. Before the grooming section was introduced in Norwegian criminal law in 2007, a preparation for the criminal act of committing a sexual offence to a child less than 16 years of age did not make the offender liable to imprisonment.

The grooming section was introduced in an attempt to protect children at an earlier stage. However, the contact itself is not a crime. There may be good reasons for adults and children to have contact using media such as the Internet. Adult and child may share the same interest in sports or games, and exchange experience and play games on the net.

An appointment is defined as place and time where adult and child have agreed to meet. It may be at the adult's location, the child's location or another location to which both have to travel.

The grooming section in Norway was inspired by legislation in the UK, where the grooming section 15 was introduced in 2003. According to this section in the UK, an adult commits an offence if the person intentionally meets a child following sexual grooming (Aas-Hansen, 2004).

Norwegian Supreme Court decisions

The described sections in the general civil penal code in Norway are applied in the Norwegian court system. The Norwegian court system consists of three levels, where the appellate court is the second highest and the Supreme Court is the highest level. The following are the most recent Supreme Court decisions in Norway (Website www.lovdata.no) concerned with sexual abuse of children by men after online grooming:

1. A man was sentenced for sexual intercourse with a girl of 13 years and 10 months with whom he achieved contact on the Internet. The case was about the amount of reparation. Even if the girl had claimed to be older than she was and participated in the act, the court decided that the reparation could not be reduced because of the victim's participation. The reparation amount was set to 40,000 Norwegian kroner (5,000 euro).
2. A 30 year-old man had sexual intercourse with a girl of 14 years and 11 months. The court decided that the appellate court had imposed too lenient a sentence. The sentence was increased to *125 days* imprisonment and 25,000 kroner in reparation to the victim.
3. A 21 year-old man was sentenced for having had intercourse on three occasions with a girl of 13 years and 10 months. The court decided that society service was an inappropriate sentence. The offender was liable to imprisonment for *two years and one month*, of which one year and four months were made conditional.
4. A 22 year-old man was liable for two cases of engaging in sexual activity with a girl 13 years and 9 months of age. The offender had admitted the act, but did not admit guilt. The court did not find grounds to impose society service, and the sentence was set to *two years and one month* imprisonment, of which six months were made conditional.

5. A 32 year-old man had sexual intercourse on three occasions with a girl of 12 years of age. The sentence was set to conditional imprisonment for *two years*. The convicted had achieved trust with the girl after chatting on the Internet, he had made a video of one incident of sexual intercourse and in two cases he did not use contraceptives. The offender admitted the crime and he stressed that he was in a very complicated personal situation. The victim received a reparation amount for psychological damage.

6. The case was about the period of imprisonment to be imposed because of sexual intercourse with a girl of 13 years and 9 months. Even if there were favourable circumstances for the offender, including immediately admitting the crime, there were also unfavourable circumstances, such as the offender giving the victim alcohol so that she got drunk. The court imposed imprisonment for *two years and one month*, of which one year and one month was conditional.

7. A 33 year-old man had sexual intercourse with a girl of 13 years and 8 months, and the Supreme Court had to decide about the period of imprisonment. The man had achieved contact with the girl on a chat page on the Internet. The fact that the girl had indicated her age was 16 years was not to be given any weight in respect of the length of imprisonment, because the convicted was to be convicted for mistake made as regards age. It was not taken into account that the girl had earlier experience of sexual intercourse. The convicted man suffered negative attention from sensational headlines in the media but the court found the media attention was to be expected and it did therefore not influence the sentence. He was sentenced to the minimum of *two years* imprisonment.

8. A 25 year-old man had sexual intercourse with two girls of 12 years and 11 months and 15 years and 8 months respectively. The convicted had established contact with the girls via Internet and SMS messages. The sentence was set to *two years and one month* imprisonment.

9. A man who was 21 years old at the time of the act was convicted to imprisonment for *30 days* for sexual activity with two girls less than 16 years of age. Since the sentence was appropriate for the seriousness of the crime, the appeal was rejected.

10. A 25 year-old man had sexual intercourse with his girlfriend of 13 ½ years of age. The sentence from the court of appeals was reduced.

11. A man, who at the time of the act was 21 years old, was sentenced to *one year and three months* imprisonment, of which ten months were made conditional, for completed sexual intercourse with two girls of 13 and 15 years. The court assumed that the man had exploited the situation to achieve sexual intercourse with the girls. It was also carried weight that no contraceptives were used. That the man has psychological problems was considered a milder circumstance.

12. A 26 year-old man was sentenced to imprisonment for *one year*. He had sexual intercourse with a young girl, with whom he achieved contact via a chat line on the Internet. The court made half of the sentence conditional. It was taken into account that the convicted had confessed immediately and agreed his guilt while interviewed by the police.

Based on these most recent cases of court decisions in Norway, it seems that a typical sentence for sexual abuse of children following online grooming is about two years. The above decisions ranged from thirty days to two years and one month imprisonment, as summarised in Table 5.1. The average age of the offender in the table is 29 years old. Victims are all between 12 and 16 years old.

In many of the sentences above, a chat line is the contact medium for offender and victim. A chat line is established within an electronic chat room, which is defined by Sheldon and Howitt (2007: 96) as follows:

> A chat room typically appears as a small window on the computer screen. Chat rooms are cyber-places where numbers of people 'chat' simultaneously to each other. Everyone's 'chat' shows on the screen in real-time. It is possible to chat in private to another person and, of course, the topics can be anything including cyber sex and arranging to meet. Users can make material available to others via file transfer or live web cam images.

While in prison convicted offenders are the responsibility of the Correctional Services in Norway. In 2008 the Norwegian government presented a white paper to the parliament formulating new policy for all correctional services. For sexual abusers of children, the new policy requires a risk assessment of all convicted paedophiles while in prison. The risk assessment should determine the likelihood and the consequence of future abuses. The purpose of the risk assessment is not to predict future behavioural crime, but rather to redirect treatment so that both likelihood and consequences are reduced (Stortingsmelding, 2008).

Norwegian Court of Appeal decisions

The function of the Courts of Justice in Norway is to settle civil disputes brought to court and to be responsible for a society's right to respond to and punish whoever breaks Norwegian Law (www.domstol.no).

The main courts of justice in Norway are: The Supreme Court, The Interlocutory Appeals Committee of the Supreme Court, The Courts of Appeal, and the District Courts. All of the latter can rule on both civil and criminal cases. The Courts of Justice have a vital role in maintaining law and order in a state based on democratic principles. The principle of the sovereignty of the people: the idea that the power resides with the people, is the basis of Norwegian constitution, with the National Assembly (the Storting) as the state's highest elected body. Courts of law have the duty and obligation to reach a decision in all the individual cases brought before them. In order for a case to be processed the concerned parties must bring the issue to court if the case is to be heard. The Courts of Justice can never commence a case on their own initiative (www.domstol.no).

All common criminal cases commence in the District Courts, which are termed 'first instance' courts of law. When the court of law pronounces a conviction or guilty verdict, this act expresses society's opinion that a law has been broken which requires punishment. The Constitution states that only a court of law has the authority or right to impose punishment on a lawbreaker (www.domstol.no).

Table 5.1 Summary of recent supreme court decisions in online victimisation cases in Norway

No.	Offender age	Victim age	Online medium	Victimisation offence	Imprisonment time	Court case
HR1	47	13	Chat line for erotic communication on the Internet	Sexual intercourse once	2 years	HR-2004-1117
HR2	30	14	Internet email invitation home to offender	Sexual intercourse once	120 days	HR-2005-207
HR3	21	13	Contact and agreed to meet using SMS	Sexual intercourse once	2 years 1 month	HR-2005-667
HR4	22	13	SMS after having found her mobile number	Sexual intercourse once	2 years 1 month	HR-2005-666
HR5	32	12	Chat line on the Internet	Sexual intercourse three times	2 years	HR-2003-428
HR6	20	13	Chat line on the Internet	Sexual intercourse once	2 years 1 month	HR-2004-803
HR7	33	13	Chat line on the Internet	Sexual intercourse	2 years	HR-2004-36
HR8	25	12 / 15	Internet / SMS	Sexual intercourse with both victims	2 years 1 month	HR-2002-1261
HR9	21	16 / 16	Internet	Sexual activity	30 days	HR-2002-296
HR10	25	13	Internet	Sexual intercourse	2 years	HR-2002-738
HR11	21	13 / 15	Internet	Sexual intercourse with both victims	1 year 3 months	HR-2002-459
HR12	26	13	Chat line on the Internet	Sexual intercourse	1 year	HR-200 1-468

There are six Courts of Appeal: the Borgarting Court of Appeal in Oslo, the Eidsivating Court of Appeal in Hamar, the Agder Court of Appeal in Skien, the Gulating Court of Appeal in Bergen, the Frostating Court of Appeal in Trondheim, and the Hålogaland Court of Appeal in Tromsø. Therefore the country is divided into six appellate districts. A senior judge president heads each Court of Appeal and each Court of Appeal has several appellate judges (www.domstol.no). There were recently 13 cases in Norwegian Courts of Appeal involving online grooming as listed in Table 5.2.

Norwegian District Court decisions
The district courts in Norway are the courts of first instance in the judiciary system. They can rule in both criminal and civil cases. There were recently five cases in Norwegian District Courts involving online grooming as listed in Table 5.3.

Convicts' online grooming behaviours
Spraydate in districts court case 1 was one of Norway's largest virtual communities. Spraydate started as a dating service on the Internet and developed slowly into a virtual community (Figure 5.1). Spraydate in its concept was not very different from more popular virtual communities today in Norway, such as Biip, Nettby, Blink and Facebook.

Members of Spraydate developed Spraydate profiles, which contained personal information, pictures and Spraydate interests. They could also participate in different kinds of Spraydate contests, exchange private and public Spraydate messages and join different Spraydate groups. Spraydate's primary target group was in the age of 18 to 32 years old. This is a slightly older segment than Biip. Spraydate was launched in Norway on February 1, 2000, and in a short while became one of Norway's most popular web services.

The court decisions provide little information on how the online grooming occurred. Here is translated text from all the court transcripts (HR – Supreme Court, LR – Courts of Appeal, TR – District Courts):

HR1. The two met the day before electronically and got in touch with each other on an erotic talking line (chat line) on the Internet. In this conversation, which also touched on sex, he said that he was 39 years old, while she said she would be 16. He asked for her phone number and called her the next day and they agreed to meet at a gas station. There she entered his car.

HR2. The victim visited the offender in his house, after he invited her via e-mail to see a movie.

HR3. Victim and offender met in a shop, where she asked him to buy cigarettes for her. Afterwards, he sent her SMS and she responded. They agreed to meet and they had sex at the offender's place.

HR4. Offender found her mobile number and sent her an SMS asking about her age.

HR5. They met on a chatting channel on the Internet. Later the victim met the offender in a hotel room for sex and video recording of sexual intercourse.

Table 5.2 Summary of recent courts of appeal decisions in online victimisation cases in Norway

No.	Offender age	Victim age	Online medium	Victimisation offence	Imprisonment time	Court case
LR1	20	15	Chat line	Sexual intercourse once	45 days	LA-1999-1264
LR2	36	15, 15	Erotic chat line	Boys sucking offender's penis	5 months	LA-2002-587
LR3	41	6–13	Internet mail with direct sexual contents	Sexual rape of several girls over a long period of time; earlier conviction	4 years minimum (custody rule)	LB-2006-102096
LR4	48	13	Chatting with a group of girls who were friends	Masturbated her; and sexual assault of several other girls	1 year 9 months	LB-2004-26490
LR5	20	15	Chat line and 30 sexually oriented e-mails and SMS	Rape with sexual abuse	2 years 9 months	LB-2004-102082
LR6	23	13–15	Internet	Rape of several girls and violence in relationships and drugs	6 years 6 month	LF-2007-54934
LR7	27	13–14	Internet: Offering actor roles in movies	Rape of several girls	9 years	LF-2006-156711
LR8	30	13, 13	Erotic chatting on the Internet	Sexual intercourse and surrogate with both victims	2 years 1 month	LF-2000-861
LR9	23	13	Chatting on the Internet	Sexual intercourse once	2 years	LG -2002-1226
LR10	19	14	Chatting on the Internet	Sexual intercourse twice	30 days	LG-2006-71563
LR11	19	13	Internet website Blink	Sexual intercourse once	2 years	LH-2006-140474
LR12	32	15	Internet and SMS	Sexual intercourse once	45 days	LH-2006-7 9242
LR13	44	13–15	Chat line on the Internet	Sexual abuse of four girls under 16 years	2 years 8 months	LA-2007-84294

Table 5.3 Summary of recent districts courts decisions in online victimisation cases in Norway

No.	Offender age	Victim age	Online medium	Victimisation offence	Imprisonment time	Court case
TR1	24 & 20*	15	Internet site Spraydate	Group sex (man and *woman) with girl	60 days	TOSLO-2002-11297
TR2	47	13	Chat on the Internet	Sexual activity with girl in chair	1 year 2 months	TOSLO-2002-10780
TR3	27	15	First chat on Blink in the Internet; then SMS	Sexual intercourse with 15 year old several times	120 days	TNHER-2007-10756
TR4	21	14	Chatting on the Internet	Sexual abuse	Case dismissed because too old (offence six years ago and police lack of investigation progress)	TKARM-2005-13086
TR5	27	14–15	Internet, said he was 18 years old	Sexual intercourse three times paid for	6 months	TAUAG-2004-80510

Figure 5.1   Internet site Spraydate where a couple (man of 24 and woman of 20) met a 15-year-old girl for group sex later (district court case TOSLO-2002-11297)

HR6. They met on a chatting channel on the Internet. Later the victim met the offender in his home where alcohol was served.

HR7. They met on a chatting channel on the Internet. They agreed to meet the same day, but the offender cancelled the meeting. They met later in the offender's car close to the victim's home.

HR8. They met on a chatting channel on the Internet and continued communicating using SMS on the mobile phone. The offender drove to the victim's home town where he booked a room in the local hotel.

HR9. They met on the Internet and agreed to meet in the offender's home where he locked the bedroom.

HR10. Internet not specified in court decision.

HR 11. Internet not specified in court decision.

HR12. They met on a chatting channel on the Internet. The chatting channel was supposed to be for persons aged 20 or more. The victim told that she was the only virgin left among her girlfriends and he responded that he could help her solve that problem. After chatting for two months, the offender went on vacation to the area where the victim lived. He contacted her via the Internet, and they agreed to meet at a shopping centre where the victim lived. She joined him in his car, and they had sex in the forest not far away. Afterwards they drove back to the shopping centre, where he let her out. They did not meet again.

LR1. They met by chatting on the Internet. They agreed to meet in a house where the victim was babysitting for a family. They had sex after the victim had argued that sex would not be smart.

LR2. They met by logging into an erotic chat line on the Internet. Both boys had sex with the man several times.

LR3. The offender sent Internet mail with direct sexual content to several girls, such as 'I want to lick yours', 'I want to see yours', and 'My cock is waiting'. They met in his car, and in the back of his car he raped each of them.

LR4. The offender started chatting on the Internet with a group of girls who were friends. He invited one of the girls to meet him at a café. They met there several times. They kissed when they met. After several café meetings, the victim joined the offender and went to his home.

LR5. He met her on an Internet chat line and exchanged at least 30 sexually oriented e-mails and SMS. The offender suggested several times to meet, and the victim finally agreed. They met at a shopping centre. They bought tickets in a movie theatre for a performance later that night. The offender said he had to pick up something in his apartment and asked the victim to join him. He raped her in his apartment and afterwards said 'sorry'. She accepted it, and they went to the movie.

LR6. Internet not specified in court decision.

LR7. The offender used false identity and false threats, as well as offering the girls the opportunity to become movie stars. He was sentenced to 9 years imprisonment, which is the longest sentence in our sample. He had sexual intercourse with 13 young girls and he carried out 6 rapes of young girls.

LR8. They met on an erotic chatting channel on the Internet.

LR9. They had met in a chat group where the minimum age was supposed to be 16 years. They agreed to meet at a shopping mall. They had sex in a handicap toilet at the mall.

LR10. Chatting on the Internet not specified in court decision.

LR11. The victim and offender had met before, but they met again on the web site Blink on the Internet. The sexual abuse took place one month after the first online contact between them.

LR 12. The victim and offender met on the Internet. Several months after their initial online meeting, they agreed on SMS to meet. The girl was at a public dance, where the offender picked her up as agreed.

LR13. Chatting on the Internet not specified in court decision.

TR1. The girl had posted a profile about herself on the website Spraydate with the correct information that she was 15 years old. The woman (20) read this information and told her boyfriend (24) about the girl. Both communicated with her on Spraydate. All three met and had sex.

TR2. The offender aged 47 claimed to be 19 years old on a chatting channel. He got in touch with a girl in wheel chair who was soon to become 14 years old. The acquaintance developed into a sexual relationship that lasted for a couple of months before it was discovered.

TR3. Offender and victim met at chat web Blink (see Figure 4.2).

Figure 5.2   Some offenders and victims (LR11, TR3) met here at Blink where it says on the right hand side. 'What is blink? girls. boys. friends. pictures. video. groups. discussions. birthdays. concerts. smile'

TR4. Chatting on the Internet as well as SMS.
TR5. Chatting on the Internet not specified in court decision.

A total of 30 court cases have been presented above. They are plotted in Figure 5.3 to identify possible relationship between the age of the victim in terms of years and the length of imprisonment for the offender.

International legislation to combat child sex abuse

Kierkegaard (2008) argues that criminal paedophiles can more easily live out their fantasies because of the lack of direct governance by an international body which could curb the illegal content and activity. Because cyberspace has no national boundary, each country has to apply its own legislation within its national border creating disparity in legislations. Most countries already have laws protecting children, but what is needed is a concerted legislation to combat child sex abuse.

With the enactment of the Convention on the Protection of Children against Sexual Exploitation and Sexual Abuse, this may soon become reality in Europe. The aim of the convention is to

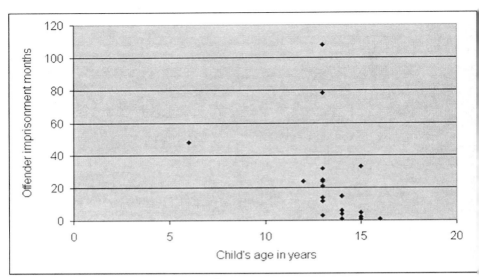

Figure 5.3   Relationship between victim age and offender sentence

prevent sexual abuse of children and to protect the rights of the child victims. This new convention, signed by the European Ministers of Justice in 2007, is the first instrument to establish the various forms of sexual abuse of children as criminal offences, as well as the grooming of children for sexual purposes and sex tourism (Kierkegaard, 2008).

Article 23 introduces a new offence of grooming or solicitation of children for sexual purposes. This has never been addressed in other existing international instruments in the field. All the elements of the offence must be committed intentionally. In addition, the purpose of the proposal to meet the child for committing any of the specified offences needs to be established before criminal responsibility is incurred. Sexual chatting does not constitute an offence (Kierkegaard, 2008).

Sexual solicitations involve requests to engage in sexual activities or sexual talk or give personal sexual information. A national random sample of young Internet users in the United States (ages 10 to 17) found 13 per cent had experienced an unwanted sexual solicitation on the Internet in the past year (Mitchell et al., 2008). Many of these incidents were confined to the Internet and relatively mild in nature. However, the potential for online sexual solicitation and harassment has raised obvious concerns among parents, teachers, and mental health professionals. Online harassment involves threats or other offensive behaviour sent online to the youth or posted online about the youth for others to see.

Sexual grooming is outlawed by the new EU convention. However, grooming is not addressed in the legislation in many member states. Also, harmonisation of legislation is needed. For example, in Greece a child is defined as such under the age of eight, while in other countries, it could be under the age of 18. Presently, Kierkegaard (2008) finds there are cultural problems associated with harmonising the law. For example, the legal age for sexual consent varies from country to country: in Spain, the legal age is 13, while it is 17 in Cyprus.

United Kingdom was one of the first EU member states with strong legislation that makes it illegal to contact and groom children with the intent of committing a sexual offence. This new offence category was included in the Sexual Offences Act 2003 in England and Wales (this section of the Act also applies to Northern Ireland). The Sexual Offences Act 2003 (England and Wales) is currently under review in Northern Ireland. Some concerns have been raised regarding a lack of clarity around the age of consent and informed consent. Currently the age of consent is 17 in Northern Ireland (it was raised from 16 to 17 under the Children and Young Persons Act 1950). The current section 15 makes 'meeting a child following sexual grooming' an offence, this applies to the Internet, other technologies such as mobile phones and to the 'real world'. The Protection of Children and Prevention of Sexual Offences (Scotland) Act 2005 includes 'meeting a child following certain preliminary contact' (s1) where a person arranges to meet a child who is under 18, having communicated with them on at least one previous occasion (in person, via the Internet or via other technologies) with the intention of performing sexual activity on the child.

Other countries are beginning to legislate against grooming behaviour. Sexual grooming has also recently been added to the Crimes Amendment Act 2005 in New Zealand. In the United States it is an offence to electronically transmit information about a child aged 16 or under for the purpose of committing a sexual offence (US Code Title 18, Part 1, Chapter 117, AS 2425). The Australian Criminal Code (s218A) makes similar restrictions, as does the Canadian Criminal Code (s172.1). The legislation in Scotland, England and Wales differs in that the sexual grooming offence applies both to the Internet and to the 'real world'; legislation in some other countries addresses only electronic grooming via the Internet and mobile phones.

The UK legislation has resulted in the arrest of several paedophiles and the rescue of many children. Kierkegaard (2008) argues that the grooming process in order to abuse a child sexually should be considered criminal and included in the EU legislation as well.

6

Knowledge Management in Policing the Internet

This chapter explores the policing of the Internet, including managing and risk assessing Internet sex offenders, drawing upon the latest research findings and current police practice in this developing area. Policing the Internet is a global problem that requires a global solution. Police forces are increasingly working together to solve the problem. As offenders' use of the Internet becomes increasingly sophisticated, policing techniques must remain current.

Risk assessment techniques play an important role in detecting and managing Internet sex offenders, presently focusing upon the use of Risk Matrix 2000 and the advice of the Sentencing Advisory Panel (SAP) in the UK on classifying categories of Internet offenders convicted for possession of indecent images of children. The Sentencing Advisory Panel system in the UK does not, however, extend to offenders grooming children.

Many police forces in Europe, Canada and the USA are working to trace Internet sex offenders and their victims. In the UK, national and local High Technology Crime Units currently investigate the grooming of children on the Internet and indecent online images of children. Successful prosecutions have been brought under the acts in the UK, both for grooming online and for the possession of indecent Internet images on the Internet following Operation Ore. This operation was launched following information provided to the UK police by the FBI in the USA regarding peer-to-peer technology in sharing indecent images of children. The National Crime Squad has made several thousand convictions since 2002 under Operation Ore (Davidson and Martellozzo, 2008).

Interpol policing crime against children

Children are the most vulnerable individuals in our society; they are also the most precious commodity that the world has and have a right to be protected from all forms of abuse. Interpol as an organisation is also committed to eradicating the sexual abuse of children and has passed several resolutions making crimes against children one of international policing's top priorities (www.interpol.int/public/children/default.asp).

Interpol's involvement in the investigation of offences against children began in 1989 following the adoption of the United Nations Convention on the Rights of the Child. To prevent a crime, and especially to prevent a child from being abused, is the goal of all law enforcement agencies. To reach this goal, Interpol is working globally with several partners raising awareness and focusing on the need to act locally and think globally so as to address the abuse of children committed by those who travel beyond borders. Interpol's specialist group on crimes against children focuses on four different arenas:

- commercial exploitation and trafficking in children
- sex offenders
- serious violent crimes against children
- child pornography

This represents a worldwide forum of specialists dealing with this type of crime (www.interpol.int/public/children/default.asp).

Interpol also have activities in different regions of the world to ensure that law enforcement officers understand the need to act upon requests involving children at risk, and create a global understanding about how to address victim identification and help rescue children being sexually abused and pornographically exploited (www.interpol.int/public/children/default.asp).

Operationally, Interpol supports member states in carrying out large operations investigating the commercial exploitation of children, paedophile networks and also supports on-going cases. The end result of the work undertaken by Interpol should be that member states see the need to share information and issue Green Notices on the offenders who travel to commit their crimes (www.interpol.int/public/children/default.asp).

Interpol keep an updated overview of legislation of Interpol member states' legislation on sexual offences against children. The legislation overview is classified under the following headings:

- ages for legal purposes
- rape
- other forms of child sex abuse
- child prostitution
- child pornography
- Internet
- extra-territorial legislation

(www.interpol.int/Public/Children/SexualAbuse/NationalLaws/Default.asp)

Cyber police

Cyber police refers to police departments and police stations in charge of policing cyber crime. The major purpose of cyber police is to fight crime on the Internet. In India, the Cyber Crime Investigation Cell is a wing of Mumbai Police set up to deal with cyber crime and to enforce Indian information technology laws. Dutch police has set up an Internet Brigade to fight cyber crime in the Netherlands, while the IWF in the UK has a similar function. Cyber crime refers to criminal activity where the electronic network is the source, tool, target, or place of a crime; an example is obscene or offensive content of websites.

Knowledge management in policing

Policing the Internet requires knowledge. Knowledge needs to be managed to support police work. This chapter explores knowledge management in law enforcement by identifying knowledge needs in policing online groomers.

Knowledge management has emerged as a critical success factor in law enforcement (Dean et al., 2008; Centrex, 2005b; ERA, 2008; Jaschke et al., 2007). Knowledge management is concerned with simplifying and improving the process of sharing, distributing, creating, capturing and understanding knowledge. Police agencies are transforming from bureaucratic organisations into knowledge organisations. Bennet and Bennet (2005) define knowledge organisations as complex adaptive systems composed of a large number of self-organising components that seek to maximise their own goals but operate according to rules in the context of relationships with other components. In an intelligent, complex, adaptive system the agents are people. The systems (organisations) are frequently composed of hierarchical levels of self-organising agents (or knowledge workers) which can take the forms of teams, divisions or other structures that have common bonds. Thus, while the components (knowledge workers) are self-organising, they are not independent from the system they comprise (the professional organisation).

Knowledge management comprises a range of practices used in an organisation to identify, create, represent, distribute and enable adoption of insights and experiences. Such insights and experiences comprise knowledge, which is defined as information combined with interpretation, reflection and context. Knowledge management efforts typically focus on organisational objectives such as improved performance, innovation, the sharing of lessons learned, and continuous improvement of the organisation. Knowledge management in law enforcement is concerned with the practices of collecting, applying and distributing knowledge in law enforcement (www.wikipedia.org).

Collier (2006) argues that effective knowledge management is as important to policing as to any other public or private sector organisation in terms of improving performance. Over the past ten years, there has been a shift from a reactive, response-led to a proactive, intelligence-led style of policing. In the UK, Norway and many other countries, the intelligence-led approach has been developed into a systematic approach such as NIM by national criminal intelligence services. The intelligence used in both strategic and tactical assessments is derived from a number of knowledge and information sources and the production of assessments represents knowledge work as well.

We have argued that policing and prosecuting has to be supplemented by development of an online environment in which children can avoid being trapped and avoid becoming victims. The field of knowledge management has much to offer in all these regards. Knowledge management by its nature is a field made up of many disciplines from information technology, information science, and artificial intelligence through to human resources management, business management, organisational culture and cognitive psychology (Davidson and Martellozzo, 2008).

For our purposes here what is important from a knowledge management perspective is the view that knowledge cannot be managed in the mechanic way envisioned by IT hardware and software systems and by the addition of parental control techniques to software and hardware. Rather, the only thing that can be managed is the context in which knowledge occurs (Davidson and Martellozzo, 2008).

Knowledge categories

A knowledge matrix is a table that lists knowledge needs (Dean and Gottschalk, 2007). The matrix shows knowledge categories and knowledge levels. Here we make distinctions between the following knowledge categories for policing the Internet:

1. *Administrative knowledge* is knowledge about police as an organisation and work place. It is knowledge about procedures, rules and regulations.
2. *Policing knowledge* is knowledge about work processes and practices in police work when fighting crime. Police knowledge is based on police science, which includes all aspects of policing internally as well as externally. It includes external factors that influence the role and behaviour of police in society.
3. *Investigative knowledge* is knowledge based on case specific and case oriented collection of information to confirm or disconfirm whether an act or no-act is criminal. Included here are case documents and evidence in such a form that they prove useful in a court case.
4. *Intelligence knowledge* is knowledge based on a systematic collection of information concerned with a certain topic, a certain domain, certain persons or any other focused scope. Collected information is transformed and processed according to a transparent methodology to discover criminal capacity, dispositions and goals. Transformation and processing generate new insights into criminality that guide the effectiveness and efficiency of policing. Included in intelligence knowledge is phenomenological knowledge, which is defined as knowledge about a phenomenon in terms of what it is about (know-what) how it works (know-how) and why it works (know-why). Phenomenological knowledge enables an intelligence officer to 'see' what 'something' is about, by understanding and not missing information when it emerges.
5. *Legal knowledge* is knowledge of the law, regulations and legal procedures. It is based on access to a variety of legal sources both nationally and internationally, including court decisions. Legal knowledge is composed of declarative, procedural and analytical knowledge. Declarative knowledge is law and other regulations. Procedural knowledge is the practice of law. Analytical knowledge is the link between case information and laws.
6. *Technological knowledge* is knowledge about the development, use, exploitation and exploration of information and communication technology. It is knowledge about applications, systems, networks and databases.
7. *Analytical knowledge* is knowledge about the strategies, tactics and actions that police can implement to reach desired goals.

In addition to this classification into knowledge categories, we also make distinctions between knowledge levels:

1. *Basic knowledge* is knowledge necessary to get work done. Basic knowledge is required for an intelligence officer and investigator as a knowledge worker to understand and interpret information and basic knowledge is required for an intelligence and investigation unit as a knowledge organisation to receive input and produce output. However, basic knowledge alone produces only elementary and basic results of little value and low quality.
2. *Advanced knowledge* is knowledge necessary to get good work done. Advanced knowledge is required for an intelligence officer and investigator as a knowledge worker to achieve satisfactory work performance, and advanced knowledge is required for an intelligence and investigation unit as a knowledge organisation to produce intelligence reports and crime analysis as well as charges that are useful in policing police crime. When advanced knowledge is combined with basic knowledge, then we find professional knowledge workers and professional knowledge organisations in law enforcement.
3. *Innovative knowledge* is knowledge that makes a real difference. When intelligence officers and investigators apply innovative knowledge in intelligence and analysis of incoming and available information, then new insights are generated in terms of crime patterns, criminal profiles and policing strategies. When intelligence units apply innovative knowledge, then new methodologies in intelligence and analysis are introduced that other parts of the police can learn.

Based on these categories and levels, our knowledge matrix consists of nine knowledge categories and three knowledge levels as illustrated in Table 6.1. The purpose of the table is to illustrate that there are a total of 27 knowledge-needs in policing online groomers. Based on the table, each intelligence unit and investigation unit has to identify and fill in the table for knowledge needs.

Knowledge levels were here defined as basic knowledge, advanced knowledge and innovative knowledge. An alternative approach is to define knowledge levels in terms of knowledge depth: know-what, know-how and know-why. These knowledge depth levels represent the extent of insight and understanding about a phenomenon. While know-what is simple perception of what is going on, know-why is a complicated insight into cause-and-effect relationships in terms of why it is going on:

1. *Know-what* is knowledge about what is happening and what is going on. A police officer perceives that something is going on that might need his or her attention. The officer's insight is limited to perception of something happening. The officer neither understands how it is happening nor why it is happening.
2. *Know-how* is knowledge about how police crime develops, how a criminal behaves or how a criminal activity is organised. The investigator's insight is not limited to a perception that something is happening; he or she also understands how it is happening or how it is.
3. *Know-why* is the knowledge representing the deepest form of understanding and insight into a phenomenon. The investigator not only knows that it occurs but how it occurs. He or she has also developed an understanding of why it occurs or why it is like this. Developing

hypotheses about cause-and-effect relationships and empirically validating causality are important characteristics of know-why knowledge.

Table 6.1 Knowledge management matrix for knowledge needs in policing online groomers

	Basic knowledge	Advanced knowledge	Innovative knowledge
Administrative knowledge	What is the role of the police?	How does the police work?	Why do the police work in this way?
Police knowledge	What do we know about online groomers?	How do we police online groomers?	Why are online groomers criminals?
Officer knowledge	What do I do?	How do I do it?	Why do I do it?
Policing knowledge	What procedures and rules are followed in policing online groomers	What procedures represent best practice in policing online groomers	How the police can be creative in understanding and policing online groomers
Investigative knowledge	Which investigative approaches are available	Which investigative approaches work best	How to select investigative approaches dependent on the situation and case
Intelligence knowledge	What information is collected and analysed for online grooming	What information is critical in policing online groomers	How is information and knowledge from intelligence analysed in a smart way
Legal knowledge	What are the legal rules making online grooming a crime?	What are the sentences in court?	How are online grooming cases argued in court?
Technological knowledge	What user behaviours can be identified?	What technology characteristics can be identified?	What are the links between user behaviours and technology characteristics?
Analytical knowledge	What segments of online grooming can be classified?	What patterns of online grooming can be classified?	How can crime mapping be applied to online grooming?

Based on these depth levels, our alternative knowledge matrix consists of nine knowledge categories and three knowledge depth levels as illustrated in Table 6.2. Again the purpose of the table is to illustrate that there are a total of 27 knowledge-needs in policing online groomers.

Knowledge management systems

When a crime reduction strategy was implemented in the UK, the following implementation lessons were learned stressing knowledge management and knowledge management systems (Homel *et al.*, 2004):

● Invest to deliver: It requires continuous development work. It goes beyond the routine processes of basic planning and priority setting. It requires a raft of preparatory work including assessments of capacity for implementation, options based on realistic risk assessments, and

Table 6.2 Alternative knowledge management matrix for knowledge needs in policing online groomers

	Know-What	Know-How	Know-Why
Administrative knowledge	What is the role of the police?	How do the police work?	Why do the police work in this way?
Police knowledge	What do we know about online groomers?	How do we police online groomers?	Why are online groomers criminals?
Officer knowledge	What do I do?	How do I do it?	Why do I do it?
Policing knowledge	What procedures and rules are followed in policing online groomers?	How do best practices work in policing online groomers?	Why should the police be creative in understanding and policing online groomers?
Investigative knowledge	What investigative approaches are available?	How do investigative approaches work best?	Why select investigative approaches dependent on the situation and case?
Intelligence knowledge	What information is collected and analysed for online grooming?	How is some information critical in policing online groomers?	Why is information and knowledge from intelligence analysed in certain ways?
Legal knowledge	What are the legal rules making online grooming a crime?	How are the sentences in court decided?	Why are court sentences the way they are?
Technological knowledge	What user behaviours can be identified?	How does technology work for online groomers?	Why do certain groomers use technology in certain ways?
Analytical knowledge	What segments of online grooming can be classified?	How can patterns of online grooming be classified?	Why should crime mapping be applied to online grooming?

the development of viable and flexible management systems, including performance management loops.

- Organise centrally to deliver locally: To support efficient local implementation, the central agency must be an active part. This means that the centre itself must be appropriately staffed with competent personnel capable of providing direct support to local initiatives.
- Separate research and evaluation from program delivery: The problem here is the different timetables for operational versus research and evaluation issues. Therefore, action to research and develop the evidence base should be undertaken as a separate but related parallel activity to the delivery of the main strategy.
- Build and maintain a knowledge management system: The management and dissemination of knowledge about implementation failures and successes, and practices and policies should be in place to stimulate learning. Effective knowledge management is basic to the continuing development and evolution of strategy implementation.

- Create flexible fund management models: Often, strategy implementation requires funding. The crime reduction strategy suffered from a variety of funding and budgeting problems. Many of these difficulties appear to have been the result of changes in the operations of central financial management in the Home Office.

Data – information – knowledge – wisdom

While data are numbers and letters without meaning, information is data in a context that makes sense. Information combined with interpretation and reflection is knowledge, while knowledge accumulated over time as learning is wisdom. In this hierarchical structure we find intelligence as more than information and less than knowledge. Intelligence is analysed information, as illustrated in Figure 6.1.

Data is considered the raw material out of which information develops. As notes, information is data endowed with relevance and purpose. The same can be said about intelligence in that it is a form of insight to which some relevance has been attached through an attempt to offer an organised analysis of the information received by a crime analyst or intelligence officer. Hence, this is why intelligence is placed between information and knowledge on the above continuum, as ideally intelligence represents as argued a form of validated information.

A core process of policing and law enforcement is investigation. It is a policing truism that information is the lifeblood of an investigation. An investigation goes nowhere if information is

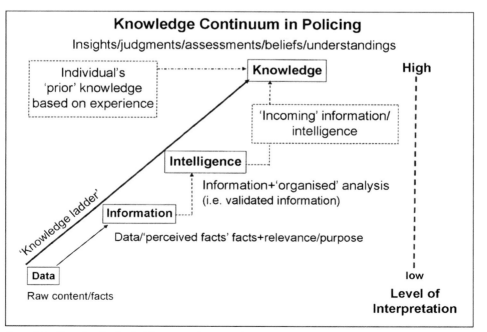

Figure 6.1   Hierarchy of police insight expressed as a continuum

not forthcoming about an incident. Information is the raw data that supplies the oxygen, which breathes life into an investigation. Information is collected by ordinary rank and file police officers either working on the street, patrolling and talking to the public, or sitting at a computer doing searches, background checks, or more sophisticated crime mapping and intelligence analysis reports.

Information, and to a similar extent, intelligence then consists of facts and other data which are organised to characterise or profile a particular situation, incident, or crime and the individual or group of individuals presumed to be involved. This organising of the data into meaningful information, of necessity involves some level of interpretation of the facts as presented. However, the role of interpretation here in information is relatively minor in comparison to its role in terms of knowledge construction. In this regard, the role of interpretation in intelligence is greater and more explicit than in information, but not as full blown as in the making of knowledge.

Knowledge helps develop relevant meaning to information in police intelligence:

> *The distinction between information and intelligence is well established, but can be difficult to grasp. Information consists of bits of data that, when combined and viewed together with relevant background knowledge, may be used to produce intelligence, which informs the actions and decisions of policing organisations.*
>
> Innes and Sheptycki, 2004: 6

Knowledge as implied operates at a higher level of abstraction and consists of judgments and assessments based in personal beliefs, truths, and expectations about the information received and how it is should be analysed, evaluated and synthesised – in short interpreted – so that it can be used and implemented into some form of action.

Classification of information sources

A variety of information sources are available to police officers involved in intelligence work. Sheptycki (2007) lists the following information sources:

- victim reports
- witness reports
- police reports
- crime scene examinations
- historical data held by police agencies (such as criminal records)
- prisoner debriefings
- technical or human surveillance products
- suspicious financial transactions reporting
- reports emanating from undercover police operations

Intelligence analysis may also refer to governmental records of other governmental departments and agencies, and other more open sources of information may be used in elaborate intelligence assessment.

However, Sheptycki (2007) found that most crime analysis is organised around existing police sector data. Intelligence analysis is typically framed by already existing institutional ways of thinking. He argues that organised crime notification, classification and measurement schemes tend to reinforce pre-existing notions of traditional police practice.

In this perspective, it is important for strategic criminal analysts to be aware of the variety of information sources available. We choose to classify information sources into the following categories in this book:

1. *Interview*. By means of *interrogation* of witnesses, suspects, reference persons and experts, information is collected on crimes, criminals, times and places, organisations, criminal projects, activities, roles, etc.
2. *Network*. By means of *informants* in the criminal underworld as well as in legal businesses, information is collected on actors, plans, competitors, markets, customers, etc. Informants often have connections with persons that a police officer would not be able to approach formally.
3. *Location*. By analysing potential and actual *crime scenes* and potential criminal scenes, information is collected on criminal procedures, preferences, crime evolution, etc. Hot spots and traces are found. Secret ransacking of suspicious places is part of this information source. Pictures, in terms of crime scene photographs, are important information elements.
4. *Documents*. Studying documents from *confiscations* may provide information on ownership, transactions, accounts, etc.
5. *Observation*. By means of *anonymous police presence* both persons and activities can be observed. Both in the physical and the virtual world, observation is important in police intelligence. An example is digital forensics, where successful cyber crime intelligence requires computer skills and modern systems in policing. Digital forensics is the art and science of applying computer science to aid the legal process. It is more than the technological, systematic inspection of electronic systems and their contents for evidence or supportive evidence of a criminal act. Digital forensics requires specialised expertise and tools when applied to intelligence in important areas such as online victimisation of children (Davidson and Gottschalk, 2008).
6. *Action*. For example, *provocation* is an action by the police to cause reactions that represent intelligence information. In the case of online victimisation of children, online grooming offenders in a paedophile ring are identified and their reaction to provocations leads intelligence officers into new nodes (persons, computers) and new actual and potential victims. While the individual paedophile is mainly concerned with combining indecent image impression and personal fantasy to achieve personal satisfaction, online organisers of sexual abuse of children are doing it for profit. By claiming on the Internet to be a boy or girl of nine years, police provoke contact with criminal business enterprises making money on paedophile customers (Davidson and Gottschalk, 2008). Undercover operations by police officers belong to the action category of information sources.

7. *Surveillance.* Surveillance of places by means of *video cameras* as well as microphones for viewing and listening belong to this information source. Police listen in on what is discussed in a room without the participants knowing. For example, police in one country identified which room was used by local Hells Angels members in their resort for crime planning and installed listening devices in that room. Harfield (2008: 64) argues that when surveillance is employed to produce evidence, such product is often considered incontrovertible (hence defence lawyers' focus on process rather than product when cross-examining surveillance officers): 'An essentially covert activity, by definition surveillance lacks transparency and is therefore vulnerable to abuse by over-zealous investigators'.

8. *Communication control.* Wire tapping in terms of *interception* belongs to this information source. Police listen in on what is discussed on a telephone or data line without the participants knowing. In the UK, the interception of communications (telephone calls, emails, letters, etc.) whilst generating intelligence to identify more conventional evidential opportunities, is excluded from trial evidence by law to the evident incredulity of foreign law enforcement colleagues (Harfield, 2008).

9. *Physical material.* Investigation of material to identify, for example, *fingerprints* on doors or bags, or material to identify blood type from blood splatters. Another example is legal visitation, which is an approach to identify illegal material. DNA is emerging as an important information source where DNA is derived from physical material such as hair or spit from a person. Police search is one approach to physical material collection.

10. *Internet.* As an *open source*, the Internet is as important for general information and specific happenings to police intelligence as to everyone else.

11. *Policing systems.* Readily available in most police agencies are *police records*, for example, DNA records may prove helpful when having DNA material from new suspects.

12. *Citizens.* Information from the *local community* is often supplied as tips to local police using law enforcement tip lines.

13. *Accusations.* Victimised persons and goods file a *claim* with the police.

14. *Exchange.* International *police cooperation* includes exchange of intelligence information. International partners for national police include national police in other countries as well as multinational organisations such as Europol and Interpol.

15. *Media.* By reading newspapers and watching TV, intelligence officers get access to *news*.

16. *Control authorities.* Cartel agencies, stock exchanges, tax authorities and other control authorities are *suppliers of information* to the police in the case of suspicious transactions.

17. *External data storage.* A number of business and government organisations store information that may be useful in police intelligence. For example, telecom firms store data about traffic, where both sender and receiver are registered with date and time of communication.

All these information sources have different characteristics. In Figure 6.2, information sources are distinguished in terms of the extent of trustworthiness and the extent of accessibility.

Prisons and other correctional environments are potential places for several information

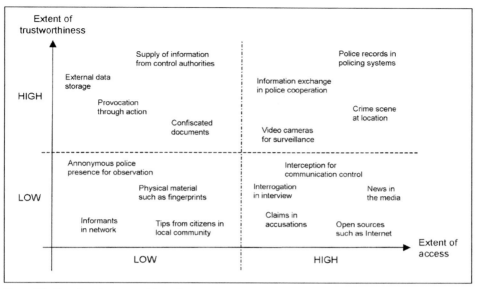

Figure 6.2   Trust in and access to information sources

sources and production of intelligence useful to law enforcement. The total prison environment, including the physical plant, the schedule regimens of both staff and inmates, and all points of ingress and egress can be legitimately tapped for intelligence purposes in countries such as the US (Maghan, 1994). Since organised criminals are often sophisticated in using the correction environment to their advantage, police and correction personnel need immersion in the intelligence operations and strategies of their respective agencies. Legal visitation and escape attempts are sources of information. Prisoners are reluctant to testify and their credibility is easily attacked. Communication control is derived from inmate use of phones, visits, mail, and other contacts.

The 17 information sources can be classified into two main categories. The first category includes all person-oriented information sources, where the challenge in police intelligence is to communicate with individuals. The second category includes all media-oriented information sources, where the challenge in police intelligence is to manage and use different technological and other media. This distinction into two main categories leads to the following classification of 17 information sources:

A. Person-oriented information sources
   1 interrogation in interview
   2 informants in network
   5 anonymous police presence undercover for observation
   6 provocation through action

12 tips from citizens in local community
13 claims in accusations
14 information exchange in police cooperation
B.*Media-oriented information sources*
  3 crime scenes at location
  4 confiscated documents
  4 confiscated documents
  7 video cameras for surveillance
  8 interception for communication control
  9 physical materials such as fingerprints
10 open sources such as Internet
11 police records in police systems
15 news in the media
16 supply of information from control authorities
17 external data storage

Fellow police officers can be the source of information in several of these categories. However, there is frequently reluctance found among police officers to turn in colleagues. Whistle blowing is not common in the police. Most Americans are familiar with whistleblowers – people who go public with information about corruption, fraud and abuse of their own organisations. Some organisations make whistle blowing very difficult and thus less probable. Johnson (2005) found that the police department is one of these organisations. She argues that the character of the police department not only makes whistle blowing less likely to occur; it ironically makes it even more necessary. In addition, she demonstrates that resistance from police departments and their retaliation against whistleblowers costs them and the public dearly.

Crime analysis

For Innes *et al.*, crime analysis is concerned with insight and understanding:

> *There has been a move away from an ad hoc, intuitive and largely unstructured mode of analytic work, to a more ordered, rationalised approach, based upon specific methodologies, on the basis that this provides a more 'objective' perspective on patterns of crime and offending. This has raised the profile and status of intelligence analysis within policing, and seen new techniques and technologies introduced, which should, at least in theory, allow police a better understanding of how, when and why crimes are occurring.*
>
> Innes *et al.*, 2005: 41

Crime analysis is described by the Council of Europe (2002) as a law enforcement function whereby data relating to crime are collected, collated, analysed, and disseminated. Crime analysis is the study of crime patterns and trends in an attempt to solve crimes or prevent their repeat occurrence.

KNOWLEDGE MANAGEMENT IN POLICING THE INTERNET

A distinction can be made between operational/tactical analysis and strategic analysis. Operational analysis is directed towards a short-term law enforcement goal with an immediate impact in mind, for example, arrest, seizure and forfeiture. The goal of strategic crime analysis is to develop a policy, to implement a policy or to evaluate the policy based on insights into the nature of a type of crime or criminal, the scope and projections of growth in types of criminal activities. But strategic analysis need not be restricted to crime; methods of strategic analysis can be used principally for all kinds of security and safety problems. Strategic analysis can deal with crime as well as with other security issues like traffic problems and public order maintenance. According to the Council of Europe (2002) it starts with the question: which information is needed, which data is lacking? A structured plan has to be developed and to be discussed. The next step is the detection of a problem, the consideration of a new phenomenon, the gathering of information.

Examples of strategic crime analysis include:

- *Crime pattern analysis*: Examination of the nature and distribution of crime within an area in order to identify emerging and current trends and patterns, linked crimes or incidents and hot spots of activity. Includes crime trend identification, crime series identification, general profile analysis and hot spot analysis. Examination of the nature and scale of crime within an area and within a time frame.

- *Crime control methods analysis*: Evaluation of investigative or preventive methods and techniques with the aim of establishing their future usefulness.

- *General profile analysis*: Identification of the typical characteristics of perpetrators of certain crimes.

- *Results analysis*: Evaluation of the effectiveness of law enforcement activities.

- *Demographic/social trends analysis*: Examination of the nature of demographic changes and their impact on criminality, as well as the analysis of social factors (for example, unemployment) which might underlie changes in trends in offending patterns. Also to describe statistically the constitution of the population of a given area and the associated economic indicators with reference to law enforcement requirements.

- *Criminal business analysis/profile*: Examination in detail how illegal operations/businesses and techniques work.

- *Market profile*: A survey of the criminal market around a given commodity (for example, illicit drugs, stolen vehicles). It can include crime pattern analysis and network analysis.

- *Strategic analysis*: Category of types of crime analysis designed to aid the formation or evaluation of crime policy. Aims to provide information which can represent a picture of a phenomenon, and which can identify trends in criminality on which management can base their decisions.

Examples of tactical/operational crime analysis include:

- *Specific profile analysis*: Identification of the specific characteristics of perpetrators of certain crimes. Construction of a hypothetical picture of the perpetrator of a serious crime or series of offences on the basis of crime scene data, witnesses' statements and other available information.

- *Offender group analysis*: Examination of the structure of a group of suspects, the significance of each member and their involvement with criminal activities.
- *Investigations/operations analysis*: Evaluation of the effectiveness of activities that are undertaken within the context of an investigation.
- *Case analysis*: Establishment of the course of events immediately before, during, and after a serious offence.
- *Comparative case analysis*: Identification of series of crimes with common offenders by seeking similarities between offences.
- *Operational crime analysis*: Category of types of crime analysis designed to support the investigation of one particular crime or one specific series of crimes with common offenders. Aims to provide an understanding of the information collected during a specific investigation.
- *Network analysis*: Provision of a detailed picture of the roles played by individuals, the nature and significance of the links between people and the strengths and weaknesses of the criminal network.

United Kingdom police forces report every three months from crime analysis of organised crime. The regional offices deal with the various law enforcement organisations and some non-government organisations. Organised criminal groups are mainly investigated by the regional police forces, sometimes assisted by national agencies. In complex cases, which most the investigations of organised crime are, analysts are involved. They apply various analysis techniques, including a large variety of charting techniques, for example, to visualise associations between entities (link charts) flows of money or other commodities (flow charts) or sequences of events in time (event charts).

In intelligence analysis, the raw material for analysis is information (based on information sources) and knowledge (based on experience). We have argued that intelligence is located on a continuum somewhere between information and knowledge. Ratcliffe has presented an alternative view by arguing that intelligence is at a higher level on the continuum than knowledge and he uses the acronym DIKI for data, information, knowledge, and intelligence to illustrate his point:

> To place the DIKI continuum in context, consider this example. At a local police station, a computer database records and retains the location of residential burglary incidents. These computer records are **data**. When a crime analyst accesses the data and recognises an emerging pattern of new burglaries in an area not normally plagued with a break-and-enter problem, then this becomes **information**. In essence, raw data have been enhanced with sufficient meaning to recognise a pattern. If the analyst subsequently talks to a detective and shares this information, and the detective remembers that a new pawnshop has just opened in the area and that known burglars have been seen entering the pawnshop, this collective wisdom becomes **knowledge**. Various information strands have coalesced to

*enable the detective and the analyst to build a picture of the criminal environment in their minds, a picture that undoubtedly has gaps, but that also has enough substance to support hypotheses and contain implications. This is the structure of knowledge. Finally, when the crime analyst and the detective take their knowledge to a senior officer who agrees to investigate the pawnshop and mount a surveillance operation to target burglars and gather further information, then this knowledge becomes **intelligence**. In other words, somebody uses it explicitly to try to reduce crime.*

Ratcliffe, 2008: 99

While this definition is certainly fascinating, it is neither mainstream nor feasible when our basic assumption is that intelligence is input to analysis. Furthermore, the definition of information does also seem a little bit strange, as information here seems to imply input from knowledge. Therefore, we continue using our stage approach in terms of data, information, intelligence, knowledge and wisdom.

Online grooming knowledge

Recent research has played a key role in raising awareness about children's use of the Internet and online risks, as have organisations such as the Virtual Global task force. However, research by Davidson and Martellozzo (2008) suggests that children are not routinely educated about sexual abuse in the context of formal education and are infrequently educated about basic safety online at school in the UK. The issue seems really much wider than online safety, as teachers participating in this work have suggested that it seems pointless to warn children about the dangers they may encounter in cyberspace unless this information is imparted in the context of wider education about sexual abuse.

Along with the police, Davidson and Martellozzo (2008) argue that schools should play an active role in educating children about sexual abuse and safety strategies in the context of the national curriculum. In order to do this effectively, training and guidance should be provided for teachers, and such work should involve parents and other care-taking persons. As mentioned earlier, children who received the Metropolitan Police Safer Surfing program appeared to be more knowledgeable about the dangers they might encounter when online.

Davidson and Martellozzo's (2008) research highlights that the Metropolitan Police Safer Surfing program designed by police is a useful and relatively effective addition to managing the knowledge that children need to know about the online environment in order to remain safe from prolonged exposure to illegal child abuse imagery on the web. This police initiative in the UK to work systematically with schools to educate children about sexual abuse in the real world and in cyberspace has potential to evolve into communities of practice internationally.

In the knowledge management literature these communities of practice are made up of members who have a professional interest in some area who seek out others with similar interests and hence a self-organising type of group evolves over time. This professional interest is largely based on the tacit knowledge of individuals and hence resides in the head and is consequently rarely made explicit or documented to the degree that such tacit knowledge requires to be of value. Such practice links often begin in an informal manner as in working together on a project like the Safer Surfing program and may become formalised at some point. However, the really key point is that whatever form such a community of practice may take in reality, it is the richness and depth of the knowledge sharing that takes place in them which is the essential element.

7

Knowledge Management in Grooming Investigations

An investigation is an effective search for material to bring an offender to justice. Knowledge and skills are required to conduct an effective investigation. Investigative knowledge enables investigators to determine if a given set of circumstances amounts to a criminal offence, to identify the types of material that may have been generated during the commission of an offence and where this material may be found. It also ensures that investigations are carried out in a manner which complies with the rules of evidence, thereby increasing the likelihood that the material gathered will be admitted as evidence.

Knowledge assists investigators to make effective and accountable decisions during an investigation. It enables them to locate, gather and use the maximum amount of material generated by the commission of an offence to identify and bring offenders to justice.

Centrex (2005a) has outlined the knowledge that investigators require to conduct competent criminal investigation. There are four areas of investigative knowledge required to conduct an effective investigation and these are:

- the legal framework.
- characteristics of crime.
- national and local force policies
- investigative skills.

Firstly, all investigators must have a current and in-depth knowledge of criminal law and the legislation, which regulates the process of investigation. Next, investigators need to understand the characteristics of crime. Crime can be placed into three broad categories: property crime, crimes against the person and crimes against society. An examination of the types of crime in each category shows that they vary widely in terms of the behaviours involved, the types of victims, the motives of offenders, the methods used to commit the crime, and the degree of planning involved. The differences between crimes are significant for investigators because the circumstances in which crimes are committed determine the volume and distribution of the material available for them to gather.

The third area of investigative knowledge is national and local police force policies. The police service is a complex organisation with its procedures and resource management. Many of these policies have a direct bearing on the conduct of investigations and investigators should have knowledge of these that are relevant to the type of investigations they are involved in.

Finally, investigative skills are required. Investigations should be conducted with integrity, commonsense and sound judgment. Actions taken during an investigation should be proportionate to the crime under investigation and take account of local cultural and social sensitivities. The success of an investigation relies on the goodwill and cooperation of victims, witnesses and the community.

Although investigators can acquire knowledge from formal training courses and the literature that exists on criminal investigation, they also need practical experience of investigations to underpin this knowledge. Centrex (2005a) argues that investigators should never rely on experience alone. This is because experience is unique to the individual, people learn at different speeds, and each will learn something different from the process.

Effective practice is generally taken to mean simply what works, but often examples of effective practice are not detailed enough for practitioners to use successfully. Practitioners do not just need to know what works, but also how and why something works if they are to understand and use the information effectively (Crimereduction, 2007). In addition to know-what, there is a need for know-how and know-why.

Police investigation is knowledge work. Investigation is the police activity concerned with the apprehension of criminals by the gathering of evidence leading to their arrest and the collection and presentation of evidence and testimony for the purpose of obtaining convictions. According to Smith and Flanagan (2000), the process begins with an initial crime scene assessment where sources of potential evidence are identified. The information derived from the process then has to be evaluated in order to gauge its relevance to the investigation. During the next stage, the information is interpreted to develop inferences and initial hypotheses. The senior investigating officer (SIO), can then develop this material into appropriate and feasible lines of enquiry. The SIO will have to prioritise actions and identify any additional information that may be required to test that scenario. As more information is collected, this is the fed back into the process until the objectives of the investigation are achieved. Providing a suspect is identified and charged, the investigation then enters the post-charge stage where case papers are compiled for the prosecution. Subsequently, the court process will begin.

Police investigation units represent a knowledge-intensive and time-critical environment. Successful police investigations are dependent on efficient and effective knowledge sharing. Furthermore, Lahneman (2004) argues that successful knowledge management in law enforcement depends on developing an organisational culture that facilitates and rewards knowledge sharing. In this context, detectives as knowledge workers are using their brains to make sense of information. Knowledge is often defined as information combined with interpretation, reflection and context. This combination takes place in the brains of detectives.

Knowledge workers in investigations

Policing is generally viewed as a highly stressful and demanding profession. Considerable research has examined stress in policing. According to Richardsen et al. (2006), most of this work has focused on the effects of the distress of police officers, the impact of police work on officers' spouses and families, police suicide, police drinking, police mortality, police fatigue, post-traumatic stress disorder, and the effects of shift work schedules on police performance and health. Although it is not clear whether police work is inherently more demanding than other professions, police officers experience work events that are associated with psychological distress.

Richardsen *et al*. (2006) studied the mediating role of both negative (cynicism) and positive (work engagement) work attitudes in the relationship between work events and work and health outcomes. The cynicism theory proposes that police officers come into the occupation with idealistic notions but quickly come to realise the hard realities of the world and of police work. Over time, they then become increasingly intolerant of faults and mistakes in others and may lose a sense of purpose. Cynicism may be a way to cope with what is perceived to be an unfriendly, unstable, and insecure world, providing a convenient explanation for constant disillusionment and a way of acting out anger and resentment in the work place.

Richardsen *et al*. (2006) found that cynicism and engagement were highly correlated with both work and health outcomes in the expected direction: that is, cynicism was associated with increased health complaints and reduced commitment and efficacy, and engagement was associated with reduced health complaints and increased commitment and efficacy.

To understand knowledge, the notion of practice and the individual as a social participant in applying knowledge is important. Knowing and learning are integrated, continuous processes for detectives in police investigations. Knowledge always undergoes construction and transformation in use. It is not simply a matter of taking in knowledge. It is an act of construction and creation, where knowledge is neither universal nor abstract but depends on context (Chiva and Alegre, 2005).

As we sometimes find knowledge competition between police organisations and criminal organisations, it is relevant to touch on the role of women in policing. While we find significant variance on a global basis, more and more countries have female officers working with male officers on a regular basis. It is not rare anymore to find a woman police officer heading a policing unit. In fact, heading a police organisation is no surprise anymore, for example in Norway, the managing director of the whole police force is a woman.

While significant barriers still confront women in policing in many parts of the world, a number of legal and cultural obstacles to women in policing have recently been removed. Some gender differences enable female and male officers to complement each other. For example, studies show that female police officers rely on a policing style that uses less physical force and are less confrontational than male officers.

Trends in arrests of online sex offenders in the United States

A study by Wolak *et al*. (2009) finds dramatic growth nationwide in the United States in arrests of online sex offenders who solicited law enforcement investigators decoyed as juveniles. The numbers nearly quintupled from 644 in 2000 to 3,100 in 2006, according to the Crimes against

Children Research Center at the University of New Hampshire. Thus, there was a 381 per cent increase in arrests of offenders who solicited undercover investigators posing as youth.

During the same period, arrests of individuals soliciting juveniles themselves grew a comparatively modest 21 per cent, from an estimated 508 arrests in 2000 to an estimated 615 in 2006, at a time when youth Internet use was growing from 73 per cent to 93 per cent. The report, *Trends in Arrests of Online Sex Offenders* (Wolak *et al.*, 2009) cautions against parents and policy makers rushing to conclude that the increasing numbers of arrests means the Internet is an especially dangerous environment for children. Online predator arrests comprise only one per cent of arrests for sex crimes against minors. The recent growth in arrests is best explained by increasing numbers of youth online, migration of crime from offline to online venues and the intensification of law enforcement activity against online crimes, according to Wolak *et al.* (2009). The growth of arrests coincided with a large expansion of federally funded Internet crimes against children task forces in the US, revisions of state statutes to criminalise online sexual solicitations, the promotion of reporting mechanisms such as the CyberTipline run by the National Center for Missing and Exploited Children, and greater public awareness about the problem.

The report by Wolak *et al.* (2009) points out that the increases in arrests of online sex offenders occurred during a time when overall sex crimes against children were declining. Although arrests of online sex offenders are increasing, especially arrests for soliciting undercover law enforcement, the study does not suggest that the Internet is facilitating an epidemic of sex crimes against youth. Rather, increasing arrests for online predation probably reflect increasing rates of youth Internet use, a migration to online sites and improved knowledge management in law enforcement.

Most victims identified by Wolak *et al.* (2009) were girls, but boys were 16 per cent of victims in 2006, compared to 25 per cent in a previous survey in 2000. In 2006, 85 per cent of offenders were open about their sexual motives, compared to 79 per cent in 2000. Sexual violence against victims was rare, 5 per cent of arrests in 2006 and 4 per cent in 2000. In 2006, 73 per cent of cases with youth victims progressed from online contact to face-to-face meetings and illegal sexual activity, as did 76 per cent in 2000. In most cases the sex was illegal because the victims were too young to consent.

According to the report, law enforcement agencies find it easy in their investigations to locate sexually predatory behaviour toward youth online. Some law enforcement officials have suggested they could easily increase the numbers of arrests even further. After six years of considerable law enforcement mobilisation in response to online sex offenders in the US, there has been a marked increase in arrests of those who would try to use the Internet to recruit minors for sexual activity. Most of these arrests have occurred through the use of undercover decoys posing online as young adolescents.

How detectives work

According to Tong (2007) the secretive nature of the detective world has attracted little attention from researchers. However, competing perspectives about detective work can be discerned from available literature. Detective work has been characterised as an art, a craft, a science, and a combination of all three. The old regime of the seasoned detective highlighted the notion of detective work as a craft. An alternative perspective highlights the scientific nature of detective work which focuses on the skills needed for crime scene management, the use of physical evidence, investigative interviewing, informant handling, offender profiling, management of the investigative process and knowledge management.

It is important for detectives to be effective in their work, as new public management is focusing closely on the effective use of resources. However, measuring effectiveness is no easy task. Measurement, in an investigative context, has focused upon the outcome of cases, often at the expense of evaluating the process of the investigation and quality of its outputs. Tong (2007) argues that not only have the police been subject to inadequate measurement criteria such as clear-up rates, there has also been a lack of recognition of good quality police work. The task of recognising good detective work involves more than providing an appropriate method of measurement; it also implies an awareness of the impact of practice as well as an awareness of the knowledge accumulation, sharing and reuse.

It follows that the most useful approach to measuring detective effectiveness will not necessarily be the measurement of specific outcomes, although such measures will be useful for resource management. Tong (2007) argues that effectiveness in the context of detective work is best measured by focusing on the key processes and decisions in which detectives engage to encourage a professional working culture based on how detectives come to decisions. In the context of the value shop for knowledge work, decisions are made in all five primary activities: understanding the problem, identifying problem solutions, prioritising actions, implementing investigation, and evaluating and controlling detective work.

Tong (2007) constructed the following profile of an effective detective after analysing the academic literature relating to detective skills and abilities:

1. *Personal Qualities.* Intelligence, common sense, initiative, inquisitiveness, independence of thought, commitment, persistence, ability to talk to people, flexibility, ability to learn, reflexivity, lateral thinking, creative thinking, patience, empathy, tolerance and interpreting uncertain and conflicting information, ability to work away from family and home, interpreting feelings, ideas and facts, honesty and integrity.
2. *Legal knowledge.* Knowledge of the law referring to police powers, procedure, criminal justice process, a good grounding in criminal law, awareness of changes to legislation, courtroom protocol, rules of disclosure, use of evidence, format of case file and awareness of defence arguments.
3. *Practical knowledge.* Technology available to detectives and used by criminals, understanding the context in which crime is committed and awareness of investigative roles of different functions of the police organisation and specialist advisors. Recognition that crime changes with time and place and may require police responses that are tailored to specific context. Forensic awareness and practical expertise (for example, crime scene preservation and packaging of evidence).

4. *Generic knowledge.* Recognition that knowledge changes. Awareness of developments in practice will allow the detective to remain up to date.
5. *Theoretical knowledge.* Understanding of theoretical approaches to investigative reasoning and theories of crime.
6. *Management skills.* The management and control of case information, implementing investigative action, formulating investigative strategies, verifying expert advice, prioritising lines of enquiry, formulating media strategies, awareness of resource availability and knowledge of the roles of personnel available to the investigation. Managing knowledge and learning through the use of research skills to enable the detective to remain up to date.
7. *Investigative skills.* Interview technique, presenting evidence, cultivating informants, extracting core information (from files, reports, victims and witnesses), file construction, appraising and evaluating information, the ability to absorb and manage large volumes of information, statement taking, problem-solving, formulating lines of enquiry, creating slow time, assimilating information from crime scene, continually reviewing lines of enquiry, questioning and challenging legal parties.
8. *Interpersonal skills.* Ability to communicate and establish a rapport with a range of people, remain open minded, awareness of consequences of actions and avoid speculation.

Stelfox and Pease (2005) argue that there has been surprisingly little empirical research into the way in which individual officers approach the task of investigating crime. In their own research they found that investigators are practical people. Assuming that the cognitive abilities of the average investigator are no more nor less than the population as a whole, it can be anticipated that he or she will remain liable to make the same cognitive errors as the rest of us. Assuming also that the decision-making environment the detective works in is unlikely to change much, it can be anticipated that errors will recur.

Intelligence has emerged as an important component of contemporary policing strategies. However, Innes *et al.* (2005) argue that crime intelligence analysis is used in line with traditional modes of policing; is a way of claiming 'scientific objectivity' for police actions; and is largely shaped by police perspectives on data. They argue that the sense of enhanced objectivity often attributed to the products of 'intelligence work' is frequently overstated. Therefore, the products of crime analysis might better be understood as an artefact of the data and methods used in their construction, rather than providing an accurate representation of any crime problems.

Added to which, Innes *et al.* (2005) found that there has been increasing frustration within certain sections of the police organisation, with the perceived failure of community-policing programs to facilitate the routine supply of high-quality information to the police from members of the community. Any such concerns with low policing have been reinforced and amplified by recent developments at the 'high policing' level, where there is a well documented shift towards trying to effect enhanced national security from threats posed by terrorist groups, drug cartels and organised-crime networks.

The presence of criminal markets and networks implies a degree of organisation in the conduct of crime. In turn, this serves to recursively justify the investment in technologies of analysis. It signals to the police themselves that simply arresting isolated individuals will have only a temporary effect on crime levels, before the adaptive qualities and replacement mechanisms of the surrounding networks and markets cause them to reform. Therefore, they need to conduct analysis so as to improve their awareness of the shape and make-up of the supporting networks and markets in which motivated criminals are located, so that any interventions taken against them are made to have more impact (Innes *et al.*, 2005).

One of the bottlenecks in international police cooperation is the targeting of the proceeds of crime. International agencies such as Interpol and Europol are sometimes involved in the interaction between the authorities and enforcement organisations of the countries concerned. Borgers and Moors (2007) studied bottlenecks in international cooperation for the Netherlands in targeting the proceeds of crime. While no bottlenecks were found in cooperation with countries such as Belgium and the United Kingdom, bottlenecks were found in relation with countries such as Spain and Turkey. In relation to Turkey, the Netherlands acts mainly as the requesting state and not the requested state:

> *Regarding the cooperative relations with Turkey, Turkish respondents state that the framing of Dutch mutual assistance requests is inadequate. On the part of the Netherlands, there are different opinions on the depth of the investigation conducted at the request of the Netherlands. As far as the way in which people address one another is concerned, it is striking that the Turkish respondents sometimes consider the Dutch manner of operation as haughty and impatient. According to Dutch respondents, communication difficulties also occur if Dutch police officials directly contact the Turkish judges involved.*
>
> Borgers and Moors, 2007: 8

To fight organised crime, law enforcement in the UK reorganised. The United Kingdom's Serious Organised Crime Agency (SOCA) commenced operations in 2006 with an annual budget of £400 million. SOCA amalgamates the National Crime Squad, the National Criminal Intelligence Service (NCIS) and investigators from Customs and the Home Office's Immigration Service (Segell, 2007).

Detective thinking styles

In criminal investigations, detectives apply different thinking styles, such as method style, challenge style, skill style, and risk style. In a survey in Norway, detectives were asked to list the five most important characteristics of effective investigators. This was done in a free format, requiring content analysis to categorise responses. Responses were categorised according to thinking styles. While creativity was the most frequently mentioned characteristic, content analysis shows that the skill style of detectives is the most effective thinking style. To be effective, detectives need to practice good empathic communication, open-minded curiosity, logical reasoning, creative thinking, and dogged determination.

Creativity is often mentioned as a characteristic of effective detectives. Detectives can be creative in their job by generating new ways to perform their work, by coming up with novel procedures and innovative ideas, and by reconfiguring known approaches into new alternatives (Perry-Smith and Shalley, 2003). Yet, detectives are often told to work by the book, forgetting the importance of creative thinking and the importance of creative persons (Dean et al., 2008).

We distinguish between four thinking styles in police investigations (Dean et al., 2008). The method style is driven by procedural steps and conceptual processes for gathering information. The challenge style is driven by the intensity of the job, the victim, the criminal and the crime. The skill style is driven by personal qualities and the ability to relate to people at different levels. The risk style is driven by creativity in discovering and developing information into evidence.

These four investigative thinking styles, as illustrated in Figure 7.1, were introduced in this book to classify characteristics of effective detectives into relevant thinking styles. Such classification enables identification of important thinking styles and learning (Garcia-Morales et al., 2006).

Our study was concerned with how police detectives experience, understand, and think about the process of doing serious and complex criminal investigations. In police investigations, the experience of investigation begins for detectives when they are given a crime to solve. When handed a case, detectives apply the basics of the procedural method they were trained in.

There are a variety of procedural steps within the criminal investigation training literature for various types of crimes but in essence all such steps follow a logical sequence that can be subsumed under a set of basic steps, referred to as the 5 Cs' of the police procedural method

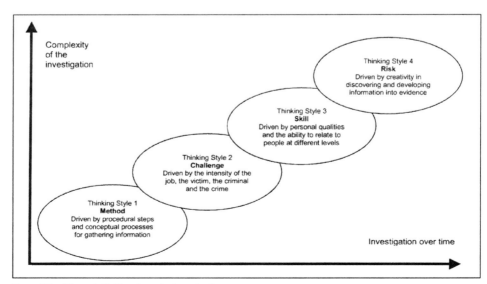

Figure 7.1   Ways of thinking about the investigation process

of investigation. The 5 Cs are the procedural steps of collecting, checking, considering, connecting and constructing – information into evidence.

Conceptually, this 'procedural method' presents a problem for detectives in that since their formal investigative training only equips them with this one way of 'thinking' investigation, the question becomes how do they learn to think in any other way or do they when investigating?

Previous empirical research has identified that apart from the above mentioned 'method' style of investigative thinking there are three other qualitatively different ways or styles of thinking that potentially can come into play when detectives investigate a crime. The three other styles or preferred ways of thinking about the investigative process that experienced detectives use with serious and complex crimes are the challenge style, the skill style, and the risk style of investigative thinking. How each of these other three investigative thinking styles works in conjunction with the basic method style is briefly outlined.

As detectives conduct a serious and/or complex investigation, they become driven by the intensity of the challenge, which motivates them to do the best job they can for the victims by catching the criminals and solving the crime through the application of the 'basic 5Cs' of the investigative style of thinking they were trained in. This challenge style of thinking is all about what motivates detectives to do the best they can. These four elements (job-victim-crime-criminal) are the key sources of intensity (Home Office, 2005b).

In meeting this investigative challenge detectives require skill to relate and communicate effectively to a variety of people to obtain information so as to establish a workable investigative focus (Kiely and Peek, 2002). Such skill also requires detectives to be flexible in how they approach people and the case, while maintaining an appropriate level of emotional involvement towards victims, witnesses, informants, and suspects. With this skill style of investigative thinking, detectives are concerned with how they relate to people. Detectives must think about how they are going to relate to the victim, witnesses, possible suspects, the local community, and the wider general public in order to get the information they need to make the case.

When exercising their investigative skills detectives seek to maximise the possibilities of a good result by taking legally sanctioned and logically justifiable risks across a wide latitude of influence. Such justifiable risk-taking requires detectives to be proactive in applying creativity to how they seek to discover new information and, if necessary, how they develop such information into evidence. This risk style revolves around how detectives think through being proactively creative enough to discover new information and if necessary develop it into evidence that will stand up to testing in a court of law.

Although experienced detectives and investigators intuitively use these four levels of thinking in an investigation, it is rare that any one detective will give equal weight to all four styles of investigative thinking in a particular case, because detectives like everyone else, have a preference for maybe one or two particular styles or ways of thinking.

This phenomenon is about the cognitive psychology of police investigators. At its core, investigation is a mind game. When it comes to solving a crime, a detective's ability to think as an investigator is everything. Four distinctively different ways of thinking are: investigation as method, investigation as challenge, investigation as skill, and investigation as risk. All four ways of describing a criminal investigation can be seen as more or less partial understandings of the whole phenomenon of investigation.

The four distinctively different ways of thinking (styles) about the investigation process by detectives is illustrated in the figure. As can be seen in the figure, there is a hierarchical structure to how investigators think. Not all cases will require the use of all four investigation-thinking styles to solve them. However, as time marches on in an investigation without a result, then other styles of investigative thinking will need to come into play to increase the likelihood of a successful outcome. In essence, the more complex the crime, the higher the investigative thinking style required to solve it.

Characteristics of effective detectives

A survey instrument was applied in this research where respondents filled in a space. In the open electronic space, respondents could write five characteristics in their own wording. To classify these responses, content analysis was needed. According to Riffe and Freitag (1997) seven features of content analysis distinguish poor studies from excellent studies. First, an explicit theoretical framework is needed. In this research, the theoretical framework of investigative thinking styles as developed by Dean et al. (2008) is applied. Second, hypotheses or research questions are needed. In this research, the research question 'what' is concerned with descriptions of characteristics. Third, other research methods should also be applied. In this research, a survey is supplemented with content analysis. Fourth, extra-media data should be incorporated. In this research, results from another investigation survey were incorporated (Glomseth et al., 2007). Fifth, inter-coder reliability should be reported. In this research, the characteristics content construct was coded by two researchers independently. Sixth, reliability based on a random sample of coded content was not relevant in this research as there is a complete set of responses. Finally, presentations of only descriptive statistics should be avoided. In this research, two independent researchers coded characteristics by respondents.

The questionnaire was sent to 325 detectives by email. With 110 responses returned, this gave a response rate of 34 per cent. However, only 71 detectives filled in the open space for characteristics of effective detectives, thereby reducing the response rate to 22 per cent. Since each detective wrote five characteristics each, a total of 355 characteristics were collected, as listed in Table 7.1.

Two raters were involved in the classification of responses. There was no need to develop key words in this research (Gottschalk, 2001) as respondents provided responses in terms of key words. Acceptable inter-rater judgment reliability (IJR) of 0.94 was achieved. Reliability is an assessment of the degree of consistency between multiple raters of a variable (Hair et al., 2006).

As can be seen in the table, 55 per cent of the respondents wrote *creativity* as one of the five characteristics of effective detectives. The word creativity comes from the Latin concept 'creare' which means 'to make' or 'to create'. Creative activity appears to be an affectively charged event, one in which complex cognitive processes are shaped by, co-occur with, and

Table 7.1 Characteristics responses (Five characteristics by 71 respondents)

Objectivity	Creativity	Involvement	Patience	Initiative
Professional	Systematic	Creative	Cooperative	Motivated
Interested	Knowledgeable	Hardworking	Collegial	Organised
Curious	Detailed	Knowledge of law	Human intelligence	Not giving up
Patience	Good writing skills	Creative	Involved	Overview
Good to communicate	Good at listening	Open mind	Social abilities	Some curiosity
Be curious	Be positive	Update oneself	Positive to new methods	Ethic attitude
Analytic abilities	Simultaneous capacity	Good judgment	Knowledge	Intelligent
Human knowledge	Professional	Objective	Honest	Flexible
Curious	Human knower	Honest	Detailed	Open mind
Open mind	Professional	Systematic	Respect for people	Logic ability
Analytic	Creative	Structured	Empathy	Working correctly
Intelligent	Structured	Offensive	Listening to ideas	Creative
Tactical	Creative	Offensive	Information seeking	Objective
Experienced	Work independent	Motivated	Analytic abilities	Cooperative
Mature thinking	Hardworking	Focus on goal	Cooperative attitude	Empathy
Organised	Honest	Knowledge	Creative	Cooperative
Structured	Communicative skills	Analytic ability	Patience	Humane
Detailed	Persistent	Creative	Judge of character	Cooperative abilities
Ability to communicate	Systematic	Ability to be objective	Positive attitude	Action oriented
Creative	Involved	Structured	Goal oriented	Social
Motivated	Detail oriented	Analytical	Systematic	Professional
Holistic	Creative	Empathetic	Involved	Good writing skills
Creative	Offensive	Human	General knowledge	Interested
Correct	Organised	Objective	Effective	Hardworking
Honest	Systematic	Thorough	Identify important issues	Empathetic
Good to cooperate	Communication	Organised	Social skills	Knowledge of task
Good to communicate	Goal oriented	Creative	Good cooperative skills	Willing to work hard
Persistent	Thorough	Open mind	Creativity	Communicative
Listening	Work in team	Curious	Think about issues	Being present
Taking responsibility	High moral	Creative	Communicative skills	Analytic
Initiative	Curious	Listening	Open mind	Fair
Creative	Engaged	Good communicator	Structured	Positive
Being objective	Analytic	Systematic	Creative	Good to communicate
Structured	Analytic	Curious	Good to formulate	Awake for new things
Objective	Creative	Patient	Offensive	Honesty

Table 7.1 *Continued*

Honest and fair	Communicating well	Awake and creative	Curious and interested	Creative
Interested in new ideas	Interested in knowledge	Concentrated	Methodical	Creative
Open	Organised	Detailed	Creative	Taking initiative
Good in communication	Observant	Human	Smart	Tactical
Knowledgeable	Open and humble	Creative	Objective	Communicative
Take good interviews	See more options	Putting question marks	Communicate	Creative
Knowledgeable	Fair	Ambitious	Patient	Thorough
Professional	Patient	Curious	Good cooperative skills	Good to communicate
Ability to socialise	Treat with respect	Patience	Interested to learn	Creative and open
Professionally interested	Good to communicate	Curious	Structured	Honest
Detailed	Trustworthy	Create confidence	Communicate	Creative
Patience	Structured	Goal oriented	Feel satisfied	Feeling sympathy
Empathy	Communication skills	Good listener	Professional	Honesty
Creative	Analytical	Staying ability	Results oriented	Personal integrity
Systematic	Analytical	Creative	Offensive	Professional
Independent	Socially skilled	Team worker	Creative	Professionally updated
Creative	Methodological	Structured	Professional competent	Social intelligence
Thorough	Professional ability	Ability to care	Moving on	Ability to cooperate
Communication skills	Empathy	Conscious ethics	Objectivity	Thorough
Professional knowledge	Thinking creatively	Independent	Learn new things	Critical reflection
Honest	Creative	Good cooperative skills	Systematically	Good formulating skills
Objective	Professionally involved	Creative	Structured	Empathy
Wide mind	Objective	Patient	Can communicate	Creative
Open	Involved	Creative	Good communicator	Independent
See connections	Active contributor	Loyal to the case	Logic thinking	Good communication
Creativity	Motivating	Professional	Investigative	Social
High integrity	Reliable	Ability to use experience	Cooperative skills	Ability to change
Structured	Objective	Professional	Curious	Creative
Knowledge	Experience	Attitude	Overview	Patience
Personal skills	See connections	Professional	Work in teams	Creative thinking
Ability to communicate	Structured	Open mind	Decision oriented	Persistent
Different perspectives	Thoroughly	Creativity	Empathy	Good communication
Ability to think logically	Ability to see pattern	Creative and intuitive	Social	Hunting instinct
Patient	Action driven	Communicative	Creative	Not conclusive
Honesty	Respect	Loyalty	Communication	Open mind

shape emotional experience (Amabile *et al.*, 2005). Novelty is a key defining criterion of creativity, which means original to the individual or team producing the idea or solution (Kaufmann, 2004).

Second to creativity, *professionalism* was mentioned by 24 per cent of the investigators. Other characteristics frequently mentioned were *objectivity*, *structured*, and *organised*.

Out of 355 characteristics, 60 characteristics were classified by the raters into the method style of thinking for detectives in police investigations. 55 characteristics were classified into the challenge style, 165 into the skill style, and 75 into the risk style.

Survey results show that the most important thinking style for effective detectives is the skill style. Examples of characteristics classified as skill style include objectivity, proficiency in communication, analytic abilities, open mind and listening skills. At the skill level of investigative thinking, detectives are concerned with how they relate to people while collecting potential evidence. Detectives must think how they are going to relate to the victim, witnesses, possible suspects, the local community, and the wider general public in order to get the information they need to make the case.

Investigation as skill emphasises the human dimension in investigative work, particularly the personal qualities of detectives. Hence, the central characteristic in this conception is relation. That is, a detective's ability to relate skilfully to a wide variety of people and, in conformity with prevailing law and regulation, collect the information vital to the matter under investigation.

Although experienced detectives and investigators intuitively use all four thinking styles in an investigation, it is rare that any one detective will give equal weight to all four styles of investigative thinking in a particular case, because detectives, like everyone else, have a preference for maybe one or two particular styles or ways of thinking.

To summarise the findings in our survey in our own words, we will argue that the five most important characteristics of a good detective are as follows:

1. *Good empathic communication (skill style)*: Detective should be a 'people person' or else will not be able to get the most valuable information out of a person (witness, victim, suspect, etc.). However, at the same time he or she must know and follow the law in detail so that the acquired information is applicable in court.

2. *Open-minded curiosity (skill style, and perhaps a bit of risk style)*: Detective should have a mind that is curious about things and open to new ways of doing things to not only discover information by making connections through being curious, but also to be open enough to avoid tunnel vision and conforming to stereotypical ideas.

3. *Creative thinking (risk style)*: Detective should be able to think creatively about the information/evidence by putting it together in different ways or looking at it from different perspectives. This outlook forms the basis for further creative thought in how to go about getting other information/evidence needed to solve a case. Creative thinking also correlates highly with curiosity and being open-minded (characteristic 2).

4. *Logical, methodical reasoning (method style)*: Detective should be able to logically derive what piece of evidence is available and useful in a particular case/situation and how legally to get

hold of it. Hence, a detective must think things through in a methodical manner without jumping to unwarranted conclusions or developing tunnel vision about a situation or person that cannot be supported with legal and logical inferences.

5. *Dogged determination, persistence (challenge style):* Detective should be able to hang in for the long haul on a difficult and protracted investigation as persistence can often crack a case. However, the reason it is the last characteristic is that just being 'determined' will not of itself necessarily find the information or evidence needed in an investigation. Hence, the reason for listing the other characteristics in priority order. If a detective has enough of the other characteristics, then determination is more likely to pass off in the long run.

From a management point of view, police investigation units need to be managed as knowledge organisations rather than bureaucratic organisations. When managed as a knowledge organisation, the skill style of detective thinking is more likely to grow and succeed in police investigations.

While the responses to the question of characteristics of good investigators indicate that the skill style is the most important, responses to another question indicate that the risk style is the one they actually apply the most, as listed in the table.

Hence, there seems to be a discrepancy between what detectives practice and what they think is a good practice. They practice the risk style most extensively, followed by the skill style. At the same time, they argue that the skill style is the most important one. This can perhaps be explained by research design limitations, assuming that it normally would seem safer to define oneself as a skilled rather than a risky detective when performing self assessment by responding to an open-ended question. Nevertheless, they are able to rate the importance of risk when it is liked to a situation and not to their own personality.

The most effective thinking style of detectives as knowledge workers was empirically found to be the skill level. While an investigation involves an evidence-gathering enterprise by human

Table 7.2 Response to thinking style items in the survey

In police investigations (1 = completely disagree, 5 = completely agree)	Mean	Deviation
Method Style of Investigative Thinking When faced with a difficult case I prefer to figure out how to solve the crime by following the basics of police procedure.	3.5	0.97
Challenge Style of Investigative Thinking I get a lot of satisfaction out of helping victims to achieve some sort of justice by bringing an alleged offender before a court.	4.1	0.92
Skill Style of Investigative Thinking I keep an open mind when investigating even when certain information suggests a possible suspect or course of action.	4.6	0.58
Risk Style of Investigative Thinking I keep an open mind and keep exploring various angles to find evidence.	4.8	0.53

beings, the conception of a detective in the knowledge organisation emphasises the quality of who is doing the gathering. Surprisingly, the same detectives claim that they apply the risk style more than the skill style. Detectives see an investigation as going nowhere unless they are able to extract good quality information out of people and their ability to do that depends on the quality of detectives' relational skill particularly with regard to communicating well with people.

8

Knowledge Management Technology

Knowledge management systems refer to a class of information systems applied to manage organisational knowledge. These systems are IT applications to support and enhance the organisational processes of knowledge creation, storage and retrieval, transfer and application.

Collier (2006) argues that technology is clearly a major impediment to progress in the intelligent application of knowledge in policing. Traditionally, inadequacies in computer systems have been evidenced in most countries in terms of the lack of national police information strategy, the inability of systems in use by different forces to communicate with each other, and the lack of integration between computer systems in any one force. There has also been a lack of confidence held by police officers in intelligence systems, suggesting that tacit rather than explicit knowledge was still fundamental to how many police officers work. This is not surprising as many police officers have considered their work a handicraft job rather than a knowledge job. The only way an inexperienced officer could learn a new policing field was to observe and join an experienced officer in their work as craftsmen.

The potential of knowledge management systems to enable new organisational forms as well as inter-organisational relationships and partnerships useful in policing will be demonstrated in this chapter by the example of geographic information systems. Partnership working is becoming an increasingly common methodology in the public sector for addressing complex social issues such as poverty, economic development and crime. According to Wastell et al. (2004) information systems have a vital role to play in enabling such inter-organisational networks and in facilitating the multi-disciplinary collaboration that is essential to joint working.

The knowledge management technology stage model presented in this chapter is a multistage model proposed for organisational evolution over time. Stages of knowledge management technology is a relative concept concerned with IT's/ICT's ability to process information for knowledge work. The knowledge management technology stage model consists of four stages. When applied to law enforcement in this chapter the stages are labelled officer-to-technology, officer-to-officer, officer-to-information, and officer-to-application.

Stages of growth model

Stages of growth models have been used widely in both organisational research and information technology management research. These models describe a wide variety of phenomena-the organisational life cycle, product life cycle, biological growth, etc. These models assume that predictable patterns (conceptualised in terms of stages) exist in the growth of organisations, the sales levels of products, and the growth of living organisms. These stages:

- are sequential in nature
- occur as a hierarchical progression that is not easily reversed
- involve a broad range of organisational activities and structures

Benchmark variables are often used to indicate characteristics in each stage of growth. A one-dimensional continuum is established for each benchmark variable. The measurement of benchmark variables can be carried out using Guttman scales. Guttman scaling is a cumulative scaling technique based on ordering theory that suggests a linear relationship between the elements of a domain and the items on a test.

In the following main part of this chapter, a four-stage model for the evolution of information technology support for knowledge management is proposed and empirically tested. The purpose of the model is both to understand the current situation in an organisation in terms of a specific stage and to develop strategies for moving to a higher stage in the future. We are concerned with the following question: Do organisations move through various stages of growth in their application of knowledge management technology over time, and is each theoretical stage regarded as an actual stage in an organisation?

Stages of growth models may be studied through organisational innovation processes. Technological innovation is considered the primary driver of improvements in many businesses today. Information technology represents a complex organisational technology, that is, technology that, when first introduced, imposes a substantial burden on would-be adopters in terms of the competence needed to use it effectively. Such technology typically has an abstract and demanding scientific base; it tends to be fragile in the sense that it does not always operate as expected; it is difficult to test in a meaningful way, and it is unpackaged in the sense that adopters cannot treat the technology as a black box.

Embodying such characteristics, organisational learning and innovation diffusion theory can be applied to explain stages of growth models. Organisational learning is sometimes placed at the centre of innovation diffusion theory through a focus on institutional mechanisms that lower the burden of organisational learning related to IT adoption. Organisations may be viewed, at any given moment, as possessing some bundle of competence related to their current operational and managerial processes. In order to successfully assimilate a new process technology, an organisation must somehow reach a state where its bundle of competence encompasses those needed to use the new technology. Innovations through stages of growth can be understood in terms of technology acceptance over time. Technology acceptance has been studied for several decades in information systems research. Technology acceptance models explain perceived usefulness and usage intentions in terms of social influence and cognitive instrumental processes.

The KMT stage model

Stages of knowledge management technology is a relative concept concerned with IT's ability to process information for knowledge work. IT at later stages is more useful to knowledge work than IT at earlier stages. The relative concept implies that IT is more directly involved in knowledge work at higher stages, and that IT is able to support more advanced knowledge work at higher stages.

Knowledge management is concerned with simplifying and improving the process of sharing, distributing, creating, capturing and understanding knowledge. Information technology can play an important role in successful knowledge management initiatives. The extent of information technology can be defined in terms of growth stages for knowledge management systems.

Here, a model consisting of four stages is presented: officer-to-technology systems, officer-to-officer systems, officer-to-information systems, and officer-to-application systems (Figure 8.1).

1. *Officer-to-Technology Stage: Tools for end users* are made available to knowledge workers. In the simplest stage, this means a capable networked PC on every desk or in every briefcase, with standardised personal productivity tools (word processing, presentation software) so that documents can be exchanged easily throughout a company. More complex and functional desktop infrastructures can also be the basis for the same types of knowledge support. Stage 1 is recognised by widespread dissemination and use of end-user tools among knowledge

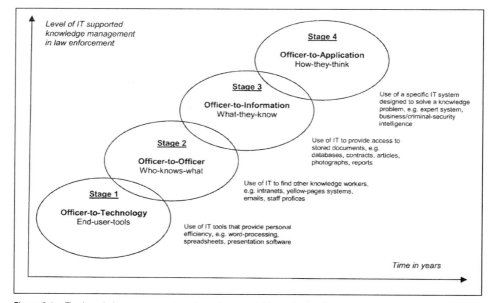

Figure 8.1   The knowledge management systems stage model for police intelligence

workers in the company. For example, lawyers in a law firm will in this stage use word processing, spreadsheets, legal databases, presentation software, and scheduling programs. Related to the new changes in computer technology is the transformation that has occurred in report writing and recordkeeping in police investigations. Every police activity or crime incident demands a report of some kind of form. The majority of police patrol reports written before 1975 were handwritten.

Today officers can write reports on small notebook computers located in the front seat of the patrol unit; discs are handed in at the end of the shift for hard copy needs. Cursor keys and spell-check functions in these report programs are useful timesaving features.

An example of an officer-to-technology system is the Major Incident Policy Document in the UK. This document is maintained whenever a Major Incident Room using HOLMES system is in operation. Decisions, which should be recorded, are those which affect the practical or administrative features of the enquiry, and each entry has clearly to show the reasoning for the decision. When the HOLMES system is used, the SIO directs which policy decisions are recorded on the system.

The basic information entered into HOLMES is location of incident, date and time of incident, victim(s), the senior investigating officer and date the enquiry commenced. During the enquiry, which has been run on the HOLMES system, a closing report is prepared and registered as another document linked to a category of Closing Report. The report will contain the following information: introduction, scene, the victim, and miscellaneous.

Stage 1 can be labelled *end-user-tools* or *people-to-technology* as information technology provides knowledge workers with tools that improve personal efficiency.

2. *Officer-to-Officer Stage:* Information about who knows what is made available to all people in the firm and to selected outside partners. Search engines should enable work with a thesaurus, since the terminology in which expertise is sought may not always match the terms the expert uses to classify that expertise.

The creation of corporate directories – also referred to as the mapping of internal expertise – is a common application of knowledge management technology. Because much knowledge in an organisation remains not codified, mapping the internal expertise is a potentially useful application of technology to enable easy identification of knowledgeable persons.

Here we find the cartographic school of knowledge management, which is concerned with mapping organisational knowledge. It aims to record and disclose who in the organisation knows what by building knowledge directories. Often called Yellow Pages, the principal idea is to make sure knowledgeable people in the organisation are accessible to others for advice, consultation, or knowledge exchange. Knowledge-oriented directories are not so much repositories of knowledge-based information as gateways to knowledge, and the knowledge is as likely to be tacit as explicit.

At Stage 2, firms apply the personalisation strategy in knowledge management. The personalisation strategy implies that knowledge is tied to the person who developed it and is shared mainly through direct person-to-person contact. This strategy focuses on dialogue between individuals: knowledge is transferred mainly in personal email, meetings and one-on-one conversations.

Electronic networks of practice are computer-mediated discussion forums focused on problems of practice that enable individuals to exchange advice and ideas with others based on common interests. Electronic networks have been found to support organisational knowledge flows between geographically dispersed co-workers and distribute research and development efforts. These networks also assist cooperative open-source software development and open congregation on the Internet for individuals interested in a specific practice. Electronic networks make it possible to share information quickly, globally, and with large numbers of individuals.

The typical system at Stage 2 of knowledge management technology in police investigations is the intranet. Intranets provide a rich set of tools for creating collaborative environments in which members of an organisation can exchange ideas, share information, and work together on common projects and assignments regardless of their physical location. Information from many different sources and media, including text, graphics, video, audio, and even digital slides can be displayed, shared, and accessed across an enterprise through a simple common interface.

Stage 2 can be labelled *who-knows-what* or *people-to-people* as knowledge workers use information technology to find other knowledge workers.

3. *Officer-to-Information Stage: Information from knowledge workers* is stored and made available to everyone in the firm and to designated external partners. Data mining techniques can be applied here to find relevant information and combine information in data warehouses:

> *Data mining is a process of extracting nontrivial, valid, novel and useful information from large databases. Hence, data mining can be viewed as a kind of search for meaningful patterns or rules from a large search space that is the database.*
>
> Srinivasa *et al.*, 2007: 4295

However, data mining like any other computer software has limitations:

> *Whenever huge masses of personal data are stored at one place, and especially when tied to a system with the intelligence to tailor this data, there is enormous privacy risk. The idea is that strict access control surround the data. Will that be the case? We can only hope. We see a risk of abuse from corrupted personnel and from hackers or other intruders. Also, there is a risk that data be overly interpreted as true, and that end users be wrongly accused. With the ease in accessing and perhaps performing data mining on huge amounts of personal data, the risk that a police investigation might take the wrong turn is much greater.*
>
> Lind *et al.*, 2007

In Stage 3, firms apply the codification strategy in knowledge management. The codification strategy centres on information technology: knowledge is carefully codified and stored in knowledge databases and can be accessed and used by anyone. With a codification strategy, knowledge is extracted from the person who developed it, is made independent from the person and stored in form of interview guides, work schedules, benchmark data etc.; and then searched and retrieved and used by many employees.

Two examples of knowledge management systems at Stage 3 in law enforcement are COPLINK and geodemographics. COPLINK has a relational database system for crime-specific cases such as gang-related incidents and serious crimes such as homicide, aggravated assault, and sexual crimes. Deliberately targeting these criminal areas allows a manageable amount of information to be entered into a database. Geodemographic profiles of the characteristics of individuals and small areas are central to efficient and effective deployment of law enforcement resources. Geocomputation is based on geographical information systems.

Stage 3 can be labelled *what-they-know* or *people-to-docs* as information technology provides knowledge workers with access to information that is typically stored in documents. Examples of documents are contracts and agreements, reports, manuals and handbooks, business forms, letters, memos, articles, drawings, blueprints, photographs, e-mail and voice mail messages, video clips, script and visuals from presentations, policy statements, computer printouts, and transcripts from meetings.

4. *Officer-to-Application Stage: Information systems solving knowledge problems* are made available to knowledge workers and solution seekers. Artificial intelligence is applied in these systems. For example, neural networks are statistically oriented tools that excel at using data to classify cases into one category or another. Another example is expert systems that can enable the knowledge of one or a few experts to be used by a much broader group of workers requiring the knowledge. Officer-to-application systems will only be successful if they are built on a thorough understanding of law enforcement.

Artificial intelligence (AI) is an area of computer science that endeavours to build machines exhibiting human-like cognitive capabilities. Most modern AI systems are founded on the realisation that intelligence is tightly intertwined with knowledge. Knowledge is associated with the symbols we manipulate.

Knowledge-based systems deal with solving problems by exercising knowledge. The most important parts of these systems are the knowledge base and the inference engine. The former holds the domain-specific knowledge whereas the latter contains the functions to exercise the knowledge in the knowledge base. Knowledge can be represented as either rules or frames. Rules are a natural choice for representing conditional knowledge, which is in the form of if-when statements. Inference engines supply the motive power to the knowledge. There are several ways to exercise knowledge, depending on the nature of the knowledge for example, backward-chaining systems work backward from the conclusions to the inputs. These systems attempt to validate the conclusions by finding evidence to support them. In law enforcement this is an important system feature, as evidence determines whether a person is charged or not for a crime.

Case-based reasoning systems are a different way to represent knowledge through explicit historical cases. This approach differs from the rule-based approach because the knowledge is not compiled and interpreted by an expert. Instead, the experiences that possibly shaped the expert's knowledge are directly used to make decisions. Learning is an important issue in case-based reasoning because with the mere addition of new cases to the library, the system learns. In law enforcement, police officers are looking for similar cases to learn how they were handled in the past, making case-based reasoning systems an attractive application in policing.

Stage 4 can be labelled *how-they-think* or *people-to-systems* where the system is intended to help solve a knowledge problem.

Information technology to support knowledge work of police officers is improving. That is, new information systems supporting police investigations are evolving. Police investigation is an information-rich and knowledge-intensive practice. Its success depends on turning information into evidence. However, the process of turning information into evidence is neither simple nor straightforward. The raw information that is gathered through the investigative process is often required to be transformed into usable knowledge before its value as potential evidence can be realised. Hence, in an investigative context, knowledge acts as an intervening variable in this transformative process of converting information via knowledge into evidence.

The extent to which knowledge management systems as described above are used by police officers is dependent on a number of factors. One important factor frequently discussed in the research literature, is the task technology fit. Task technology theory argues that the use of a technology may result in different outcomes, depending upon its configuration and the task for which it is used. Four elements are part of the theory: task characteristics, technology characteristics, which combine to affect the fit, and which affects the outcome in terms of performance or utilisation. Tasks are broadly defined as the actions carried out in turning inputs to outputs in order to satisfy information needs. Perceived technology fit depends on the agreement between the perceived capabilities of the technology, the needs of the task and the competence of the users (Lin and Huang, 2008).

Kappos and Rivard (2008) argue that culture plays an increasingly important role in information system initiatives. Depending on cultural values, information systems initiatives will be stimulated or prevented. For example if legality is more important than effectiveness, and if formal is more important than informal, then initiatives will emerge more easily.

Knowledge management systems have created incentives for promoting knowledge sharing among organisational members and for fostering innovation within public and private institutions. Knowledge management systems can support four knowledge management processes:

- Knowledge creation is a process of proactively determining what knowledge is desired and needed.

- Knowledge development is the process of establishing valuable knowledge.
- Knowledge reuse is the process of putting knowledge in a reusable form.
- Knowledge transfer is the process of disseminating knowledge effectively.

Hsiao, 2008

It is important to stress here that stages of growth models are very different from life cycle models. While stage models define and describe accumulated improvements in knowledge management technology to support policing the police, life cycle models represent a cycle of birth, growth, decline and eventually death of information technology.

In future research there is a need to validate the stage model both theoretically and empirically. Furthermore, there is a need for benchmark variables that will have different content for different stages. In the current presentation of our model, the stages are lacking both theoretical background and practical situations. While Stage 4 may seem understandable and viable, the remaining stages are in need of further conceptual work. Core questions in future research will be whether officer-to-technology, officer-to-officer, officer-to-information and officer-to-application are valid, practicable, and accountable concepts.

In future research, pros (strengths) and cons (weaknesses) to the suggested model have to be taken into account. We need to provide a more critical analysis of a stage model such as the one suggested. It is not at all intuitively obvious that the progression over time is from end-user-tools, via who-knows-what and what-they-know, to how-they-think. Why not what-they-know, via who-knows-what and end-user-tools, to how-they-think; or end-user-tools via what-they-know and who-knows-what to how-they-think? The conceptual research presented here is lacking empirical evidence. Only a questionnaire based on Guttman scaling rather than Likert scaling can verify the suggested sequence or alternatively identify another sequence.

The important contribution of this model is the introduction of the stage hypothesis to knowledge management technology in policing the police. Rather than thinking of knowledge management technology in terms of alternative strategies, we suggest an evolutionary approach where the future is building on the past, rather than the future being a divergent path from the past. Rather than thinking that what was done in the past is wrong, past actions are the only available foundation for future actions. If past actions are not on the path to success, direction is changed without history being reversed.

Unified communication in knowledge management

While knowledge resides in the heads of knowledge workers in knowledge organisations such as intelligence and investigation units in the police, knowledge sharing is dependent on individuals communicating with each other. Communication between individuals in an organisation as well as between individuals in cooperating organisations occur to a growing extent by the use of information and communication technology (ICT). However, electronic communication so far has tended to be fragmented.

Unified communication (UC) refers to a trend in organisations to simplify and integrate all forms of communications. It is typically a software program as well as technical infrastructure. The idea is for an individual to be able to send a message on one medium to be received on another. For example, a voice mail message can be read in a text mail message using a unified communication program. The typical UC software program unifies different communication mediums such as phone, e-mail, chat, voice mail, and fax.

Unified communication is sometimes confused with unified messaging. Unified communication refers to a real-time delivery of communications based on the preferred method and location of the recipient, while unified messaging collects messages from several sources (such as e-mail, voice mail and faxes) and holds those messages for retrieval at a later time. With unified messaging all types of messages are stored in one system.

UC can include a variety of elements, such as instant messaging, telephony, video, e-mail voice mail, short message services, and white boarding. UC is concerned with integration of sound, picture, text and video. All of these elements are brought into real time and coordinated. The concept of presence is a factor implying knowledge of one's intended recipients' locations. For example, unified communication technology could allow a user to seamlessly collaborate with another person on a project, even if the two users are in separate locations. The user could quickly locate the necessary person by accessing an interactive directory, engage in a text messaging session, and then escalate the session to a voice call, or even a video call – all within minutes. In another example, an employee receives a call from a customer who wants answers. Unified communication could enable that worker to access a real-time list of available expert colleagues, then make a call that would reach the necessary person, enabling the employee to answer the customer faster, and eliminating rounds of back-and-forth emails and phone-tag according to Wikipedia:

> *Unified communication helps organisations, small and large alike, to streamline information delivery and ensure ease of use. Human delays are also minimised or eliminated, resulting in better, faster interaction and service-delivery for the customer, and cost savings for the business. Unified communication also allows for easier, more direct collaboration between co-workers and with suppliers and clients, even if they are not physically on the same site. This allows for possible reductions in business travel, especially with multi-party video communications, reducing an organisation's carbon footprint.*

www.wikipedia.org

Unified communication (UC) seems very useful for knowledge workers, as many of them may cross the lines between different knowledge sectors on a daily or hourly basis depending on the task and the client. With an increasingly mobile workforce, businesses are rarely centralised in one location. Unified communication facilitates this on-the-go, always-available style of communication. In addition, unified communications technology can be tailored to each person's specific job or to a particular section of a company. Successful UC stimulates efficient and effective collaboration and communication between knowledge workers beyond telephone conversations and electronic mail.

One of the vendors of unified communication is Microsoft. According to Microsoft, organisations can improve individual and team results by using Microsoft solutions to communicate and collaborate faster with team members, partners, and customers across geographies and time zones to achieve benefits and business value such as (www.microsoft.com/businessvalue/improve.mspx):

- *Improved User and Team Productivity.* Microsoft unified communications solutions help users to be more productive by making it easier to contact colleagues for information, check for messages, and stay productive while out of the office.
- *Faster Project Completion.* Improved communication within project teams improves efficiency and reduces completion time, as does the ability to reach out to subject-matter experts beyond the project team, allowing teams to complete more projects. These capabilities can also bring the same benefits to product development time resulting in decreased time to market for new products.
- *Shortened Sales Cycle Times.* Microsoft unified communications solutions promote collaboration on sales presentations and help speed responses to customer questions. Presence awareness allows salespeople to find the subject-matter experts they need to answer questions quickly and easily, which can reduce the time spent on proposals and responding to customer questions. These advantages can increase the number of proposals delivered and won.
- *Faster Resolution of Customer Issues.* Enhanced communication between customer service and subject-matter experts through presence awareness, call forwarding, and other tools means customer issues can be resolved more quickly, reducing the cost required to field calls and handle customer interactions.
- *Attract and Retain Employees.* Microsoft unified communications can be used to provide a flexible working environment for workers, helping reduce turnover and costs associated with hiring. Furthermore, being able to provide the latest tools can have a positive effect on attracting new talent.

Unified communication is not only confused with unified messaging (UM). Since UC is a new term and concept that has not yet found its permanent contents, it is also confused with other terms such as instant messaging. Instant messaging (IM) are technologies that create the possibility of real-time text-based communication between two or more participants over the Internet or some form of internal network/intranet. It is important to understand that what separates chat and instant messaging from technologies such as e-mail is the perceived synchronicity of the communication by the user. Chat happens in real-time before your eyes. Some systems allow the sending of messages to people not currently logged on (offline messages) thus removing much of the difference between IM and e-mail. From a definitional point of view, IM might be considered part of UC, where UC is a system-based approach to unifying telephony, instant messaging, presence, and web (www.wikipedia.org).

According to Riemer and Frössler (2007) the idea behind UC is to relieve the user of the burden to juggle with a large number of devices and channels in different contexts. Unified communication can thus be defined as the integration of communication technologies to improve workers' ability to interact, where UC systems aim to integrate different information and communication channels, such as e-mail, telephone, SMS, instant messaging and voice mail in order to reduce the fragmentation and complexity of today's information and communication landscape. Schauer (2008) argues that unified communication is a practical business and technology approach removing barriers to enable people-to-people communication.

UC is an emerging IT industry term used to describe all forms of call and multimedia and cross media message management functions controlled by an individual user for both business and social purposes. This includes any enterprise informational or transactional application process that emulates a human user and uses a single, content-independent personal messaging channel (mailbox) for contact access (www.wikipedia.org).

From a theoretical point of view, UC is concerned with media synchronicity. Media synchronicity theory focuses on the ability of media to support synchronicity, a shared pattern of coordinated behaviour among individuals as they work together. Dennis et al. (2008) argue that communication is composed of two primary processes: conveyance of information and convergence on meaning. These two processes are needed to generate shared understanding. All work requiring more than one individual is composed of different combinations of conveyance of information and convergence on meaning. The successful completion of most tasks involving more than one individual requires both conveyance and convergence processes, where communication performance will be improved when individuals use a variety of media to perform a task.

Media synchronicity theory proposes that for conveyance processes, use of media supporting lower synchronicity should result in better communication performance. For convergence processes, use of media supporting higher synchronicity should result in better communication performance. Dennis et al. (2008: 596) argue that communication performance will be improved when media capabilities that affect information transmission, individual information processing, and synchronicity are matched to fundamental communication processes in terms of conveyance and convergence:

> Most tasks require individuals both to convey information and to converge on shared meanings. Media with capabilities that support low synchronicity best serves conveyance processes, while convergence media with capabilities that support high synchronicity best serves processes. Thus choosing one single medium may prove less effective than choosing a set of media. Face-to-face communication is not always the richest medium, and, richer is not necessarily better.
>
> Dennis et al., 2008: 596

In order to perform conveyance and convergence, an individual must engage in two individual processes: information transmission (preparing information for transmission, transmitting it through a medium, and receiving information from a medium) and information processing (understanding the meaning of information and integrating it into a mental model). Dennis et al.'s

(2008) focus is among individuals for information transmission and within individuals for information processing.

The case of geographic information systems

Police crime mapping might be a useful tool in identifying online groomers and their behaviours. Most of the activities of the police have explicitly spatial consequences (Ashby *et al.*, 2007) and geographic information systems (GIS) can be a valuable tool at Stages 1, 3 and 4 in the KMT Stage Model for policing the police.

GIS are applied in a variety of electronic government situations, from tracing the origins and spread of foot and mouth disease on farms to locating crime hot spots for law enforcement. GIS have become indispensable to effective knowledge transfer within both the public and private sector. High-ranking issues among the defining purposes of e-government are highly agile, citizen-centric, accountable, transparent, effective, and efficient government operations and services (Scholl and Klischewski, 2007). For reaching such goals, the integration of government information resources and processes, and thus the interoperation of independent information systems are essential. Yet, most integration and interoperation efforts meet serious challenges and limitations.

Improved interoperability between public organisations as well as between public and private organisations is of critical importance to make electronic government more successful (Cabinet Office, 2005a). In this section, stages of GIS representing levels of interoperability are presented. In law enforcement agencies such as the Independent Police Complaints Commission (IPCC) concerned with enforcing law on the police, the application of GIS will serve two main purposes:

- pattern recognition in police complaints and police crime
- information exchange with the police and other public and private organisations

As pointed out by Gottschalk and Tolloczko (2007), the level of sophistication varies among agencies applying GIS. Also, the extent to which GIS interoperate with each other are subject to substantial variation. A survey on interoperability for GIS in the UK was conducted by the e-government unit of the Cabinet Office (2005b).

According to this survey, 49 per cent of the surveyed government organisations participated in data sharing projects for GIS, indicating that half of the organisations were working at the lowest level for e-government interoperability. The fractions at higher levels were not identifiable from the survey. Many different application packages were in use, such as ESRI, Mapinfo, Intergraph, GGP, CadCorp, INNOgistic and Autodesk.

To improve interoperability of such systems for GIS and other e-government systems, the UK Cabinet Office (2005b) developed an e-government interoperability framework. The framework is mostly technical in nature, stressing alignment with the Internet and adoption of the browser as the key interface. The framework intends to stimulate government agencies to work more easily together electronically; make systems, knowledge and experience reusable from one agency to another, and reduce the effort needed to deal with government online by encouraging consistency of approach.

Geographic information systems have become an important tool for crime measures and spatial analysis of criminal activity. Classical and spatial statistics have been merged to form more comprehensive approaches in understanding how crime is related to social problems. According to the National Institute of Justice (NIJ, 2006) these methods allow for the measurement of proximity effects on places by neighbouring areas that lead to a multi-dimensional and less static understanding of factors that contribute to or repel crime across space.

Geographic information systems in law enforcement represent digital repositories for e-government. Crime mapping is concerned with knowledge management in e-government for change management in policing. The diffusion of information technology in policing is accelerating as technology to support knowledge work in law enforcement is improving. The diffusion of computerised crime mapping in policing is part of this IT revolution in law enforcement.

The theoretical framework for crime mapping in law enforcement is often based on the theory of problem-oriented policing. A broad and popular definition of problem-oriented policing is as follows: Problem-oriented policing is designed to identify and remove the causes of recurring crime and disorder problems that harm communities. The concept of problem-oriented policing places a high value on developing, within that strategy, new responses that are preventive in nature, that are not dependent on the use of the criminal justice system, and that draw on the potential contributions of other public agencies, the community, and the private sector.

Problem-oriented policing can be associated with police effectiveness and crime prevention. Crime prevention, as well as crime, is hard to define, but problem-oriented policing is most closely related, but not limited, to situational crime prevention. Since problem-oriented policing is more of a theoretical concept, not a theory of crime, it is suitable for the use of the study of processes in crime prevention initiatives in the police and their effectiveness. Still this concept needs a more practical and manageable framework to be used in the research. The well-known SARA model has been widely used as a framework for problem-oriented policing and has almost become synonymous with problem-oriented policing. Research studies by the Home Office (2000) in the UK have applied the SARA model for assessing problem-oriented initiatives. Norwegian police literature also uses the SARA model as a framework for carrying out problem-oriented policing. Scanning, analysis, response, and assessment are the four stages in the SARA model.

Problem-oriented policing relies on collaboration with partners at the various stages in the SARA model. Some of the weaknesses in the UK were failure to involve partners and insensitivity to others' agendas, styles, constraints or ideologies (Home Office, 2000).

Police complaints and crime is not spread evenly across maps. It clumps in some areas and is absent in others. People use this knowledge in their daily activities. According to NIJ (2005), they avoid some places and seek out others. Their choices of neighbourhoods, schools, stores, streets, and recreation are governed partially by the understanding that their chances of being a victim are greater in some of these places than in others. In some places people lock their cars and secure their belongings. In other places they do not.

Crime mapping is concerned with advancing spatial understanding. Areas of concentrated crime are often referred to as hot spots. NIJ (2005) identified several crime hot spot theories. For example, place theories explain why crime events occur at specific locations. Street theories deal with crimes at slightly larger geographic areas than specific places; that is, over small, stretched areas such as streets or blocks. Neighbourhood theories attempt to explain neighbourhood differences. Still other theories attempt to explain differences in crime patterns at much higher levels of aggregation for example, theories of crime differ among cities and among regions. On the city level, suggested actions may include citywide changes in economic, transportation, education, welfare, and recreation policies.

There are many GIS that are applied in law enforcement organisations. Here are some examples of systems in the UK that were reviewed by the Home Office (2006): Amethyst: Devon and Cornwall, CADDIE: Sussex, COSMOS: Birmingham, GMAC: Greater Manchester, JUPITER: East Midlands Government Office region, LASS: London Government Office region, NERISS: North East Government Office region, North West Regional Crime Mapping System: North West Government Office region, Project DRAGON: Welsh Assembly, and SCaDIS: Surrey.

Ashby and Longley (2005) conducted an empirical study of the Devon and Cornwall Constabulary. They found that geo-demographic analyses, including people and places of local policing environments, crime profiles, and police performance, provided a significantly increased level of community intelligence for police use. This was supplemented and further enhanced by the use of penetration ranking reports where neighbourhood types were ranked by standardised crime rates, and cumulative percentage of the crime was compared with the corresponding population at risk.

An example of GIS in policing in Norway is illustrated in Figure 8.2. In the centre of Oslo, pocket thieves were becoming very active. Application of GIS revealed a pattern, and one of the hot spots was identified. The hot spot was the restaurant Uncle Donald in the University Street. Police officers contacted the owner of the restaurant as well as the doormen. One action taken was to install hangers for clothes underneath each guest table. Another action was a wardrobe for guest clothes. In addition, policing information was shared with people employed in the restaurant. As a consequence, the number of pocket thefts dropped in this restaurant as well as in the city as a whole.

NIJ (2005) argues that moving beyond the manual pin-mapping approaches of the past, desktop GIS technologies have introduced crime analysts to new ways of visualising and mapping crime. Specifically, tools for dynamic visualisation and mapping in a GIS environment make it possible to inductively describe and visualise spatial distributions, identify unusual observations or spatial outliers, and discover patterns of spatial association, including clusters and hot spots.

Weisburd and Lum (2005) studied diffusion of computerised crime mapping in policing. They found that diffusion is dependent on the importance of hot spots policing approaches and is linked strongly to those approaches in police agencies with computerised crime mapping capabilities. We will organise such research findings into the stages of growth model.

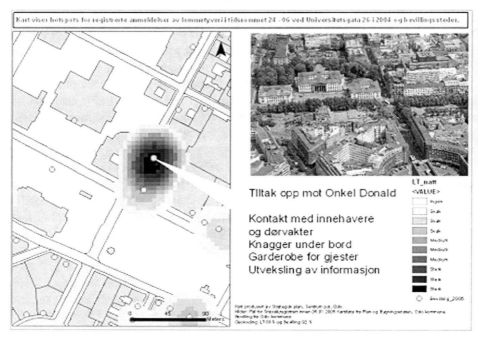

Figure 8.2   Geographic information system applied to pocket theft in Oslo

The diffusion of an innovation such as crime mapping can be conceptualised as a process in each law enforcement agency. In the following, we conceptualise the process in terms of maturity levels as suggested by Gottschalk and Tolloczko (2007). The purpose of this maturity model is to help practitioners and researchers study organisational evolution and determine future direction in a police organisation's use of electronic systems when mapping crime.

Maturity models assume that predictable patterns exist in the growth of an organisation. This is conceptualised in terms of levels of maturity. These stages:

- are sequential in nature
- occur as a hierarchical progression that is not easily reversed
- involve a broad range of organisational activities and structures
- are dependent on contingent actions at each stage of progress to the next stage

In the case of crime mapping, levels of maturity represent the extent to which geographic information systems are innovating law enforcement.

In this section, we present a maturity model for geographic information systems applications consisting of eight maturity levels as illustrated in the figure. Gottschalk and Tolloczko (2007) define the following maturity levels (Figure 8.3):

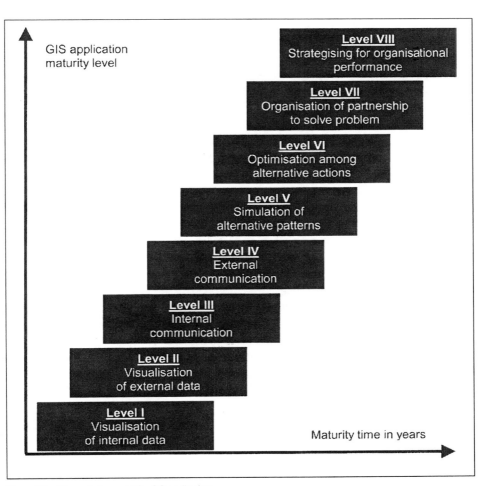

Figure 8.3   The maturity model for GIS applications

1. *Visualisation of internal data.* An electronic map is used to visualise geographic areas using police data. A typical example is the mapping of hot spots. Hot spots are areas of concentrated crime (NIJ, 2005, 2006). Crime analysts look for concentrations of individual events that might indicate a series of related crimes. Computerised crime mapping is central to the development of a hot spots approach to policing (Weisburd and Lum, 2005).

2. *Visualisation of external data.* An electronic map is used to visualise both police data and external data. For example, the Vancouver Police Department obtained data from the LandScan Global Population Database for spatial analysis of criminal activity. The LandScan Global Population Database has been adopted by many US and international government

agencies, as well as the United Nations, for estimating populations at risk from criminal activity.

3. *Internal communication*. The electronic map is shared with officers at different locations. For example, COSMOS (COmmunity Safety Mapping On-line System) in Birmingham is an Internet GIS-based community safety tool, designed as a central point of contact for crime and disorder reduction. It provides access to multi-agency data through interactive mapping and data query tools and through interactive tabular and graphical profiles.

4. *External communication*. The electronic map is shared with other public agencies and private organisations that join the problem-solving task. For example, CADDIE (Crime and Disorder Data Information Exchange) in Sussex is an Internet-based solution designed to ensure that all 13 CDRPs (Crime and Disorder Reduction Partnerships) and partners in the county have access to relevant, accurate and timely information about crime and disorder.

5. *Simulation of alternative patterns*. Registered hot spots and other items on the map are statistically correlated with each other, so that different crime patterns will emerge from computer simulations. A typical example is prospective hot spotting, where future locations of crime are predicted. For example, Bowers *et al.* (2004) used a moving window technique to generate prospective risk surfaces.

6. *Optimisation among alternative actions*. Based on targets and other inputs, the system suggests an optimal solution to the problem. For example, the Devon and Cornwall Constabulary apply geo-demographics for resource allocation in policing. According to Ashby and Longley (2005), geo-demographic profiles of characteristics of individuals and small areas are important in tactical and strategic resource management in many areas of business and are becoming similarly central to efficient and effective deployment of resources by public services.

7. *Organisation of partnership to solve problem*. The police agency is reorganised to work according to problem-oriented policing. For example, the Project Dragon provides timely daily exchange of information between Probation, the Prison Service and the Police to monitor prison releases and supports partnerships prevention responses to re-offending.

8. *Strategising for organisational performance*. The police agency makes its policing strategy based on GIS results. To be successful, Ratcliffe (2004) argues that there are fundamental training needs for managers to enable a greater understanding of the analyses presented to them, and how to use mapping to further crime prevention and reduction. At this level, executive training of police chiefs is more important than increasing the technical ability of crime analysts. According to Ratcliffe (2004) the challenge for the future of crime reduction practice in law enforcement is less to worry about the training of analysts, and more to address the inability of law enforcement management to understand and act on the crime analysis they are given. An emerging example of this maturity level is GMAC (Greater Manchester Against Crime), which operates through a business process model that is changing organisational structures and strategies. GMAC is a structure and process

framework for delivering partnership working, utilising a strategic analytical capability across Manchester.

The Norwegian Police Directorate set out a new strategy for crime prevention and community safety to be implemented by all Norwegian police districts in 2002. It was called problem-oriented policing and was initiated because of the Parliamentary White Paper no. 22 — Police Reform 2000. The police Directorate defines problem-oriented policing as a work philosophy. The intention of this philosophy is to make the police more efficient in crime prevention and crime reduction (CPOP, 2005).

Problem-oriented policing has since been taught and implemented on several maturity levels in police agencies. There are 27 police districts in Norway, each headed by a chief of police. The chief of police has full responsibility for policing within their district. Oslo police district is the largest with more than 2,300 employees. The Norwegian Police Directorate is managing all police districts and reporting to the Department of Justice. Since 2002, the directorate has arranged seminars and workshops for top-level police management in the theory and practice of problem-oriented policing.

An important practical implication of problem-oriented policing is electronic mapping of crime. An example of crime mapping is pocket thefts in Oslo as illustrated in Figure 8.4. Based on

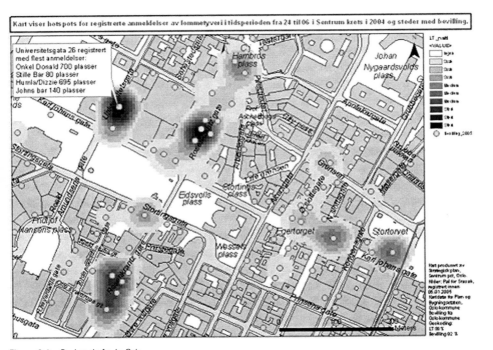

Figure 8.4   Pocket thefts in Oslo

visualisation of both internal (Level 1) and external (Level 2) data as well as internal communication (Level 3) and external communication (Level 4) with city authorities, simulations were performed (Level 5), actions were discussed (Level 6) and partnerships (Level 7) were initiated.

Restaurants were important partners since the GIS-based analysis showed that pocket theft was found near and in restaurants. The problem of pocket thefts was solved by restaurants opening wardrobes and installing hangers under guest tables.

We find that the Oslo Police District has reached maturity Level 7. Other police districts in Norway are found at lower levels. One reason for the variation in maturity is the variation in population density. Oslo being the capital and the largest city in Norway with a population of 550,000 inhabitants will typically have more geographically concentrated crimes than other police districts.

The diffusion of computerised crime mapping is based on widely available technologies. Technology is an important factor in explaining the rapid adoption of geographical information systems in mapping crime. However, the availability of a new technology is not enough to explain its widespread adoption. Weisburd and Lum (2005) found three more explanations. First, diffusion of a new technology generally begins with the wide recognition of a need for change. Second, the identification of a need, through some type of crisis or reassessment, is followed by a period of research and development. Finally, research and development concluded that law enforcement should be more focused on crime hot spots. Computerised crime mapping became central to the creation of crime hot spots by identifying clusters of addresses which evidenced high rates of recorded crime.

After adoption of computerised crime mapping, police organisations develop in terms of crime mapping maturity as suggested by our maturity model. In an evaluation of geographical profiling software, Rich and Shively (2004) found limitations in all compared software applications, for example, only CrimeStat is able to export results to other mapping software, while only Rigel Analyst has the ability to generate reports. Both Dragnet and Rigel Analyst have the ability to manually add crime data. Based on this evaluation of software applications, mature police organisations will have to struggle to find software applications which support Levels 7 and 8 in the maturity model.

The use of geographic information systems (GIS) and spatial data analysis techniques have become prominent tools for analysing criminal behaviour and the impacts of the criminal justice system on society. According to NIJ (2006) classical and spatial statistics have been merged to form more comprehensive approaches in understanding social problems from research and practical standpoints. These methods allow for the measurement of proximity effects on places by neighbouring areas that lead to a multi-dimensional and less static understanding of factors that contribute to or repel crime across space. As stressed by researchers such as Ashby and Longley (2005) it is important that law enforcement keep pace with new developments in effective crime prevention and crime investigation.

In the maturity model by Gottschalk and Tolloczko (2007), interoperability challenges occur at all levels. In particular, Level 7 for organisation of partnership to solve problem requires electronic information from a variety of sources, such as customs, municipalities, hospitals, agricultural authorities, and schools. For example, in the struggle tracing the origins of foot and mouth disease in the UK, geographic information systems have become indispensable to effective knowledge transfer within both the public and private sector.

9

Police Performance Management

In this chapter, we will introduce an empirical study of performance measurement in the police value shop. Also, we will present results from the survey on intelligence strategy implementation.

An empirical study of police investigations

To measure performance in the primary activities of the value shop, a survey instrument was developed. The questionnaire was e-mailed to police officers in charge of criminal investigations in Norway in 2005. A total of 101 questionnaires were returned. This represents an approximate response rate of 20 per cent. We have to write approximate, as police chiefs were contacted to have them distribute the link with the questionnaire to their managers of police investigations. The sample consisted of police officers in charge of criminal investigations in Norway with personnel responsibility, budget responsibility, outcome responsibility, knowledge responsibility, and investigation responsibility.

The primary activities of the intelligence and investigation value shop were all measured on multiple item scales as listed in Table 9.1. We developed all items by interviewing senior investigation officers in Norway. Therefore, an exploratory factor analysis had to be conducted before the confirmatory factor analysis. The exploratory factor analysis suggested only three factors rather than five. However, since the statistically suggested three-factor model was found to be without theoretical implications, confirmatory factor analysis with five factors was conducted.

All five scales had acceptable reliability in terms of Cronbach alpha. Therefore, means for each item were averaged into means for each primary activity. Out of the five primary activities in the value shop, performance in police investigations was best in problem understanding (5.0) and alternative solutions (5.0), while evaluation achieved the lowest score (4.0).

An empirical study of intelligence work

The national strategy for intelligence and analysis in Norway was to be implemented in 2007. In the survey research, organisation structure and organisation culture were applied as predictors of implementation extent. In separate regressions it was found that both structure and culture have a significant influence on implementation, where a knowledge-oriented structure and a knowledge-oriented culture lead to more implementation than a bureaucracy-oriented structure and bureaucracy-oriented culture. When the two predictors were combined in one regression, the explanatory power of structure was stronger than culture, making culture a non-significant predictor in the regression analysis.

Table 9.1 Investigation performance in value shop activities

Police investigation performance in the value shop (Scale from 1 = not clever to 7 = very clever)	Average	Alpha
Understanding the case, what it is all about: problem finding and acquisition	5.0	.934
Channel the case to the right investigator	5.1	
Assess initial case information and other relevant information	5.2	
Collect additional historical information	4.3	
Evaluate whether there is suspicion of a criminal offence	5.5	
Assess the police task in the case	5.4	
Inform parties and stakeholders of the case	4.6	
Identifying investigation alternatives, which investigative steps are potentially relevant to be the case: problem solutions	5.0	.956
Determine the purpose of the investigation	5.1	
Assess the extent to which there is experience from similar cases	5.0	
Discuss with colleagues what potential investigation schemes are appropriate	4.9	
Assess the seriousness of the criminal offence	5.1	
Find methods for investigative steps	5.0	
Plan for alternative investigative steps	4.6	
Investigation plan derived from alternatives by use of criteria for success: choice of solution to the problem	4.8	.942
Identify criteria for choice of investigation program	4.6	
Discuss with colleagues which investigation program is the best	4.8	
Check routines and guidelines for police work	4.4	
Check resources for investigative actions	4.7	
Find a qualified investigation leader	4.8	
Determine what the police must do in the case	5.2	
Work on the case, carrying out the investigation plan: execution of solution to solve problem	4.8	.915
Collect information from files	4.6	
Collect information from persons	5.0	
Secure leads	4.9	
Interrogate potential suspects	5.4	
Interrogate potential witnesses	5.3	
Inform involved persons (such as relatives) about the future	4.3	
Determining how the investigation has progressed so far and possible changes in the future: control and evaluation	4.0	.926
Evaluate the quality of police work in the case	4.1	
Evaluate the quality of legal work in the case	4.0	
Involve in the evaluation everyone who has participated in the investigation	3.7	
Assess how the investigation of the case was managed	3.7	
Control the use of resources in the case	4.0	
Learn from the case	4.6	
Average overall performance in the value shop	4.7	.965

When looking at empirical results concerning intelligence work from this study, we can select some items from the questionnaire as listed in Table 9.2. The scale ranges from 1 (completely disagree) to 7 (completely agree). The highest score can be found for the statement 'We have

Table 9.2   Measurement of strategy implementation

No.	Statement about implementation of national strategy	Mean	Dev
01	We have implemented intelligence and analysis unit	4.11	1.986
02	We have implemented operational analysis function	3.98	2.099
03	We have implemented operational intelligence function	4.33	1.957
04	We have implemented strategic analysis function	3.99	2.064
05	We have implemented strategic intelligence function	3.70	1.895
06	We prioritise now knowledge-based police work	3.91	1.681
07	We have adapted the strategy to our own strategy	3.74	1.671
08	We have created environment to succeed with the strategy	3.41	1.568
09	A change process according to the strategy is going on	3.90	1.657
10	We have planned when to evaluate the implementation	2.30	1.506
11	Critical success factors for implementation have been identified	2.54	1.500
12	Goals have been set for the implementation process	2.76	1.707
13	Deadlines for implementation have been set	2.42	1.697
14	Resources have been allocated to strategy implementation	2.70	1.634
15	Measurement parameters according to strategy are developed	2.49	1.496
	Average	3.33	1.332

implemented operational intelligence function' with a score of 4.33. The lowest score can be found for the statement 'We have planned when to evaluate the implementation' with a score of 2.30.

On a scale from 1 to 7, the median is 4. All scores below 4 represent disagreement, while all scores above 4 represent agreement. Only two statements have an average score above 4, i.e. 'We have implemented intelligence and analysis unit' and 'We have implemented operational intelligence unit'. The average score for all items is 3.33, which indicates slight disagreement.

All statements have a standard deviation above 1, which indicate substantial variation among respondents. The greatest variation among respondents can be found for the statement 'We have implemented operational analysis function' with a standard deviation of 2.064.

The significant determinant of implementation extent of the national strategy for intelligence and analysis was organisational structure. A more knowledge-oriented organisational structure leads to a greater extent of implementation. A more bureaucratic structure leads to a lower degree of implementation. Items measuring organisation structure are listed in Table 9.3.

The reliability of this scale was not satisfactory with all eighteen items included. An acceptable reliability was achieved by eliminating items 1, 2, 5, 6, 9 and 10. By eliminating these six items, thirteen items with a reliability of 0.885 remained.

Other performance indicators

Police performance is a complicated construct. The police reform in the UK has developed some performance indicators for policing within an assessment framework. The policing performance assessment framework is an initiative led by the Home Office (2005a) with the support of the

Table 9.3   Measurement of organisation structure

No.	Statement about implementation of national strategy	Mean	Dev
01	We do not work sequentially with a case at a time	4.66	1.748
02	We are free to choose how to solve our assignments	3.34	1.748
03	We have good routines for transferring knowledge internally	3.80	1.546
04	We have good routines for transferring knowledge externally	3.53	1.486
05	We do not always follow institutional routines	4.42	1.400
06	We do not always have to follow lines of command	3.87	1.622
07	Program management is important in our organisation	3.35	1.325
08	We do not have a bureaucratic decision-making system	3.77	1.746
09	There is not always consistency between authority and responsibility	4.64	1.499
10	We are not always dependent on superiors' decisions	3.85	1.468
11	We change organisation structure in pace with the environment	3.68	1.602
12	Our organisation is not characterised by hierarchy	3.32	1.594
13	In our organisation is it not always formal authority that counts	3.75	1.674
14	Our organisation changes continuously	4.01	1.688
15	We are a knowledge organisation	4.31	1.743
16	We have a flexible organisation structure	3.54	1.584
17	We have an integrated cooperation internally	3.96	1.526
18	We have an integrated cooperation with partners externally	4.03	1.419
	Average	3.76	1.029

Association of Chief Police Officers and the Association of Police Authorities. Here are some examples of performance indicators for 2005/2006:

- satisfaction of victims of domestic burglary, violent crime, vehicle crime and road traffic collisions
- using the British Crime Survey, the percentage of people who think their local police do a good job
- satisfaction of victims of racist incidents with respect to the overall service provided
- using the British Crime Survey, the risk of personal crime
- domestic burglaries per 1,000 households
- number of offences brought to justice
- percentage of offences resulting in a sanction detection
- percentage of domestic violence incidents with a power of arrest
- number of people killed
- using the British Crime Survey, fear of crime
- percentage of police officer time spent on frontline duties
- delivery of cashable and non-cashable efficiency target
- average number of working hours lost per annum due to sickness per police officer

The guidance on statutory performance indicators for policing includes user satisfaction measures, confidence measures, fairness, equality and diversity measures, measures of crime level, offences brought to justice measures, sanction detection measures, domestic violence measures, traffic measures, quality of life measures, frontline policing measures, and resource use measures.

One of the resource use measures is delivery of cashable and non-cashable efficiency target. A cashable gain is where a particular level of output of a particular quality is achieved for less cost. A non-cashable gain is where more output and/or output of better quality is achieved for the same cost.

In 1993, there was a debate in the UK whether to allow and stimulate direct entry into police management. According to Leishman and Savage (1993) it was a fundamental fact of the British police service that everyone had to start at the bottom, at the 'lowest' rank of constable, in which office all entrants must serve a minimum period of two years. On the surface, then, the police service may appear to occupy a unique position among public sector organisations, as an apparently egalitarian meritocracy in which all confirmed constables could be said to have the opportunity to aspire to senior management positions.

At that time, chief constables were the first generation of completely self-made chiefs, lacking even the middle-class socialisation of university, although most went to grammar schools. Leishman and Savage (1993) argue that there are two important reasons in favour of direct entry. First, direct entry offers potential for the active furtherance of equal opportunities in the British police service. Whereas in Britain, target attainment would depend on the numbers of officers remaining in the service beyond their two-year probationary period and then progressing through the rank of sergeant, this was not the case in Holland. Its system of direct entry, coupled with an explicit policy of positive action, allowed the recruitment and training of sufficient numbers of women and ethnic minority candidates directly into the rank of inspector, to achieve minimum targets within the time-scale agreed.

A second argument in favour of direct entry followed, in a sense, part of the rationale for 'civilianisation' within the service. While much of this process had been driven by the pursuit of economies, behind it also was the question of competences and specialist skills. For example, staff with backgrounds in personnel management have been appointed to head the personnel department in place of police officers (Leishman and Savage, 1993).

According to Jackson and Wade (2005), the understanding of police behaviour, especially proactive behaviour, has been pursued throughout policing history. Researchers have examined the impact of environmental factors (weapons, crime, etc.) individual factors (attitude, personality, etc.) police subculture, and organisational and departmental management on police behaviour. Despite all of these research efforts, most if not all of the authors contributing to this line of research have concluded that the categorisation, understanding, and predicting of police behaviour is arduous (if not impossible) or that the relationship between police attitudes and their behaviour is weak at best.

Researchers have examined empirically and conceptually the impact of social capital and police sense of responsibility on police behaviour. For example, community social capital has been identified in the literature as having a significant impact on police behaviour mainly because social capital serves as a measure of the community's ability to solve its own problems. In communities with low social capital, police may perceive themselves as the only form of social order and may therefore develop a higher sense of responsibility towards protecting citizens, themselves, and preventing crime.

Jackson and Wade (2005) suggest that the examination of police sense of responsibility towards the community may be important in understanding police behaviour. This assertion implies that police sense of responsibility may serve as an influential variable in explaining why police may demonstrate higher levels of proactive policing in communities with low social capital in comparison to those with high social capital. Police sense of responsibility toward the community seems important for understanding how police function in areas under their command. In communities where crime is commonplace, police can become overwhelmed and may therefore focus on more serious crimes that pose a greater threat to police and citizen safety and ignore the lower level crimes that do not.

Given these arguments, the major purpose of the study conducted by Jackson and Wade (2005) was to examine the relationship between police perception of their community's social capital and their sense of responsibility toward the provision of public safety and in turn to assess empirically the impact of sense of responsibility on their propensity to engage in proactive policing.

By studying police perceptions of social capital and their sense of responsibility, it was possible to not only understand why community policing is or is not successful but more importantly it was possible to understand police behaviour in environments that by their structural and demographic make-up, complicate the task of effective policing.

Jackson and Wade's (2005) findings support the hypothesis that police who indicate a more negative perception of community social capital are more likely to indicate a higher sense of responsibility towards the community. This finding suggests that as the police perception of community social capital becomes negative, they are more likely to rely upon their own resources to solve community problems. Generally, the only real resources that police possess in low social capital communities are their law enforcement powers.

Another finding was police who express a more negative perception of community social capital were more likely to indicate higher levels of proactive behaviour. This finding suggests that in communities with low social capital, police may utilise their law enforcement powers more in comparison to communities that posses higher levels of social capital.

The data gathered through a questionnaire distributed among the Kansas City Police Department in the US, suggested that the amount of crime occurring within the community is the most important variable for the explanation of police proactive behaviour. Police proactive behaviour includes new patrol techniques, increased utilisation of technology, the organisation of specialised units, and the use of criminal profiling. By being more proactive, police are conducting more stop-and-frisk contacts, requesting proof of identification more frequently, conducting more drug sweeps, and dispersing citizens who gather to protest public policies of various kinds (Jackson and Wade, 2005).

Proactive policing might perpetuate and exacerbate the social distance rift between the police and their community and it also increases the likelihood that an officer may abuse his or her authority. In a time period of three years, Prince George's County in the US paid out eight million dollars in jury awards and settlements in lawsuits that involved police misconduct and excessive force. The increasing costs resulting from payouts in police litigation cases and liability claims, coupled with increased pressure from public insurance pools to cut losses, are a few of the reasons that some US law enforcement agencies are beginning to implement risk management programs (Archbold, 2005).

Risk management is a process used to identify and control exposure to potential risks and liabilities in both private and public organisations. Almost all of the basic duties of police work expose police officers to liability incidents on a daily basis. One aspect of police work that makes it unique to all other professions is the ability of police officers to use lethal and non-lethal force. This unique aspect of police work also contributes to police officer exposure to high levels of risk, which could lead to litigation, liability claims or citizen complaints (Archbold, 2005).

Police personnel face some of society's most serious problems, often work in dangerous settings, are typically expected to react quickly, and at the same time correctly. They must adapt to an occupation in which one moment may bring the threat of death, while other extended periods bring routine and boredom. They are expected to maintain control in chaotic situations involving injustice, public apathy, conflicting roles, injuries and fatalities. Yet they are expected by both the public and their peers to approach these situations in an objective and professional manner, to be effective decision makers and independent problems solvers while working in a system that encourages dependency by its quasi-military structure (Kelley, 2005).

The nature of work in police professions requires optimal mental health. When their mental functioning are comprised, police professionals can lose touch with the common sense and resilience they need to minimise stress, enjoy their work, and operate at peak performance. Over time, Kelley (2005) finds that poor mental health can dramatically increase police officers' proneness to physical illness, emotional disorders, accidents, marital and family problems, excessive drinking and drug use, suicide, and litigation ranging from excessive force and false arrest, to failure to provide appropriate protection and services.

Performance leadership

Although the appropriate measurement of police performance has long perplexed police practitioners, Coleman (2008) found that there has been a growing consensus that the traditional measurement of only outputs is insufficient. Authorities in Britain, the USA, and Canada have concluded that traditional police organisations have been focused mainly on the processes and outputs achieved through rigid adherence to bureaucratic processes and the finite measurement of easily determined performance indicators.

Coleman (2008: 307) phrased the question: 'Managing strategic knowledge in policing: do police leaders have sufficient knowledge about organisational performance to make informed strategic decisions?' He argues that there is a need for strategic management and, thus, the strategic performance measurements necessary to generate knowledge with which to make strategic decisions. Consequently, his study explored the extent to which Canadian police organisations have strategic performance measurement systems in place that are congruent with modern policing.

Because the goal of his study was to determine the extent to which Canadian police organisations were operating strategically and had implemented a Strategic Performance Measurement (SPM), a self-report survey of 128 questions was derived from the literature. The questions were created to identify whether respondents understood the concept of strategic management and SPM; whether they designed output measures and outcome measures to assist in organisational decision-making; whether they collected and analysed the appropriate data so that knowledge can be generated to assist strategic decision-making, and whether they used this resultant knowledge when making strategic decisions.

The resulting comprehensive survey was distributed to leaders – chiefs of police, chief constables or the equivalents – of 75 Canadian police organisations. All of these organisations, which were selected from the Police Resources in Canada, 2004 report, were police agencies staffed with 50 or more police officers. Of the 75 surveys distributed, 39 responses were received (52 per cent) from police leaders in all provinces.

In order to determine the extent of the implementation of strategic management and the establishment of SPM in Canadian policing, the questions and responses were grouped into categories. Because policing must be implemented and managed strategically, the first category that was analysed related to respondents' perception of what is meant by policing as organisational strategy. Most respondents did not appear to understand the concept of organisational strategy or to have only a partial understanding. The second category addressed the question of whether the police organisation had a corporate business plan. According to the literature, organisations that are led and managed strategically have a corporate plan or business plan with which to communicate the strategy and to guide their achievement of organisational goals. When respondents were asked to articulate the organisational strategy of their organisation, half of the responding police leaders whose organisations reportedly had a corporate business plan suggested that they did not understand the concept of an organisational strategy.

Of the 23 organisations represented in the study (n = 39) that reportedly had a performance measurement system to determine organisational success, 21 of these used community surveys. Because the perception of the prevalence of crime and disorder, and thus the extent of the fear of crime and disorder, in a community is considered a potential crime factor that affects the outcome of policing, an important component of a community survey is the opportunity to determine the extent to whuch respondents have a fear of crime and disorder. Whether or not a police organisation determines the extent of the fear of crime in the community seems to be another indication of the organisation's focus on outcomes. The study found that most of those which reported they used surveys also measured the fear of crime.

$$\boxed{10}$$

Approach to Educational Awareness and Internet Safety

This chapter will describe and evaluate international moves to protect children online and outline the role of educational awareness programs. There have already been considerable efforts to increase online child protection internationally. The G8 countries have agreed a strategy to protect children from sexual abuse on the Internet. Key aims include the development of an international database of offenders and victims to aid victim identification and offender monitoring and the targeting of those profiting from the sale of indecent images of children. Internet service providers and credit card companies, such as the UK's Association for Payment Clearing Services, have also joined the international movement against the production and distribution of sexually abusive images of children online. Their efforts have focused primarily on attempting to trace individuals who use credit cards to access illegal sites containing indecent images of children. There has also been an attempt to put mechanisms into place which would prevent online payment for illegal sites hosted outside the UK (Davidson and Martellozzo, 2008).

Organisations like the Virtual Global Taskforce (VGT) and the Internet Watch Foundation (IWF) are making some headway in attempting to protect children online. VGT is an organisation that comprises several international law enforcement agencies from Australia, Canada, the United States, the United Kingdom and Interpol. Through the provision of advice and support to children, VGT aims to protect children online and has recently set up a bogus website to attract online groomers (Davidson and Martellozzo, 2008). A report to VGT by a child has recently led to the conviction of a sex offender for online grooming and the possession of indecent images. The IWF is one of the main government watchdogs in this area. Although based in the UK, the IWF is part of the US's Safer Internet Plus Program.

IWF's core function is as an Internet hotline service for the public to report their inadvertent exposure to potentially illegal online content, as a notice-and-take-down body for that content. As a result of work by IWF analysts, potentially illegal sexual abuse content URLs are regularly added to the foundation's list. Blocking of web sites is facilitated by this list.

Educational context of Internet safety

Children and young people make extensive use of the Internet using interactive services such as games, chat rooms, and instant messages. Davidson and Martellozzo (2008) emphasise the importance of encouraging appropriate and safe use of the Internet by assisting children and young people to feel comfortable navigating the information highway. Technology, it is suggested, should be combined with education to raise awareness amongst children, parents, and teachers and to promote effective inter-agency partnership working.

Some researchers have suggested that all children should undertake life skills education programs at school on appropriate and inappropriate sexual behaviour. Such programs could certainly incorporate Internet safety. Davidson and Martellozzo's (2008) study suggests that not enough is currently being done in the UK to educate children about sexual abuse or to safeguard them from the dangers of the Internet. Similarly, the Institute for Public Policy Research in the UK have argued that there is a need for greater cooperation between the government, the police, and schools in properly protecting children from sexual abuse. With the explosion of illegal child abuse images over the Internet on the increase and the inherent difficulties from a legislative point of view in identifying and successfully prosecuting offenders, it becomes imperative that a strong educational focus on safety-proofing children against such images, as far as possible, is where the emphasis needs to be placed by governments. In other words, the focal point should be the management of the online environment in which children can potentially be trapped and become victims through risk of being exposed to abusive images or to being groomed.

It is suggested that it is preferable to raise awareness among young people about the potential dangers they may encounter online than to attempt to monitor their online behaviour. This point is particularly relevant for teenage users who may resent any such action and who may well have sufficient computing knowledge to disable any such controls. Hence, a strategic partnership between police and educational agencies like schools and parent groups forms part of the online environmental context that must be managed well through establishing quality safety programs for children and young people. Therefore, Davidson and Martellozzo's (2008) study sought to explore the extent to which the first interactive Internet UK safety program designed by the Metropolitan Police was effective in raising children's knowledge about Internet safety.

Williams (2005) argues that there are many facets of child safety on the Internet. For example, protection of children using the Internet from viewing pornographic images is needed as well as prevention of damage to children through adults viewing child pornography disseminated via the Internet. Warnings, particularly official warnings, seem to have little part to play in either situation. Warnings are sometimes counterproductive, eliciting the 'forbidden fruit' response.

The Metropolitan Police safer surfing program and Internet safety

The Metropolitan Police Program was one of the original Internet safety programmes to be offered in the UK. It no longer runs but differed from other educational Internet programs in that it was interactive and delivered directly to children in schools. It was unique in this respect. The

Child Exploitation and Online Protection Centre (CEOP) now runs the THINKUKNOW programme in some UK schools, the programme is currently being evaluated by the Centre for Abuse and Trauma Studies (Davidson, report forthcoming 6/2009).

The Safer Surfing program was designed in 2002 for use with 12 to 14-year-old children as this age group has been identified as active, independent users of the Internet. The first stage of Davidson and Martellozzo's (2008) research sought to explore the context in which the police and schools work to educate children about sexual abuse and Internet safety. This issue was explored via a literature review and semi-structured interviews with a small sample of safer schools police officers, teachers and head teachers in London schools. Findings from this element of the research are limited given the small sample size. The second stage of their research sought to explore children's experiences on the Internet and to evaluate the effectiveness of the Metropolitan Police Safer Surfing Program. A non-random convenience sample of 188 children aged 10–14 participated in observations of program delivery. The observational data provided a valuable insight into program delivery, children's responses as well as children's Internet use.

Concerning program delivery, children did not always recall the safer (SAFER) mnemonic. However, children who had participated in the program did appear much more knowledgeable about safety (80 per cent mentioned safety) than children who had not yet participated (34 per cent mentioned safety). The post-program group also appeared much more knowledgeable about the dangers of private chat rooms. Some of these children mentioned the benefits of staying in public chat areas. Children in the post-program group also raised an important point about using a false personal identity online in order to protect themselves. The pre-program group did not raise these issues (Davidson and Martellozzo, 2008).

Children who had received the program appeared much more knowledgeable about Internet dangers and the majority of the children had clearly learnt the key program messages and were able to discuss safety strategies. It would seem to Davidson and Martellozzo (2008: 283) that children have some basic knowledge about the possible dangers of chatting online gained from peers and from news coverage based on answers they collected, such as: 'it's just what you hear on the news' and 'you know about Jessica and Holly, we saw what happened on TV'.

The police program served to reinforce such impressions and memories and to educate the children about safety strategies. It was, however, of concern to Davidson and Martellozzo (2008) that the children in their study did not appear to have discussed the program with their parents. Only 31 per cent of the post-program group children had informed their parents about the police program and few had given the leaflet to their parents. Some of the children who had not received the police program had a basic understanding about the dangers of chat rooms. This knowledge was, however, very limited and when questioned further it was clear to Davidson and Martellozzo (2008) that some of these children would be willing to provide personal information and on some occasions meet with an online acquaintance.

In the study by Davidson and Martellozzo (2008) some teachers believed that sexual abuse and Internet safety should be covered in the national curriculum. The Department for Education and Skills (DfES) in the UK leads work across government to ensure that all children and young people stay healthy and safe, to ensure that they receive an education at the highest possible standards of achievement, and that they live a safe and healthy childhood (www.dfes.gov.uk). Thus, DfES might issue guidance that sexual abuse and Internet safety should be covered in the national curriculum.

Teachers welcomed the involvement of safer schools police officers on this topic suggesting that presentations on sensitive issues such as sexual abuse delivered by the police had greater impact upon the children than those given by teachers:

> If we try and teach them about abuse and staying safe on the Internet they probably will not listen, I'm not saying we shouldn't, but we need training really and we need the police to support us with this sort of program. I think we need to be working with the police on this one.

> Davidson and Martellozzo, 2008: 284

In their responses, teachers emphasised the importance of taking the social and cultural context into account when educating children about sexual abuse and safety. It was suggested that police officers working in this context would have to consider the possibility that they may be working with vulnerable children, who are sexually aware and sexually experienced, and who may have been sexually abused. This would presumably also apply to any teacher raising issues about sexual abuse in the context of lessons (Davidson and Martellozzo, 2008).

Norwegian actions for awareness and safety

Again, we will use Norway as the case in this chapter. Faremo (2007) described the following actions for educational awareness and Internet safety in Norway:

- *More research on magnitude and consequences.* More research on Internet related abuse of children, such as experiences with contact initiatives from adults, children's use of web cameras in relation to abuses and research into the market for sexual services from children on the Internet.
- *More knowledge for childcare and health care personnel.* Health care institutions, schools and other places that children visit need to teach children how to use the Internet in a safe way.
- *Guidelines for authorities and service providers.* Government agencies and authorities need to work with Internet service providers (ISPs) to develop guidelines for development and operation of Internet sites that offer communication such as chatting. Internet sites that comply with the guidelines might have an official approval mark on their home page.
- *A forum for all business and government actors on the Internet.* Both chatting service providers and other service providers on the Internet should join in a forum to exchange experiences and ideas with each other and with government agencies.
- *Reporting directly to the police.* On each relevant Internet site, there should be a button to click, which causes the creation of a message directly to the police.

- *A central point for information registration in the criminal police*. Information from citizens in the local community that are supplied as tips to the police should be registered, stored, processed and retrieved at one central point in the national criminal police force.
- *Political and government backing*. All approaches concerned with Internet related abuses of children should be coordinated at the political and government level between ministries and agencies.
- *Norwegian version of 'Task Force on Child Protection on the Internet'*. A Norwegian version of the British Task Force on Child Protection and the Internet should be supported at the national government level. The task force should work across agencies and professions.
- *Virtual police station*. The virtual police station should be like any other police district, with constables doing surveillance, observations, and interviews on the Internet and having informants on the Internet.
- *Victim identification*. Children, who are sexually abused and exposed on the Internet, should be identified, to stop ongoing abuses, prevent more victimisation and bring offenders to justice.
- *Registration of sex offenders*. A new intelligence database should contain registered sex offenders in the national criminal police.
- *Preventive measures*. Parents, children, teachers and other important stakeholder groups need information, support and attitudinal stimulation by relevant authorities. Learning packages, lectures and media attention is needed.
- *International law enforcement initiative*. The Norwegian practice of police information handling might be exported to other countries and international police cooperation should be established. The role of non-government organisations should not be in the area of crime handling, as practiced in some countries.
- *Export of Norwegian filter technology*. The Norwegian technology to filter, stop and eliminate distribution of indecent images should be promoted internationally. Foreign Internet service providers (ISPs) should be encouraged to use effective filtering systems.
- *Develop Nordic collaboration*. Police and other authorities have a long tradition of collaboration in Norway, Sweden, Denmark, Finland and Iceland. A joint Nordic task force should be established for intelligence and investigation of online victimisation of children.
- *Norway joining The Virtual Global Taskforce*. The Virtual Global Taskforce (VGT) is a supplement to already existing police cooperation that Norway should join.
- *Strengthen competence at Norwegian embassies*. When Norwegians engage in sexual activity with children in other countries, Norwegian embassies need the necessary competence to cooperate closely with local authorities to fight sexual abuse of children and arrest Norwegian offenders overseas.
- *International Internet sites to be studied by Norwegian law enforcement*. International law enforcement organisations as well as national law enforcement agencies all over the world publish insights and information on their web sites. Norwegian law enforcement officials should study such official web sites from all over the world. Such sites should be studied on a continuous basis to keep up to date on developments in the field of online grooming behaviours and law enforcement practices globally that may affect Norwegian practice.

Internet safety in chatting rooms is currently focusing on three issues. Firstly, anonymity of users leads to the situation that an excluded user may reappear under a new user name. Second, both potential offenders and potential victims move their communication away from open chatting rooms into closed environments such as personal e-mail. Finally, when an Internet service provider discovers something potentially criminal, the provider is reluctant to report it to the police as the police do not seem to respond to the information supplied by the provider.

Since 1997, 'Mimmi' has had the job of excluding persons who write indecent things on the Norwegian web site chat. no as shown in Figure 10.1. She often sees adults trying to attract young people. Mimmi is a moderator on the web page.

They are smart, and they know what they are doing. They come back again and again. 'It is obvious that they know what they are hunting, and what age groups they want to talk to' Mimmi said to Døvik (2008).

A new book in Norwegian in 2008 represented an important educational awareness initiative (Høstmælingen et al., 2008). The book entitled Child Convention: Children's Rights in Norway is based on the Convention on the Rights of the Child from the United Nations in 1989 and ratified in Norway in 1991. The convention became part of Norwegian law in 2003. Only Somalia and the US have not yet ratified the convention. The Norwegian book discusses the current situation

Figure 10.1   Web site for chat.no

in Norway, including the grooming section introduced in Norwegian criminal law in 2007. The book is written by lawyers and other scholars on subjects such as disabled children's rights, refugee children's rights, and minority children's rights.

An important educational awareness resource is the web page BliSikker.net (BeSure.net) for parents, children, youngsters and teachers. In addition to their presence on the Internet, they also run courses in schools all over the country. More than 24 schools were visited in 2007. BliSikker.net is financed by a number of public and private institutions. Persons involved include Suhail Mustaq, a police officer working for the Norwegian Police Security Services (PST).

A potential action by Norwegian police is to close down web sites. Norwegian police have closed down websites for prostitution, such as www.e-zone.no, but cases of websites for online groomers are not known.

One of the actions listed above is *export of Norwegian filter technology*. The Norwegian technology to filter, stop and eliminate distribution of indecent images should be promoted internationally. Foreign Internet service providers (ISPs) should be encouraged to use effective filtering systems. A child sexual abuse filter is a technical barrier that blocks websites containing child sexual abuse content to a mobile phone or computer. Following the introduction of the filter by telecompanies such as Telenor in Norway, Telenor and others are joining forces with other mobile operators to expand the global outreach of the filter.

Telenor was a pioneer within this field and became the world's first telecom operator to cooperate with law enforcement authorities in creating such a filter. In 2004, Telenor in Norway entered into a cooperative agreement with the Norwegian National Criminal Police Investigation Service (Kripos). In 2005 this partnership extended to include not only Internet subscribers, but also to block prohibited content from the mobile customers.

As part of the service, Kripos provides a hotline where people can tip off the authorities about illegal sites containing child sexual abuse material, as described in the next chapter. Professionals at Kripos perform the content screening and continuously provide Telenor and other telecom firms with an updated list of web sites that should be blocked. The role of Telenor is limited to provide technical solutions and manage filtering processes based on a list of prohibited web sites provided by Kripos. Telenor does not engage in any kind of censorship or evaluation of the legality of contents distributed by others. The partnership therefore clearly states that Kripos is responsible for making all assessments as to legal issues related to content.

11

Recent Initiatives to Protect Children Online

Davidson and Martellozzo (2008) explored the impact of a police programme in the UK designed to educate children about online safety and the extent to which teachers informally and formally educate secondary and primary school children about sexual abuse both in the real world and in cyberspace. Their study indicated that teachers felt untrained in this sensitive area which was addressed by safer schools police officers in England and Wales. They argue that teachers should be educating children about sexual abuse as part of their general sexuality education.

Protecting vulnerable young people

However, Davidson and Martellozzo stress that this is a sensitive area, and the delivery of such education is dependent upon building teachers' confidence and understanding through effective training in collaboration with the police:

> Whilst there are some difficult areas to confront given that much sexual abuse is perpetrated by people known to children and often from within their immediate families, this is an important aspect of crime prevention. There are clearly enormous benefits to be gained from systematically informing parents about their children's sex education and strategies for safety.

> Davidson and Martellozzo, 2008: 284

While people known to children such as uncles or other relatives tend to be the perpetrators and the responsible adults for much sexual abuse, sexual abuse after online grooming is more likely to be committed by people who are strangers to children. If the goal is sexual abuse, then online grooming is a means to that end for strangers by using the Internet to identify potential targets and victims. Thus the role of parents and other family members might be more important in educating children against online grooming than educating children generally against sexual abuse, since online groomers are strangers rather than people known to children.

It is certainly a difficult issue. A core difficulty of teaching children about online safety, where the threat is largely from strangers or virtual friends, is when sexual abuse issues have not been addressed first by either parents or in the school curriculum.

According to Davidson and Martellozzo (2008) intervention programs operate successfully in the context of the formal education system in other countries, for example, in New Zealand the

Keeping Ourselves Safe (KOS) program was developed by the police and the Department of Education and is delivered to all children in schools by trained teachers and the police also have a significant input to this program. Other similar programs are operating in the USA; the Safe-T program, for example, operates in middle and junior schools in Vermont. This program aims to prevent sexual victimisation and to promote healthy relationships in young people (www.pcavt.org). Some research suggests that such programs are successful in raising knowledge levels amongst children and others have suggested that older children are better able to act upon such knowledge (Davidson and Martellozzo, 2008).

In the USA, the Internet Crime Against Children (ICAC) Task Force has created a program to help both children and parents to understand the importance of the Internet but also the danger that may be encountered whilst using it. NetSmartz Workshop has developed the program. NetSmartz is an interactive, educational safety resource from the National Centre for Missing and Exploited Children and Boys & Girls Clubs of America (BGCA) that uses age appropriate, 3-D activities to teach children and teens how to be safer when using the Internet. NetSmartz has been implemented in more than 3000 BGCA Clubs nationally, serving more than 3.3 million young people (Davidson and Martellozzo, 2008).

The program provides parents, children, and teachers with an overview of online risks. More recently CEOP (Child Exploitation and Online Protection Centre) in the UK have designed an Internet safety presentation that is delivered to children. The 'Getting it Right' presentation led to children's awareness of key safety issues arising following the presentation (Davidson and Martellozzo, 2008).

Parental controls and firewalls can also be set up on home computers but a degree of technical knowledge is needed to do so. Parents do not, however, necessarily have this knowledge. Whilst children are well protected on the Internet at school given the knowledge of computing staff and technological advancement in this area, they are most vulnerable at home and ensuring that parents have some basic knowledge about Internet protection is of paramount importance. This issue could be addressed via a simple leaflet when a home computer is purchased. It could be argued that the dissemination of this information is the responsibility of Internet service providers and companies responsible for the production, sale, and distribution of equipment (Davidson and Martellozzo, 2008).

The police in the UK have worked in primary and secondary schools in the past to educate children about safety and sexual abuse, but it is clear from Davidson and Martellozzo's (2008) study that the challenge is for education providers, Internet service providers and the police to work together in systematically informing children and their parents about sexual abuse and safety strategies both in cyberspace and in the real world. The findings from their research also suggest that there is a need for governments to provide clear guidance and possibly training for teachers on educating children about sexual abuse. The police and social services should also be involved in this process (Davidson and Martellozzo, 2008).

It may seem that international efforts to protect children online are largely failing as the number of indecent images of children on the Internet continues to increase, and the images become ever more disturbing involving a greater degree of violence and increasingly younger children. It is suggested that governments are failing to make the growing trade in indecent images of children a high enough political priority and that the hidden nature of online grooming and the lack of public awareness make this possible. According to Davidson and Martellozzo (2008), recent research conducted in the UK suggests that child victimisation and protection issues are not a high priority for the criminal justice agencies involved in the investigative process.

Initiatives in Norway

The first initiative to mention is a recent initiative in Norway where the opening of children's houses is carried out. The minister of justice is opening *children's houses* ('barnehus') all over Norway in 2008 and 2009 (www.regjeringen.no). More than 160 children visited the Children's House in the city of Bergen from it's opening in November 2007 until August 2008. The target audience is children who have been exposed to violence or sexual assault. They also have children who have witnessed threats and violence. The environment in each house is adapted to children. Help is available and activities take place. It addition, each house is suited for police work, childcare work as well as court work, such as interviewing a child for a criminal court case. Children up to 16 years of age can talk about what they have experienced, and the conversation is recorded on video. Six persons are working at the 'barnehus' in Bergen. The personnel have backgroundsin child psychology, qualitative research, school education and police training.

The second initiative in Norway is *digital forensics* in intelligence and analysis by law enforcement agencies (Gjerde, 2008). Successful cyber crime intelligence requires computer skills and modern systems in policing. Digital forensics is the art and science of applying computer science to aid the legal process. It is more than the technological, systematic inspection of electronic systems and their contents for evidence or supportive evidence of a criminal act. Digital forensics requires specialised expertise and tools when applied to intelligence in important areas such as online victimisation of children (Davidson and Gottschalk, 2008).

While the expansion of the Internet and the proliferation of information technology have created new opportunities for those who engage in illegal activities (Taylor and Quayle, 2003), the area of digital forensics has grown rapidly as well (Ferraro and Casey, 2005). This has helped in the discovery of new ways of criminal activities. Sex offenders use the Internet to access indecent images of children, to select victims for abuse and to communicate with other sex offenders. This activity has expanded so much that law enforcement agencies have difficulty tracking down the child victims and perpetrators involved unless they have the capability of professional digital forensics and intelligence (Smith, 2008).

As a term, digital forensics refers to the study of technology, the way criminals use it and the way to extract and examine digital evidence (Ferraro and Casey, 2005). Digital forensics is an approach to identifying evidence from computers that can be used in trials. A typical forensics investigation consists of two main phases, exploration and evidence respectively. During the exploration phase, investigators attempt to identify the nature of the problem and what exactly happened or is expected to happen at the crime scene. The evidence phase takes place after the exploration has been concluded. It consists of accumulating all documentation which will be introduced in court as evidence.

From a data viewpoint, this two-phase procedure can be broken down into six stages: preparation, incident response, data collection, data analysis, presentation of findings and incident closure. Some of these stages may be so complex in certain circumstances that they are divided into sub-stages. The most time consuming tasks in digital forensics investigation are searching, extracting and analysing. Therefore, a need exists for a forensics model that allows formalisation of the digital forensics process, innovative data mining techniques for the forensics process and a dedicated infrastructure for digital forensics. Digital detectives are now educated by the Norwegian Police University College to use such techniques, tools and methods (Gjerde, 2008).

Norway was the first country to establish a commissioner, or ombudsman, with statutory rights to protect children and their rights. Since 1981, the Ombudsman for Children in Norway has worked continuously to improve national and international legislation affecting children's welfare. The duties of the Ombudsman are to promote children's interests to public and private authorities and to investigate the developments of conditions under which children grow up (www.barneombudet.no/english/). The new grooming section 201a in Norwegian criminal law was initiated and acclaimed by the Ombudsman, which argued that the section gives a strong signal to society that children's rights for protection are critical and that the new section might have a preventive effect on those who plan sexual assaults against children.

The third initiative to mention is thus the ombudsman who launched an initiative to establish an *emergency telephone* number for children and for adults who have observed children in need.

The fourth initiative is concerned with the protection of personal information about children that is published on the Internet. Some parents tend to publish sensitive information about their children and pictures from vacations and other occasions without considering the potential dangers involved. The principle of *child consent* will imply that parents will have to ask their children and get their permission before publishing material involving them. The principle of child consent is an initiative to be included when Norway is to revise its Child Law ('barnelov') in 2009.

The fifth initiative stems from the organisation Save the Children Norway, which has developed and published chatting rules. There are four important *chatting rules* in their pamphlet (Redd Barna, 2007):

1. Be anonymous. Never give away your name, address or telephone number.
2. Leave if you do not like the chat. You are in charge!
3. Never meet someone from the chat alone. Always bring an adult the first time.
4. If you are to meet someone from the chat, choose a public place with many people.

The sixth initiative is to implement the data storage directive from the EU in Norway. Police argue that it will help investigate online grooming of children. The directive says that traffic data has to be stored by telecom service providers between six and 24 months (Høgetveit and Ingerø, 2008).

The Norwegian red police button

The seventh initiative is the *red button* that was introduced in September 2008. The red button is located on web pages for children where grooming may occur. The red button can be pressed by children and others who experience abuse behaviour on that web site. When the button is pressed, an automatic message is sent to the national criminal police (Kripos) in Norway (Døvik, 2008). Kripos is open day and night. The red button is shown in Figures 11.1 and 11.2.

Figure 11.1   Red button on children web sites for reporting misuse to police

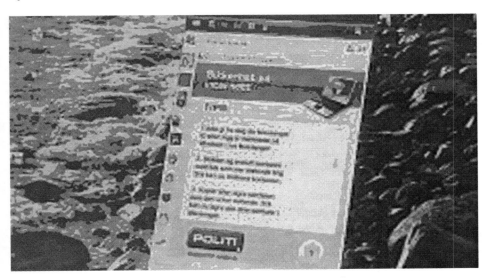

Figure 11.2   Red button located on the chatting program *Messenger* from Microsoft

It is Microsoft in Norway who has taken the lead to install this system, which is to be found on all web sites used by children. By pressing the red button marked police, abuse can easily be reported directly to the police (Døvik, 2008).

When the red button is pressed, the police page tips.kripos.no automatically opens on the screen as shown in Figure 11.3. Three alternatives emerge on the screen: Sexual exploitation of

Figure 11.3   This police page automatically opens when a red button has been pressed

children ('Seksuell utnytting av barn'), human trafficking ('Menneskehandel') and racial expressions on the Internet ('Rasistiske ytringer pa internett').

If sexual exploitation of children is ticked, then instructions on the screen say that the tip registration will occur in three steps (Figure 11.4):

Step 1: What is the tip about?
Step 2: Where did the act occur?
Step 3: Who is the sender of the tip?

Next, there is a choice between ticking (Figure 11.5):

- web pages that have pictures or films sexualising children
- sexual exploitation of children on the Internet (grooming)
- sexual offence against children

Child exploitation and online protection centre in the UK

CEOP was established in April 2006 in response to a growing concern about child abuse predominantly online and to provide support for investigations into online offenders. Ceop's (2008) remit is defined in the following way:

Figure 11.4   The police tip page when sexual exploitation of children has been ticked

- to provide a single 24/7 point of contact for the reporting of online child abuse for the public, law enforcers, industry and other organisations
- to offer information and advice to victims and potential victims of abuse and to parents
- to receive, assess and disseminate international and domestic intelligence coming into the UK on online and offline offenders, including paedophiles and other serious sex offenders
- to support, co-ordinate and assist national and international investigations into suspects and victims of online child abuse
- to provide – in the medium to longer term – specialist forensic services, including forensic support to forces
- to undertake some proactive investigations into online child abuse
- to identify and recover criminal assets from those profiting from online child abuse
- to deliver proactive crime prevention and crime reduction strategies to reduce the harm caused by online child abuse
- to commission and undertake research, including research into the nature of the crime, criminal and environment
- to deliver and contribute to comprehensive and effective educational programs

Figure 11.5   The first registration page when sexual exploitation of children has been ticked

- to maintain and manage the national database of child abuse images (ChildBase) and implement and manage appropriate links to VISOR and other relevant systems
- to collect, maintain and manage information on serious sex offenders (the so-called serious sex offenders register)
- to provide the secretariat to the Virtual Global Taskforce

CEOP is an affiliate of the Serious Organised Crime Agency (SOCA). This means that it is ultimately accountable to the SOCA Board but enjoys full operational independence.

Information privacy concerns protective responses

Information privacy refers to an individual's ability to control when, how, and to what extent their personal information is communicated to others. Past research into issues associated with information privacy has focused on understanding what motivates Internet users to divulge personal information and what inhibits them from divulging it. Internet users' concerns for information privacy have received considerable attention as a salient belief that determines their willingness or unwillingness to divulge personal information in online, virtual environments (Son and Kim, 2008).

In a study, Son and Kim (2008), introduce the notion of information privacy-protective responses and define it as a set of Internet users' behavioural responses to their perception of information privacy threats that results from web sites information practices. Their set of responses consists of six types: refusal, misrepresentation, removal, negative word-of-mouth, complaining directly to website, and complaining directly to third-party organisations:

- *Refusal*. Refuse to give information to online groomer because you think it is too personal.
- *Misrepresentation*. Falsify some of your personal information asked for by online groomer.
- *Removal*. Take action to have your information removed from online website when your personal information was not properly handled.
- *Negative word-of-mouth*. Speak to your friends and/or relatives about your bad experience with online website when your personal information was not properly handled.
- *Complaining directly*. Write or call online website organisation to complain about the way they use personal information when your personal information was not properly handled.
- *Complaining indirectly*. Write or call an elected official or consumer organisation to complain about the way online companies use personal information when your personal information was not properly handled.

Children may use all these responses when their privacy is threatened.

12

Online Sex Offending Prevention

According to the free encyclopaedia Wikipedia (www.wikipedia.org), crime prevention is any initiative or policy which reduces or eliminates the aggregate level of victimisation or the risk of individual criminal participation and the rate of victimisation, as well as efforts to change perceptions. Crime prevention is the attempt to reduce victimisation and to deter crime and criminals. It is applied specifically to efforts made by governments to reduce crime, enforce the law, and maintain criminal justice.

It is agreed in police science that governments must go beyond law enforcement and criminal justice to tackle the risk factors that cause crime because it is more cost effective and leads to greater social benefits than the standard ways of responding to crime.

Norwegian National Crime Prevention Council

As an example of a prevention organisation, the Norwegian National Crime Prevention Council (KRÅD, 2008) functions as the Norwegian government's body of expertise within the judicial system. It is a government agency working under the Ministry of Justice. The council is free and independent in selecting matters to focus on and what kind of advice it chooses to give. It cannot be instructed as long as it works within the limits of its mandate.

The Norwegian crime policy's main aim is to prevent crimes taking place. By accumulating information and disseminating knowledge on crime and crime prevention work, the council works to reduce crime and improve levels of safety in society. The council also evaluates reforms, conducts survey research to develop new insights and provides support for local crime prevention projects. The council works on commission from the Norwegian government, often in collaboration with other organisations and public sector agencies.

The council's primary target groups are decision makers and employees within the justice system, as well as operatives in the field of crime prevention and members of the general public with an interest in and a need for the knowledge that is possessed by the members of the council.

The mandate for the council states that the council is to contribute to the coordination of crime prevention ventures between official authorities and private organisations. The council focuses on young people and is given the following primary tasks:

- Initiate cooperation with other authorities and organisations, giving advice and guidance to crime prevention strategies and actions and initiate research related to this.
- Initiate and support crime prevention work centrally and locally.

- Work on tasks, give advice and attend hearings in cooperation with or on assignment from the Ministry of Justice or other ministries.
- Contribute to the understanding of the importance of crime prevention at all levels in Norwegian society.
- Participate in the criminology debate.

New offender treatment approaches

The treatment of Internet sex offenders is a very new area, and there are few programs focusing specifically on this issue. The chapter will provide an overview of current treatment practices in Europe, the US and Canada.

Treatment approaches with sex offenders whose offending is Internet related tend to be based on the cognitive behavioural treatment (CBT) model. However, the structure and delivery of such programs differ. In England and Wales, there has been a recent attempt to centrally develop and organise a CBT program for Internet sex offenders that is now in use by the National Probation Service and will possibly be introduced to prisons. The Internet Sex Offender Treatment Program (i-SOTP) runs alongside the existing sex offender treatment program. Another CBT treatment program is currently operational at a local level at the Forensic Department, University Hospital, Basel, Switzerland. This inpatient and outpatient clinic for sex offenders includes those remanded in custody, on probation, post release from prison, and some self-referring. Approximately 15–20 per cent of all Internet offenders are self-referring.

Forty men have attended the program so far in Switzerland. Therapy lasts for one year with weekly sessions of 1.5 hours. It is based upon relapse prevention models adapted for use with Internet sex offenders. The majority of offenders have been charged with possession of child Internet pornography. The program has been running for four years, and the CBT model used is based upon work which has been adapted for use with sex offenders using indecent Internet images of children.

Theory-based crime prevention

Online grooming of children for sexual abuse is a crime that can be explained by a number of criminology theories. Depending on the relevant theory, situational crime prevention emerges. For example, the rational choice theory of crime and its cognate field of study, situational crime prevention, have exerted a considerable influence in criminal justice policy and criminology. When discussing rational choice theory, Hayward (2007) argues that the growing tendency among many individuals to engage in certain forms of criminal decision-making strategies for crimes such as online grooming may be the result of a series of subjectivities and emotions that reflect the material values and cultural logic associated with late modern consumerism. Thus, prevention should be concerned about changing material values and cultural logic that will change decision-making strategies.

It is difficult to overstate the importance of theory to law enforcement understanding of crime and criminals. Theory allows analysts to understand and predict outcomes on a probabilistic basis

(Colquitt and Zapata-Phelan, 2007). Theory allows analysts to describe and explain a process or sequence of events. Theory prevents analysts from being confused by the complexity of the real world by providing a linguistic tool for organising a coherent understanding of the real world. Theory acts as an educational device that creates insights into criminal phenomena.

Rational choice theory suggests that people who commit crimes do so after considering the risks of detection and punishment for the crimes, as well as the rewards of completing these acts successfully. Examples of this theory include a man who discovers that his wife is having an affair and chooses to kill her, her lover, or both; the bank teller who is experiencing personal financial difficulty and decides to embezzle funds from the bank to substantially increase her earnings; and an inner-city youth who decides that social opportunities are minimal and that it would be easier to make money by dealing crack cocaine (Lyman and Potter, 2007).

Some theorists believe that crime can be reduced through the use of deterrents. The goal of deterrence as crime prevention is based on the assumption that criminals or potential criminals will think carefully before committing a crime if the likelihood of getting caught and/or the fear of swift and severe punishment are present. Based on such belief, *general deterrence theory* holds that crime can be thwarted by the threat of punishment, while *special deterrence theory* holds that penalties for criminal acts should be sufficiently severe that convicted criminals will never repeat their acts (Lyman and Potter, 2007).

Furthermore, *learning theories* have been used to explain the onset of criminal activity. The body of research on learning theory stresses the attitudes, ability, values, and behaviours needed to maintain a criminal career (Lyman and Potter, 2007).

Next, *cultural deviance theories* assume that slum dwellers violate the law because they belong to a unique subculture that exists in lower-class areas. The subculture's values and norms conflict with those of the upper class on which criminal law is based (Lyman and Potter, 2007).

Yet another criminology theory is *social control theory*, where social control refers to those processes by which the community influences its members toward compliance with established norms of behavior:

> *Social control theorists argue that the relevant question is not, Why do persons become involved in crime, organised or otherwise? but, rather, Why do most persons conform to societal norms? If, as control theorists generally assume, most persons are sufficiently motivated by the potential rewards to commit criminal acts, why do only a few make crime a career? According to control theorists, delinquent acts result when an individual's bond to society is weak or broken. The strength of this bond is determined by internal and external restraints. In other words, internal and external restraints determine whether we move in the direction of crime or of law-abiding behavior.*

Abadinsky, 2007: 22

All kinds of theories should be applied cautiously. Hayward (2007) argues that as long as crime prevention theorists continue to prioritise rational choice theory of crime over and above any concern with the multifarious subjective experiences of the offender, their usefulness when it comes to the control of the growing number of crime types will inevitably be limited.

Crime prevention and the British planning system

There is a national policy in the UK attempting to bring crime prevention into the centre of the planning process. In research conducted by Morton and Kitchen (2005: 419), the operational relationship between planners and Police Architectural Liaison Officers (ALOs) was studied. This relationship is at the heart of British Government's desire to make crime prevention a key objective for planning:

> As a factor which the British planning system is expected to take into account, crime prevention is a relatively late arrival on the scene. The first formal guidance from the Government about the relationship was contained in DoE Circular 5/94 (Department of the Environment, 1994) which was notable mainly for the emphasis it placed on consultation with Police Architectural Liaison Officers or equivalent rather than for solid advice about how planners should handle crime prevention issues in their everyday work. Since that point, crime prevention, public safety, and the contribution that attention to these matters can make to the achievement of sustainable communities have risen rapidly up the planning agenda as issues for consideration.

There have been four stages in the process of bringing crime prevention issues higher up the planning agenda in the UK (Morton and Kitchen, 2005):

- *Stage 1: Crime and Disorder Act, 1998*. This act had two impacts on the planning process. First, the high profile element was the requirement for the creation of crime and disorder reduction partnerships between local authorities, the police and other key players to identify and tackle problems in the field, which are now operational in various forms in local authority areas across England. What these provide is a strategic approach to crime prevention together with an action plan, both of which are agreed between the police, local authorities and other partners. Second, the less high profile element was the new duty imposed on local planning authorities to take account of crime prevention issues in their work and to do all they reasonably can to reduce crime and disorder.
- *Stage 2: Urban Policy White Paper, 2000*. This paper was issued by the Department of the Environment, Transport and the Regions. Based on an understanding of new urbanism, planning should include prevention of emerging crime trends in urban areas.
- *Stage 3: Safer Places Document, 2004*. This document on planning system and crime prevention was issued by the Office of the Deputy Prime Minister and the Home Office. What went into the planning process was both urban design advice stressing the value of permeable approaches to housing layouts and advice from reviews of the available research to the effect that permeable layouts consistently demonstrate higher crime rates than do less permeable layouts. The new guidance raised the profile of planning for crime prevention via a substantial document.

- *Stage 4: Delivering Sustainable Development, 2005*. This document from the Deputy Prime Minister's office takes as its central theme the proposition that the primary task of the planning system is to deliver sustainable development, which it expects the fresh round of plan-making ushered in acts to address. The role of the planning system in helping to achieve public safety is clearly established here.

However, Morton and Kitchen (2005) conducted an empirical study among planners which revealed that the planning community tended not to read guidelines and other documents from the Government. The proportion of planners that had actually read a specific guidance under a year after publication was relatively small, and thus its impact on their work must be limited. It seems clear that publication of documents is not enough. If the planning community is going to take on board the key messages in this field, then they need to be actively promoted to do so.

It is not only the UK that is attempting to bring crime prevention into the centre of community planning processes. Similar efforts are found in other European countries such as Germany and the Netherlands. In these countries, crime prevention committees are institutions which mainly initiate, support and reinforce inter-institutional cooperation. Several forms of cooperation exist between the police, municipal authorities, private security services and citizens as well (Schulze and Brink, 2006).

In 2002, the Dutch government launched a program called 'Towards a Safer Society'. Its goal was to achieve a 20 to 25 per cent reduction in violent crimes in public areas between 2002 and 2010. However, the number of violent crimes has continued to increase. Thus, the Dutch government became interested in accumulating knowledge on violence prevention and in developing evidence-based crime prevention plans (Leeuw *et al.*, 2007).

In the end, the proof of good prevention planning lies in crime statistics for crime prevention efficiency. Here, efficiency in crime prevention includes technical efficiency. Technical efficiency is a relative measure of how well the inputs are processed to achieve desired outputs (Barros, 2007).

Theory and practice for crime prevention

As we will see in the next chapter, research is being launched to develop more knowledge about online grooming. Such research is initiated to increase theoretical understanding as well as empirical results, all of which with the purpose of saving children from victimisation. The ambiguity that comes from the use of a virtual identity needs to be better understood.

Any research initiated will need a scoping study before the main research fieldwork with offenders begins, given the absence of literature or comparative legislation and approaches to online child safety in different countries and on the characteristics and behaviour of online groomers. This scoping phase will equip researchers with vital information to help refine the main research design and aid the development of robust data collection tools before extensive resources are deployed in the filed. A scoping phase might gather information on issues encompassing: the legislative context of work with Internet sex offenders in different countries;

each country's approach to educational awareness and Internet safety and any recent initiatives to protect children online; the techniques and methods offenders use to groom people online; the extent of any barriers professionals have experienced in gaining clinical or research interviews with these men; online groomers general presentation and extent of openness to discuss their offending behaviour at interview; and the location of convicted online groomers in each country.

Qualitative research aims to explore the process of online grooming and victim selection, focusing upon the behaviours of men who target children and young people online. Interviews will be undertaken with convicted online groomers in the prison system in many countries.

While such important research is going on, the practice of prevention cannot wait for research results. Activities have to be implemented and monitored continuously. For example, the red button of the Norwegian criminal police needs to be monitored and evaluated. Already in the first few months, the monthly rate reached 350 complaints, or more than ten per day. The police confirmed in an interview with Stokke (2009) that they had already received some valuable tips for further police investigations.

New insights into theory and practice will influence legislation. Many jurisdictions do already have legislation in place that criminalises online child grooming for the purposes of sexual contact. Examples include the UK, Norway and Australia. For example, in Queensland a 25-year-old man had groomed what he thought to be a 13-year-old girl ('Becky boo 13') in an IRC room by sending emails inviting her to engage in sexual activity. In fact, the emails were to a police officer pretending to be the child in question. The defendant was convicted and sentenced to imprisonment for two-and-a-half years, with parole after nine months. This was reduced on appeal to an 18-month term, suspended from the time of the appeal, the defendant having already served 90 days in custody. In a more recent incident in Australia, a man was sentenced to two years imprisonment for using online chat rooms to proposition children to engage in sexual acts on the Internet. This sentence was suspended after the offender served three months in jail, with a condition that he not re-offend for three years (AIC, 2008).

Again from these two examples, it is apparent that a real child need not be involved in the commission of the offence, as child grooming can be viewed as an act preliminary to commission of a sexual abuse. It does not matter that the person is a fictitious person represented to the adult as a real person. Successful prosecutions of cases involving covert sting operations where investigators pose online as children have been achieved in other countries as well (AIC, 2008).

Information and communication technology enables offenders to target children individually or collectively. Possible motives include personal gratification of the offender, often by the way of sexual exploitation. Future legislation might move law enforcement into cyberspace, where cyber policing will prevent grooming initiatives reaching their destinations. As much as technology can enable offenders, technology can enable police in cyberspace. Paedophiles will become visible as individuals on the Internet. It is not only their actions, such as flattery and gifts, that are visible. The individuals as such are also visible.

Individuals can become visible by police application of intelligent search engines. By combining typical phrases used by paedophiles, their presence might be discovered. Examples of phrases include 'let's go private', 'where's your computer in the house', 'who's your favourite band', 'I know someone who can get you a modelling job', and 'I know a way you can earn money fast' (SafeTeens, 2009).

But, first and foremost, children must watch out for themselves.

The case of online sexual grooming in Sweden

In Sweden, and particularly in the Swedish media, the term grooming has become synonymous with discussions of the online sexual solicitation of children and youth:

> *The use of the term in the literature on the sexual abuse of children predates the phenomenon of online sexual solicitation by some considerable time, however. The sexual grooming concept refers to a process whereby an offender creates the opportunity to sexually abuse or exploit a child by first winning the victim's trust. Typical depictions describe a (male) perpetrator who presents himself as the child's adult friend, as someone who shares the child's interests, perhaps giving the child gifts, and providing appreciation, comfort, and understanding for the child's problems. Over time, sexual grooming further involves developing a relationship of exclusivity with the child, by means of which the perpetrator simultaneously creates a distance between the child and his or her parents, or other persons who would otherwise function as a protection against various forms of abuse. This serves also to reduce the likelihood that the planned abuse will be detected or reported.*
>
> Shannon, 2008: 161

With this definition in mind, we will now look into empirical results obtained by Shannon (2008) in Sweden. The findings are based on police data relating to reported sexual offences against persons below 18 years of age where the perpetrator and the victim had been in contact with one another online. A total of 315 relevant police reports were identified, which were broken down into four categories:

1. cases where perpetrator and victim had only been in contact online (n = 179)
2. cases where perpetrator and victim had been in contact both online and offline (by phone), but where the material provides no sure indication of a sexual offence having taken place at an offline meeting (n = 45)
3. cases where an adult perpetrator who already knew the child offline had used the Internet to develop the existing relationship for sexual purposes (n = 22)
4. cases where the perpetrator and victim came into contact with one another online, and where the perpetrator had subsequently committed a sexual offence against the victim at an offline meeting (n = 69)

In our perspective of sexual abuse after online grooming, the cases in the fourth category are of main interest, where online contacts resulting in offline sexual offences are described on the basis of the different approaches employed by the perpetrators to persuade the victims to meet them offline:

Three general approaches were identified in the material: cases where the child had been promised work as a model, cases where they had been offered payment for sexual services, and cases where the perpetrator had used online contacts to develop a friendship or romantic relationship with the child.

Shannon, 2008: 172

The largest group of offline offences (29 out of 69 cases in category 4) related to cases where the perpetrators had developed friendship and some kind of romance with the victims, first online and then frequently also by means of mobile phone contacts. The victims were mostly under 15 years and the youngest victim was aged 11 at the time of the offence. All victims, with one exception, were girls. The perpetrators' ages ranged from 17 to 44 years. In one-third of the cases, the perpetrator was more than 20 years older than the victim.

The duration of the Internet contacts varied to a great extent:

In approximately one-third of cases the online contact had continued for over six months (and for up to over two years) prior to the commission of the offline offence. Many of these longer online contacts involved children who described having problems in school, with bullying for example, or at home and having felt a need to talk to someone about these problems.

Shannon, 2008: 173

Virtually all of the offences resulting from these longer-term contacts had been committed in the perpetrators' homes. Even in the cases where intercourse took place against the child's will, it was not always the case that the child broke off contact with the perpetrator as a result.

The data presented in the article by Shannon (2008) provide an illustration of the substantial range of types of online sexual contacts from adults that children in Sweden are currently being exposed to. At the same time, they indicate that the nature of these contacts, the range of types of online offences currently being committed, and the strategies employed by adult perpetrators to persuade children to meet them offline are all similar to those found in other countries, such as the UK, the US, Norway and Australia.

13

Future Research into Online Grooming

The extent of any barriers professionals have experienced in gaining clinical or research interviews with these men is quite unknown. Similarly, online groomers' general presentation and extent of openness to discuss their offending behaviour at interview is quite unknown. The location of convicted groomers in a country is quite unknown. To achieve access to convicted groomers for interviews in prisons, we need letters of recommendation from relevant criminal justice services, prison governors and prison officials. Evidence of cooperation is needed from prison management so that interviews are possible. We, as researchers, assume this will happen, but we do not provide evidence.

Research interviews with online grooming sexual offenders

As discussed, the process of finding interviewees and setting up interviews is central to the outcomes of much empirical research. There are four key areas around recruitment of interviewees:

- initially finding a knowledgeable informant
- getting a range of views
- testing emerging themes with new interviewees
- choosing interviewees to extend results

Once an interview has been arranged, issues to be covered with this specific interviewee have to be considered. The list of questions is initially generated in negotiation with the relevant academic and non-academic literature, alongside research thoughts about what areas might be important to cover in the interview (Rapley, 2004).

For example, when Hanoa (2008) interviewed inmates in Norwegian prisons about violence and threats among inmates, she recruited interviewees who had personal experiences in the area. Her study took an exploratory and qualitative approach. An appropriate method was therefore to interview inmates and let them provide insight into their experiences and perceptions of why and how threats occur. She interviewed 13 inmates in four different prisons.

For interviews with convicted sexual offenders in Norway, letters were sent to the Norwegian Correctional Services. To identify inmates, there is a need to find the birth date identification numbers of convicted persons. Sentences from courts do not include these numbers, so identification of individuals is made difficult. Therefore, letters were sent to the services.

The first round of requests consisted of some letters of agreement from the criminal justice services that we will use to undertake the scoping exercise and case analysis. Relevant collaborators in these services should sign it as proof of contact (on headed paper).

The second round of letters asks for approval to access inmates. In these application letters, the background and the purpose of the interviews are explained, and we ask that an invitation letter to potential inmates who have been convicted for sections in criminal law (195, 196, 200, 201 as well as 201a, to be included, given that the available sample is very small) is handed over to relevant inmates in each region's prisons with the aim of achieving consent to interview given that they meet the desired characteristics in terms of having used the Internet for grooming. A stamped, addressed envelope has to be included with the invitation, which is handed to each target inmate with the invitation, and prison warders are not to open this letter.

The invitation letter has to tell who will conduct the interviews; that interviewers have to treat the information as confidential, and that inmates are to deliver their consent to the wing warders or contact warders in a sealed envelope, which is not to be opened before mailing. In their reply, inmates should write their name or inmate number, wing and what prison they reply from. Invitation letters to inmates should be short, as many inmates are not used to reading.

Norwegian Correctional Services have published guidelines as to how applications for research on correctional services are to be formulated:

http://web3.custompublish.com/getfile.php/607466.823.tbcsrqafsc/retningslinjer_ forskning.pdf?return = www.kriminalomsorgen.no

Initially, letters were sent to regions east and northeast. Region east has few inmates convicted of sexual abuse. Region northeast has almost 100 inmates convicted of sexual abuse (half of them rape) and all prisons are easily accessible from Oslo for interviews. Applications were not sent to all six regions, only two of them, because coordination between regions takes time, which could lead to late responses. All letters have to present why the research is important and how the research results are to be used. Arguing how the correctional services can benefit from this research and that all interested parties will receive a copy of the final research report strengthens the application.

Each correctional service region will need to consider whether they have to present the application to an ethics committee. Since participation is based on consent, it should not be necessary according to current rules.

Research project: understanding the process of online grooming

The Commission of the European Communities, Directorate-General Information Society and Media, supports its safer Internet plus program including knowledge enhancement projects. One of the knowledge enhancement projects launched in 2009 is concerned with understanding the process of online grooming in terms of the behaviour of men who target young people online.

Participating researching institutions in this project are the National Centre for Social Research (UK), Kingston University (UK), Royal Holloway University of London (UK), Norwegian School of Management (Norway), University of Palermo (Italy) and the University of Mons-Hainaut (Belgium).

The rationale for the project is the fact that sexual abuse of children via the Internet is an international problem, a crime without geographical boundaries. Solutions both to perpetrators use of the Internet and to the safety of children and young people online must be sought and found at a broad level and will necessarily involve agencies working to protect children at local, national and international levels. The police have suggested that an increasing number of online sex offenders are grooming children and young people on online social networks, making such sites important research issues. However, it is difficult to measure how many offenders are attracted to these sites. While a great deal is known about sex offender behaviour, and there is an increasing body of pioneering work addressing those accessing indecent child images, little is known about online groomers and the way in which they select victims.

To this end, the safer Internet plus program invited proposals for projects that aim to enhance the knowledge of the online sexual abuse of children, with a particular focus on online grooming – defined as the process by which a person befriends a young person online in order to facilitate a meeting with the goal of committing sexual abuse. However, due to the insignificant amount of elapsed time since legislation targeting grooming was introduced in countries such as Norway and the UK, and the absence of specific legislation in other countries, online groomers are a small, hidden and hard-to-reach research population.

The project for increased understanding of the process of online grooming in terms of the behaviours of men who target young people online will be the largest study of online grooming commissioned to date and will take place in the UK and three more European sites. Depth interviews will be conducted with a purposive sample of thirty online groomers in the UK and at least seven online groomers in each of the partner sites. This sample size and regional distribution is specified as it is attainable given the two key legislative and logistic challenges associated with identifying this research population and in encouraging participation in the research.

First, the sample is naturally skewed towards UK offenders due to the elapsed years since specific legislation was introduced in 2003 (compared to other European states). It is also pertinent to note that reaching thirty online groomers in the UK may in fact be approaching the extent of the population rather than a selected sub-sample currently in prison. Second, sampling and recruitment is far more challenging for non-UK research partners. Here the lack of legislation outside of the UK means that there are naturally fewer online groomers in the respective prison systems to recruit into the research. Norway is the exception where legislation was passed in 2007, but there are still very few Internet sex offenders in the criminal justice system.

In addition, those offenders who have groomed young people online will only be identifiable through conversations with key stakeholders and analysis of individual offender case files. To conclude, the research population is essentially 'hidden' and increasing the sample size is not possible for the reasons outlined above.

Depth interviews will focus on exploring and describing all phases of the online grooming process. In particular, the study will:

- Describe the behaviours of both offenders who groom and young people who are groomed and explore differences (for example in demographics, behaviour and profiles) within each group and how these differences may have a bearing on offence outcome
- describe how information and communication technology (ICT) is used to facilitate the process of online grooming
- further the current low knowledge base about the way in which young people are selected and prepared for abuse online
- make a significant contribution to the development of educational awareness and preventative initiatives aimed at parents and young people
- contribute to the development of online sex offender risk assessment and management knowledge

This study represents the first European attempt to explore Internet offending behaviour with perpetrators.

Project work plan to study the process of online grooming

The project consists of several phases:

- *Phase 1: Scoping Study – Literature Review, Interviews with Stakeholders and Content Analysis of Police Offender Case Files.* Phase 1 of the research aims to explore the background and context of Internet abuse in each country and to gather data from key stakeholders working with Internet sex offenders in the criminal justice system. Information from this phase will inform the literature review and the development of the offender interview guide.
- *Phase 2: Offender Interviews.* During Phase 2 individual in-depth interviews will be conducted with a sample of 30 men convicted of online grooming who are serving a custodial sentence in England and Wales and a further sample of sex offenders whose offending has included online grooming in each of the European countries, with seven interviews from each of the remaining countries applying the same interview guide. A total of approximately 50 interviews will be conducted with online groomers.
- *Phase 3: Teacher/Parent Focus Groups and Dissemination.* The aim of Phase 3 is (i) to hold focus groups with educators and parents about how to 'translate' findings for professionals working with children and to the children themselves and (ii) to ensure that key findings are disseminated to practitioners in each participating country, and also to disseminate the findings to young people and their parents via educators and the media, and to a wide international audience.

Given that potential participants for this research will probably be incarcerated, the selection and recruitment of online groomers is a particularly challenging aspect of the qualitative work. A number of arrangements for consent may have to be considered.

Conclusions

The International Corporation for Assigned Names and Numbers (ICANN) is currently the most powerful force in global Internet governance. ICANN regularly makes policies fundamental to any potential for protecting children online now or in the future; to stopping the flow of child pornography and hardcore obscenity; to thwarting sex offenders and sex traffickers; and to controlling under-age access to harmful materials. Preston (2008) argues that now is a tremendous opportunity to influence policies affecting the development of the Internet. Individuals and organisations that support the protection of children and families must come to the table. ICANN can do more to encourage effective participation by a much broader cross-section of non-commercial Internet users. The ICANN ambition is to fulfil the promise of seeking and supporting broad, informed participation of all Internet stakeholders by reflecting the functional, geographic, and cultural diversity of the Internet at all levels of policy and legislation development and decision-making.

References

Aas-Hansen, A. (2004) *Barn som møter overgriper på internett – Fokus på rettspraksis (Children Who Meet Offenders on the Internet: Focus on Legislative Practice)* Redd Barna (Save the Children Norway) www.reddbarna.no.

Abadinsky, H. (2007) *Organised Crime.* 8th edn, Belmont, CA: Thomson Wadsworth.

Abel, G.C. and Becker, J.V. (1984) *The Treatment of Child Molesters.* Treatment Manual, unpublished.

Abel, G.C. and Becker, J.V. (1987) Self Reported Sex Crimes of Non-Incarcerated Paraphilliacs. *Journal of Interpersonal Violence,* 2: 6, 3–25.

Abel, G.C., Cunningham-Rathner, J., Becker, J.V. and McHugh, J. (1983) Motivating Sex Offenders for Treatment. In Finkelhor, D. (Ed.) *A Sourcebook on Child Sexual Abuse.* California: Sage.

Abel, G.C., Cunningham-Rathner, J., Becker, J.V. and McHugh, J. (1988) The Nature and Extent of Sexual Assault. In Marshall, W.L. (Ed.) *Handbook of Sexual Assault.* New York: Plenum.

Afuah, A. and Tucci, C.L. (2003) *Internet Business Models and Strategies.* 2nd edn. New York: McGraw-Hill.

Amabile, T.M., Barsade, S.G., Mueller, J.S. and Staw, B.M. (2005) Affect and Creativity at Work. *Administrative Science Quarterly,* 50: 367–403.

Andersson, I.T. (2002) *Från barndom till brott – Om 20 män dömda för sexualla övergrepp mot 38 barn (From Childhood to Crime: 20 Men Convicted of Sexual Abuse of 38 Children)* Sweden: Department of Psychology, Göteborg University.

Archbold, C.A. (2005) Managing the Bottom Line: Risk Management in Policing. *Policing: An International Journal of Police Strategies and Management,* 28: 1, 30–48.

Ashby, D.I. and Longley, P.A. (2005) Geocomputation, Geodemographics and Resource Allocation for Local Policing. *Transactions in GIS,* 9: 1, 53–72.

Ashby, D.I., Irving, B. and Longley, P. (2007) Police Reform and the New Public Management Paradigm: Matching Technology to the Rhetoric. *Environment and Planning: Government and Policy,* 25: 2, 159–75.

Australian Institute of Criminology (2008) *Online Child Grooming Laws.* Canberra: AIC. Australian Government www.aic.gov.au.

Baartz, D. (2009) *Australians, the Internet and Technology Enabled Child Sex Abuse.* unpublished document.

Bagley, C. (1992) Development of an Adolescent Stress Scale for use of School Counsellors. *School Psychology Int.,* 13, 31–49.

Barros, C.P. (2007) Efficiency in Crime Prevention: A Study of Lisbon's Police Precincts. *International Review of Applied Economics,* 21: 5, 687–97.

BBC (2007) *MySpace Bars 29,000 Sex Offenders.* 25th July http://news.bbc.co.uk/2/hi/technology/6914870

Becerra-Fernandez, I., Gonzalez, A. and Sabherwal, R. (2004) *Knowledge Management: Challenges, Solutions and Technologies.* Upper Saddle River, NJ: Prentice Hall.

Beckett, R.C., Beech, A., Fisher, D. and Fordham, A.S. (2004) *Community-based Treatment for Sex Offenders: An Evaluation of Seven Treatment Programmes.* London: Home Office.

Beckett, R.C., Beech, A., Fisher, D. and Fordham, A.S.(1994) *Community-based Treatment for Sex Treatment Programmes.* London: Home Office.

Beech, A. and Elliot, I. (2009) Understanding the Online Sexual Exploitation of Children: How Useful are Theories of Contact Sexual Offending in Understanding Risk? Global Symposium for Examining the Relationship between Online and Offline Offenses and Preventing the Sexual Exploitation of Children, University of North Carolina, April 6–7.

Beech, A., Fisher, D., Beckett, R., Scott-Fordham, A. (1998) *STEP 3: An Evaluation of The Prison Sex Offender Treatment Programme.* London: Home Office.

Bennet, A. and Bennet, D. (2005) Designing the Knowledge Organization of the Future: The Intelligent Complex Adaptive System. In Holsapple, C.W. (Ed.) *Handbook of Knowledge Management.* Netherlands: Springer Science and Business Media.

Borgers, M.J. and Moors, J.A. (2007) Targeting the Proceeds of Crime: Bottlenecks in International Cooperation. *European Journal of Crime, Criminal Law and Criminal Justice*, 1–22.

Bowers, K.J., Johnson, S.D. and Pease, K. (2004) Prospective Hot-Spotting: The Future of Crime Mapping? *British Journal of Criminology*, 44, 641–58.

Brå (2007) *Vuxnas sexualla kontakter med barn via Internet (Adults' Sexual Contacts With Children Via Internet)* Stockholm: Brottsförebyggande radet (Crime Prevention Council) www.bra.se.

Brantsæter, M.C. (2001) *Møter med menn dømt for seksuelle overgrep mot barn (Meetings With Men Convicted of Sexual Offences Against Children)* Institutt for sosiologi og samfunnsgeografi (Institute for Sociology and Society Geography) Norway: Universitetet i Oslo (University of Oslo).

Cabinet Office (2005a) *e-Government Interoperability Framework*, e-Government Unit, London: Cabinet Office.

Cabinet Office (2005b) *Geographic Information: An Analysis of Interoperability and Information Sharing in the United Kingdom.* London: Cabinet Office.

Calder, M.C. (2004) The Internet: Potential, Problems and Pathways to Hands-on Sexual Offending. In Calder, M.C. (Ed.) *Child Sexual Abuse and The Internet: Tackling The New Frontier.* Lyme Regis: Russell House Publishing.

Canter, D. and Heritage, R. (1990) A Multivariate Model of Sexual Offence Behaviour: Developments in 'Offender Profiling'. *Journal of Forensic Psychiatry*, 1: 2, 185–212.

Carr, J. (2006) *Out of Sight, Out of Mind: Tackling Child Sexual Abuse Images on The Internet – A Global Challenge.* NCH.

Centrex (2005a) *Practice Advice on Core Investigative Doctrine.* Bedford: National Centre for Policing Excellence.

Centrex (2005b) *Guidance on the National Intelligence Model.* Bedford: National Centre for Policing Excellence.

Child Exploitation and Online Protection Centre (2006) *Understanding Online Social Network Services and Risks to Youth.* London: CEOP. www.ceop.gov.uk.

Child Exploitation and Online Protection Centre (2008) *Business Plan 2008–2009*, London: CEOP. www.ceop.gov.uk.

Child Online Protection Act 2000 (COPA) United States

Chiva, R. and Alegre, J. (2005) Organizational Learning and Organizational Knowledge. *Journal of Management Learning*, 36: 1, 49–68.

Civic Government (Scotland) Act 1982

Coleman, T.G. (2008) Managing Strategic Knowledge in Policing: Do Police Leaders Have Sufficient Knowledge About Organizational Performance to Make Informed Strategic Decisions? *Police Practice and Research*, 9: 4, 307–22.

Collier, P.M. (2006) Policing and the Intelligent Application of Knowledge. *Public Money and Management*, April, 109–16.

Colquitt, J.A. and Zapata-Phelan, C.P. (2007) Trends in Theory Building and Theory Testing: A Five-Decade Study of The Academy of Management Journal. *Academy of Management Journal*, 50: 6, 1281–303.

Conrad, C. (2006) Measuring Costs of Child Abuse and Neglect: A Mathematical Model of Specific Cost Estimations. *Journal of Health and Human Services Administration*, Summer, 103–23.

Cook, N. (2008) *Enterprise 2.0: How Social Software Will Change the Future of Work.* Aldershot: Gower.

Coulborn-Fuller, K. (1993) *Sex Offenders and their Victims.* NSPCC conference proceedings.

Council of Europe (2002) *Crime Analysis: Organized crime – Best practice survey no. 4.* Strasbourg: Department of Crime Problems, Directorate General – Legal Affairs, Council of Europe.

CPOP (2005) *Centre of Problem-oriented Policing*, http://www.popcenter.org/default.htm (accessed 9th December, 2005).

Craig, L., Browne, K. and Beech, A. (2004) *Identifying Sexual and Violent Re-offenders.* British Psychological Society Conference, 22nd March 2004, Leicester University.

Craissati, J., Webb, L. and Keen, S. (2008) The Relationship Between Developmental Variables, Personality Disorder and Risk in Sex Offenders. *Sexual Abuse: A Journal of Research and Treatment*, 20: 2, 119–38.

Crimereduction (2007) *Improving Performance Through Applied Knowledge.* Home Office. crimereduction, www.crimereduction.gov.uk.

Crimes Amendment Act 2005 New Zealand

Criminal Code Australia (s172.1)

Criminal Code Australia (s218A)

Criminal Code Canada (s172.1)

Criminal Courts and Services Act (Scotland) 2000

Criminal Justice (Scotland) Act 2003

Croy, J. (2006) *From Operation Hamlet to Operation Video Child.* Droit Fundamental. http://droitfondamental.eu.

Davidson, J. (2002) *The Sentencing and Treatment of Convicted Child Sexual Abusers in The Criminal Justice System in England and Wales.* PhD Thesis London School of Economics and Political Science.

Davidson, J. (2004) Child Sexual Abuse Prevention Programmes: The Role of Schools. In Giotakos, O., Eher, R. and Pfafflin, F. (Eds.) *Sex Offending is Everybody's Business.* Conference of the International Association for the Treatment of Sexual Offenders, 6–9 Oct. Pabst, Lengerich.

Davidson, J. (2006) Victims Speak: Comparing Child Sexual Abusers and Child Victims Accounts, Perceptions and Interpretations of Sexual Abuse. *Victims and Offenders.* 1: 2, 159–74.

Davidson, J. (2007) *Current Practice and Research into Internet Sex Offending.* Department of Social and Political Studies, University of Westminster.

Davidson, J. (2008) *Child Sexual Abuse: Media Representations and Government Reactions.* Abingdon: Routledge.

Davidson, J. and Gottschalk, P. (2008) Digital Forensics in Law Enforcement: The Case of Online Victimization of Children. *Electronic Government – An International Journal,* 5: 4, 445–51.

Davidson, J. and Martellozzo, E. (2004) *Educating Children About Sexual Abuse and Evaluating The Metropolitan Police Safer Surfing Programme.* http://www.saferschoolpartnerships.org/ssp-topics/evaluations/documents/ssfindingsreport.pdf

Davidson, J. and Martellozzo, E. (2005) *Policing the Internet and Protecting Children from Sex Offenders Online: When Strangers Become 'Virtual Friends'.* www.oii.ox.ac.uk/research/cybersafety/extentions.pdfs/papers/julia_davidson.pdf

Davidson, J. and Martellozzo, E. (2008) Protecting Vulnerable Young People in Cyberspace From Sexual Abuse: Raising Awareness and Responding Globally. *Police Practice and Research,* 9: 4, 277–89.

Davidson, J., Bifulco, A., Thomas G. and Ramsay, M. (2006) Child Victims of Sexual Abuse: Children's Experience of The Investigative Process in The Criminal Justice System. *Practice Journal.*

Dean, G. and Gottschalk, P. (2007) *Knowledge Management in Policing and Law Enforcement: Foundations, Structures, Applications.* Oxford: Oxford University Press.

Dean, G., Fahsing, I.A., Glomseth, R. and Gottschalk, P. (2008) Capturing Knowledge of Police Investigations: Towards a Research Agenda. *Police Practice and Research,* 9: 4, 341–55.

Dean, G., Fahsing, I.A., Gottschalk, P. and Solli-Sæther, H. (2008) Investigative Thinking and Creativity: An Empirical Study of Police Detectives in Norway. *International Journal of Innovation and Learning,* 5: 2, 170–85.

Dennis, A.R., Fuller, R.M. and Valacich, J.S. (2008) Media, Tasks, and Communication Processes: A Theory of Media Synchronicity. *MIS Quarterly,* 32: 3, 575–600.

Dombrowski, S.C., Gischlar, K.L. and Durst, T. (2007) Safeguarding Young People from Cyber Pornography and Cyber Sexual Predation: A Major Dilemma of the Internet. *Child Abuse Review,* 16, 153–70.

Døvik, O. (2008) Rød knapp skal stanse overgripere (Red Button Shall Stop Offenders) *NRK* (Norwegian Broadcasting Corporation) www.nrk.no, published 11.08.2008.

Dunaigre, P. (2001) Paedophilia: A Psychiatric and Psychoanalytical Point of View. In Arnaldo, C.A. (Ed.) *Child Abuse on the Internet: Ending the Silence.* Oxford: Beghahn Books.

Earl, M.J. (2000) Evolving the E-business. *Business Strategy Review,* 11: 2, 33–8.

Elliot, M. (1993) *The Ultimate Taboo.* London: Longman.

ERA (2008) *Combating Fraud and Financial Crime.* Trier: Academy of European Law. www.era.int.

Eurobarometer (2007) *Eurobarometer on Safer Internet for Children: Qualitative Study 2007.* ec.europa.eu/information_ society/activities/sip/eurobarometer/.

European Commission (2008) *Safer Internet Plus: A Multi-Annual Community Programme on Promoting Safer Use of The Internet and New Online Technologies.* Information Society and Media Directorate-General, European Commission http:/ /ec.europa.eu/saferinternet.

Fagin, J. and Wexler, S. (1988) Explanations of Sexual Assualt amongst Violent Delinquents. *Journal of Adolescent Research*, 3: 2, 363–85.

Faremo, G. (2007) *Forebygging av internettrelaterte overgrep mot barn (Prevention of Internet Related Abuse of Children)* Justis – og politidepartementet (Ministry of Justice and the Police) Oslo, www.regjeringen.no.

Ferraro, M.M. and Casey, E. (2005) *Investigating Child Exploitation and Pornography: The Internet, the Law and Forensic Science.* New York: Elsevier.

Finkelhor, D. (1984) *Child Sexual Abuse: New Theory and Research.* New York: Free Press.

Finkelhor, D. (1984) *Four Conditions: A Model. Child Sexual Abuse: New Theories and Research*, New York: Free Press.

Finkelhor, D., Araji, S., Baron, L., Browne, A., Doyle Peters, S. and Wyatt, G. (1986) *A Sourcebook on Child Sexual Abuse.* California: Sage.

Folkvord, M. (2008) Treng personvern (Need Identification Protection) *Klassekampen* (daily newspaper, Saturday 30 August, page 5.

Frankfort-Nachmias, C. and Nachmias, D. (2002) *Research Methods in the Social Sciences.* 5th edn. UK: Arnold.

Garcia-Morales, V., Llorens-Montes, F. and Verdu-Jover, A. (2006) Organizational Learning Categories: Their Influence on Organizational Performance. *International Journal of Innovation and Learning*, 3: 5, 518–36.

Gillan, A. (2003) Race to Save New Victims of Child Pornography. *Guardian*, November 4.

Gillespie, A.A. (2005) Indecent Images of Children: The Ever-Changing Law. *Child Abuse Review*, 14, 430–43.

Gjerde, M. (2008) Digital etterforsking (Digital Forensics) *Politiforum* (Norwegian Police Journal) 8, 30–3.

Glomseth, R., Gottschalk, P. and Solli-Sæther, H. (2007) Occupational Culture as Determinant of Knowledge Sharing and Performance in Police Investigations. *International Journal of the Sociology of Law*, 35, 96–107.

Gottschalk, P. (2001) Descriptions of Responsibility for Implementation: A Content Analysis of Strategic Information Systems/Technology Planning Documents. *Technological Forecasting and Social Change*, 68, 207–21.

Gottschalk, P. (2006) *E-Business Strategy, Sourcing and Governance.* Hershey, PA: Idea Group Publishing.

Gottschalk, P. (2008) Maturity Levels for Criminal Organizations. *International Journal of Law, Crime and Justice*, 36, 106–14.

Gottschalk, P. (2009) Maturity Levels for Interoperability in Digital Government. *Government Information Quarterly*, 26, 75–81.

Gottschalk, P. and Solli-Sæther, H. (2006) Maturity Model for IT Outsourcing Relationships. *Industrial Management and Data Systems*, 105: 6, 685–702.

Gottschalk, P. and Tolloczko, P. (2007) Maturity Model for Mapping Crime in Law Enforcement. *Electronic Government, an International Journal*, 4: 1, 59–67.

Graves, R.B., Openshaw, K., Ascione, F. and Ericksen, S. (1996) Demographic and Parental Characteristics of Youthful Sex Offenders. *International Journal of Offender Therapy and Comparative Criminology*, 40: 4, 300–17.

Gudjonsson, G. (1991) The Attribution of Blame and Type of Crime Committed: Transcultural Validation. *Journal of the Forensic Science Society*, 31: 3, 349–52.

Hair, J.F., Black, W.C., Babin, B.J., Anderson, R.E. and Tatham, R.L. (2006) *Multivariate Data Analysis.* 6th edn, Upper Saddle River, NJ: Prentice Hall.

Hammer, E.F. and Gleuck, B.C. (1957) Psycho-dynamic Patterns in Sex Offenders: A Four Factor Theory. *Psychiatric Quarterly*, 31, 325–45.

Hammond, S. (2004) The Challenge of Sex Offender Assessment: The Case of Internet Offenders. In: Calder, M.C. (Ed.) *Child Sexual Abuse and the Internet: Tackling the New Frontier.* Lyme Regis: Russell House Publishing.

Hanoa, K. (2008) *Vold og trusler mellom innsatte (Violence and Threats Among Inmates)* Rapport, Kriminalomsorgens Utdanningssenter (Correctional Service of Norway Staff Academy) Oslo, www.krus.no.

Harfield, C. (2008) Paradigms, Pathologies, and Practicalities: Policing Organised Crime in England and Wales. *Policing*, 2: 1, 63–73.

Hart, S., Kropp, P., Laws, D., Klaver, J., Logan, C. and Watt, K. (2003) *The Risk for Sexual Violence Protocol: Structured Professional Guidelines for Assessing Risk of Sexual Violence.* Vancouver: Simon Fraser University.

Hayward, K. (2007) Situational Crime Prevention and its Discontents: Rational Choice Theory Versus the 'Culture of Now'. *Social Policy and Administration*, 41: 3, 232–50.

Hegg, K. (2008) *Internettrelaterte overgrep mot barn (Internet Related Abuses of Children)* Redd Barna (Save the Children), www.reddbarna.no.

Hernandez, A. (2009) *Psychological and Behavioral Characteristics of Child Pornography Offenders in Treatment.* Global Symposium for Examining the Relationship between Online and Offline Offenses and Preventing the Sexual Exploitation of Children, University of North Carolina, April 6–7.

Higgins, D.J. (2004) The Importance of Degree versus Type of Maltreatment: A Cluster Analysis of Child Abuse Types. *The Journal of Psychology*, 138: 4, 303–24.

Higuchi, H. (2008) Trafficking in Women and Children in Japan. In Ebbe, O. and Das, D. (Eds.) *Global Trafficking in Women and Children.* Boca Raton, FL: Taylor and Francis.

Høgetveit, E. and Ingerø, O.O. (2008) Datalagring må til (Data Storage is Needed) *Aftenposten* (daily newspaper in Norway) debattinnlegg (debate article) Monday 8 September, page 5.

Home Office (2000) *Not Rocket Science.* Crime Reduction Research Series, London: Home Office.

Home Office (2002) *Protecting the Public: Strengthening Protection Against Sex Offenders and Reforming The Law on Sexual Offences.* London: Home Office.

Home Office (2004) *Risk Management and Policy Strategy: A Guide for Probation Areas and NPD.* London: HMSO.

Home Office (2005a) *Guidance on Statutory Performance Indicators for Policing 2005/2006.* Police Standards Unit, Home Office, www.policereform.gov.uk.

Home Office (2005b) *Senior Investigating Officer Development Programme.* Police Standards Unit, Home Office, www.policereform.gov.uk.

Home Office (2006) *Review of GIS-Based Information Sharing Systems*, Home Office Online Report.

Homel, P., Nutley, S., Webb, B. and Tilley, N. (2004) *Investing to Deliver: Reviewing the Implementation of The UK Crime Reduction Programme.* London: Home Office. www.policereform.gov.uk.

Høstmælingen, N., Kjørholt, E. and Sandberg, K. (Eds.) (2008) *Barnekonvensjonen: Barns rettigheter i Norge (Child Convention: Children's Rights in Norway)* Oslo: Universitetsforlaget.

Housel, T. and Bell, A.H. (2001) *Measuring and Managing Knowledge.* New York: McGraw-Hill Irwin.

Hsiao, R.L. (2008) Knowledge Sharing in a Global Professional Service Firm. *MIS Quarterly Executive*, 7: 3, 123–37.

http://www.publications.uk/pa/id200304/ldhansard/vo041013/text/41013-31.htm

http://www.supremecourtus.gov/oral_arguments/argument_transcripts/03-218.pdf

Innes, M. and Sheptycki, J. (2004) From Detection to Disruption: Intelligence and The Changing Logic of Police Crime Control in the United Kingdom. *International Criminal Justice Review*, 14, 1–24.

Innes, M., Fielding, N. and Cope, N. (2005) The Appliance of Science: The Theory and Practice of Crime Intelligence Analysis. *British Journal of Criminology*, 45, 39–57.

Internet Watch Foundation (2006) *Remove Online Images of Child Abuse.* Press Release and Conference, Tuesday 24th October, Central Hall, Westminster.

Internet Watch Foundation (2007) *2007 Annual and Charity Report.* Cambridge: IWF. www.iwf.org.uk.

Jackson, A.L. and Wade, J.E. (2005) Police Perceptions of Social Capital and Sense of Responsibility. *Policing: An International Journal of Police Strategies and Management*, 28: 1, 49–68.

Jaschke, H., Bjørgo, T., Romero, F., Kwanten, C., Mawby, R. and Pogan, M. (2007) *Perspectives of Police Science in Europe*, Final Report, European Police College, Hampshire: CEPOL.

Jewkes, Y. (Ed.) (2003a) *Dot.cons.: Crime, Deviance and Identity on the Internet.* Cullompton: Willan.

Johnson, R.A. (2005) Whistleblowing and the Police. *Rutgers University Journal of Law and Urban Policy*, 1: 3, 74–83.

Justis (2007) *På vei imot et tryggere Norge – noen tall og fakta (On the Road to a Safer Norway: Some Numbers and Facts)* Justis – og politidepartementet (Ministry of Justice and Police) Oslo, www.regjeringen.no.

Kaplan, M.S. (1985) The Impact of Parolees Perceptions of Confidentiality on the Reporting of their Urges to Interact Sexually with Children. In Morrison, T. *et al.* (Eds.) *Sexual Offending Against Children.* London: Routledge.

Kappos, A. and Rivard, S. (2008) A Three-Perspective Model of Culture, Information Systems and their Development and Use. *MIS Quarterly*, 32: 3, 601–34.

Kaufmann, G. (2004) Two Kinds of Creativity: But Which Ones? *Creativity and Innovation Management*, 13: 3, 154–65.

Kazanjian, R.K. (1988) Relation of Dominant Problems to Stages of Growth in Technology-Based New Ventures. *Academy of Management Journal*, 31: 2, 257–79.

Kazanjian, R.K. and Drazin, R. (1989) An Empirical Test of a Stage of Growth Progression Model. *Management Science*, 35: 1, 1489–503.

Kear-Colwell, J. (1996) Guest Editorial: A Personal Position on the Treatment of Individuals who Commit Sexual Offences. *International Journal of Offender Therapy and Comparative Criminology*, 40: 4, 259–62.

Kelley, T.M. (2005) Mental Health and Prospective Police Professionals. *Policing: An International Journal of Police Strategies and Management*, 28: 1, 6–29.

Kelly, L., Regan, L. and Burton, S. (1991) *An Exploratory Study of the Prevalence of Sexual Abuse in a Sample of 16–21-Year-Olds.* London: Polytechnic of North London.

Kiely, J.A. and Peek, G.S. (2002) The Culture of the British Police: Views of Police Officers. *The Service Industries Journal*, 22: 1, 167–83.

Kierkegaard, S. (2008) Cybering, Online Grooming and Ageplay. *Computer Law and Security Report*, 24, 41–55.

King, W.R. and Teo, T.S. (1997) Integration Between Business Planning and Information Systems Planning: Validating a Stage Hypothesis. *Decision Sciences*, 28: 2, 279–307.

Klaine, E., Davis, H. and Hicks, M. (2001) *Child Pornography: The Criminal Justice System Response.* Washington DC: National Centre for Missing and Exploited Children. www.missingkids.com/en_us/publications/NC81.pdf

KRÅD (2008) *The National Crime Prevention Council.* Det kriminalitetsforebyggende råd, Oslo, www.krad.no

Krone, T. (2004) *A Typology of Online Child Pornography Offending. Trends and Issues in Crime and Criminal Justice, No. 279.* Canberra: Australian Institute of Criminology.

Lahneman, W.J. (2004) Knowledge-Sharing in the Intelligence Community After 9/11. *International Journal of Intelligence and Counterintelligence*, 17: 614–33.

Lankester, D. and Meyer, B. (1986) *Relationship of Family Structure to Sex Offender Behaviour.* Unpublished paper.

Laulik, S., Allam, J. and Sheridan, L. (2007) An Investigation into Maladaptive Personality Functioning in Internet Sex Offenders. *Psychology, Crime and Law*, 13, 523–35.

Lauvanger, R. (1997) *Psykologiske karakteristika ved menn som har begått eller er redde for å begå seksuelle overgrep mot barn og ungdom (Psychological Characteristics of Men who have Committed or are Afraid of Committing Sexual Abuse of Children and Teenagers)* University of Oslo.

Leeuw, F.L., Knaap, L.M. and S. Bogaerts. (2007) Reducing the Knowledge-Practice Gap: A New Method Applied to Crime Prevention. *Public Money and Management*, June, 245–50.

Leishman, F. and Savage, S.P. (1993) Officers or Managers? Direct Entry into British Police Management. *International Journal of Public Sector Management*, 6: 5, 4–11.

Lillywhite, R. and Skidmore, P. (2006) Boys Are Not Sexually Exploited? A Challenge to Practitioners, *Child Abuse Review*, 15, 351–361.

Lin, T.C. and Huang, C.C. (2008) Understanding Knowledge Management System Usage Antecedents: An Integration of Social Cognitive Theory and Task Technology Fit. *Information and Management*, 45, 410–7.

Lind, H., Hjelm, J. and Lind, M. (2007) Privacy Surviving Data Retention in Europe? *W3C Workshop on Languages for Privacy Policy Negotiation and Semantics-Driven Enforcement*, www.w3.org.

Lord Hansard Debates (2004) *Extreme Pornography.* London: HMSO.

Lyman, M.D. and Potter, G.W. (2007) *Organized Crime.* 4th edn. Upper Saddle River, NJ: Pearson.

Maghan, J. (1994) Intelligence Gathering Approaches in Prisons, *Low Intensity Conflict and Law Enforcement*, 3: 3, 548–57.

Management of Offenders Act (Scotland) 2005.

Marshall, W.L. (1996) Assessment, Treatment and Theorizing about Sex Offenders: Developments over the Last Twenty Years and Future Directions. *Criminal Justice and Behaviour*, 23: 162–99.

Marshall, W.L. and Mazzucco, A. (1995) Self-esteem and Parental Attachments in Child Molesters. *Sexual Abuse: A Journal of Research and Treatment*, 7: 279–85.

Marshall, W.L., Laws, D.R. and Barbaree, H.E. (1990) *Handbook of Sexual Assault: Issues, Theories, and Treatment of the Offender*. New York: Garland.

Marshall,W.L. and Barbaree, H.E. (1990) An Integrated Theory of the Etiology of Sexual Offending. In Marshall, Laws and Barbaree (1990).

Martellozzo, E. (2009) *Preliminary PhD findings: Policing Practice and Online Grooming*. Global Symposium for Examining the Relationship between Online and Offline Offenses and Preventing the Sexual Exploitation of Children, University of North Carolina, April 6–7. 2009

Martellozzo, E. (2004) Child Pornography on the Internet: Police Strategies. In Giotakos, O., Eher, R. and Pfafflin, F. (Eds) *Sex Offending is Everybody's Business*.

Medietilsynet (2008) *Trygg bruk undersøkelsen 2008 (Safe Use Survey 2008)* Medietilsynet (Norwegian Media Authority) Fredrikstad, Norway.

Mercado, C.C., Alvarez, S. and Levenson, J. (2008) The Impact of Specialized Sex Offender Legislation on Community Re-entry, *Sexual Abuse: A Journal of Research and Treatment*, 20: 2, 188–205.

Middleton, D., Elliott, I., Manderville-Norden, R. and Beech, A. (2006) An Investigation into the Applicability of the Ward and Siegert Pathways Model of Child Sexual Abuse with Internet Sex Offenders. *Psychology, Crime and Law*, in press.

Mitchell, K.J., Wolak, J. and Finkelhor, D. (2005) Police Posing as Juveniles Online to Catch Sex Offenders: Is it Working? *Sexual Abuse: A Journal of Research and Treatment*, 17: 3, 241–67.

Mitchell, K.J., Wolak, J. and Finkelhor, D. (2008) Are Blogs Putting Youth at Risk for Online Sexual Solicitation or Harassment? *Child Abuse and Neglect*, 32, 277–94.

MMI (2007) *Safer Internet for Children: Qualitative Study in 29 European Countries*. Oslo: MMI Univero.

Monck, E., Bentovim, A., Goodall, G., Hyde, C., Lewin, R., Sharland, E. and Elton, A. (1996) *Child Sexual Abuse: A Descriptive and Treatment Study. Studies in Child Protection*, London: HMSO.

Morton, C. and Kitchen, T. (2005) Crime Prevention and the British Planning System: Operational Relationships between Planners and the Police. *Planning, Practice and Research*, 20: 4, 419–31.

Nash, C.L. and West, D.J. (1985) Sexual Molestation of Young Girls: A Retrospective Study. In West, D.J. (Ed.) *Sexual Victimisation*. Aldershot: Ashgate.

National Institute of Justice (2005) *Mapping Crime: Understanding Hot Spots*. Washington, DC: NIJ. Office of Justice Programs, www.ojp.usdoj.gov/nij

National Institute of Justice (2006) *Mapping and Analysis for Public Safety (MAPS)*. NIJ. http://www.ojp.usdoj.gov/nij/maps/.

National Offender Management and the Scottish Executive (2005) *Consultation Possession of Extreme Pornographic Material*.

National Probation Service Sex Offender Strategy (2004) www.probation2000.com/pit/circulars/pc20

Nicolaisen, H. (2008) *Nettrelaterte overgrep og rettspraksis – Overgrep som følge av kontaktetablering på internett (Net Related Offences and Legislative Context: Offences Following Contacts on the Internet)* Redd Barna (Save The Children Norway) Oslo, www.reddbarna.no.

Nolan, R.L. (1979) Managing the Crises in Data Processing. *Harvard Business Review*, Mar-Apr. 115–26.

Northern Ireland Office (2006) *Reforming the Law on Sexual Offences in Northern Ireland: A Consultation Document*. July 2006, Vol 2, NI Sex Crime Unit.

Northern Ireland Research Team (1991) *Child Sexual Abuse in Northern Ireland*.Belfast: Geystone.

NRK (2008) Etterlyser pedofil mann (Searching Paedophile Man) *Norsk rikskringkasting (Norwegian Broadcasting Corporation)* www.nrk.no.

O'Brien, M.D. and Webster, S.D. (2007) The Construction and Preliminary Validation of the Internet Behaviours and Attitudes Questionnaire. *Sex Abuse*, 19, 237–56.

Obscene Publications Act (1959, 1964) England and Wales

O'Callaghan, D. and Print, B. (1994) Adolescent Sexual Abusers: Research Assessment and Treatment. In Morrison *et al. Sexual Offending Against Children*. London: Routledge.

O'Connell, R. (2003) *Be Somebody Else But be Yourself at All Times: Degrees of Identity Deception in Chatrooms*. Cyberspace Research Unit, University of Central Lancashire. http://www.once.uclan.ac.uk/print/deception_print.htm.

O'Connell, R. (2004a) *A Typology of Child Cybersexploitation and Online Grooming Practices*. Cyberspace Research Unit, University of Central Lancashire, www.fkbko.net.

O'Connell, R. (2004b) From Fixed to Mobile Internet: The Morphing of Criminal Activity On-line. In Calder, M.C. (Ed.) *Child Sexual Abuse and The Internet: Tackling the New Frontier*. Lyme Regis: Russell House Publishing.

Oftedal, H. (2008) Overgrepstiltalt var 'Stian 15' (Offender in Court Was 'Stian 15') *Fædrelandsvennen* (daily newspaper), www.fvn.no.

Oliver, D. (1993) *A Comparison of the Personality Characteristics of Adolescent Sex Offenders and Other Adolescent Offenders*. California: Sage.

Parliamentary Research Paper (2005) 05/19 http://www.parliament.uk/commons/lib/research/rp200505-019.pdf

Peplau, L.A. and Perlman, D. (1982) *Loneliness: A Sourcebook of Current Theory, Research and Therapy*. New York: John Wiley.

Perry-Smith, J.E. and Shalley, C.E. (2003) The Social Side of Creativity: A Static and Dynamic Social Network Perspective. *Academy of Management Review*, 29: 1, 89–106.

Pfarrer, M., DeCelles, K., Smith, K. and Taylor, M. (2008) After the Fall: Reintegrating the Corrupt Organization. *The Academy of Management Review*, 33: 3, 730–49.

Pithers, W.D. (1999) Empathy, Definition, Enhancement and Relevance to the Treatment of Sexual Abusers. *Journal of Interpersonal Violence*, March.

Police, Public Order and Criminal Justice (Scotland) Bill, 2006

Preston, C.B. (2008) Internet Porn, ICANN and Families: A Call to Action. *Journal of Internet Law*, October, 3–15.

Probation Circular (2005) *Launch of New Internet Sex Offender Treatment Programme*. National Probation Service.

Probation Circular (2005) *Sex Offender Programmes: Management Update*. National Probation Service.

Probation Circular (2006) *Implementation Plans For Internet Sex Offender Treatment Programme*. National Probation Service.

Quayle, E. (2009) *Abuse Images of Children: Identifying Gaps in Our Knowledge*. Global Symposium for Examining the Relationship between Online and Offline Offenses and Preventing the Sexual Exploitation of Children, University of North Carolina, April 6–7, 2009.

Quayle, E. and Taylor, M. (2001) Child Seduction and Self-Representation on the Internet. *Cyberpsychology and Behaviour*, 4: 5, 597–607.

Quayle, E. and Taylor, M. (2002) Paedophiles, Pornography and the Internet: Assessment Issues. *British Journal of Social Work*, 32: 863–75.

Quayle, E. and Taylor, M. (2003) Model of Problematic Internet Use in People with a Sexual Interest in Children. *Cyberpsychology and Behaviour*, 6: 1, 93–106.

Quayle, E., Loof, L. and Palmer, T. (2008) *Child Pornography and Sexual Exploitation of Children Online*. World Congress III against Sexual Exploitation of Children and Adolescents, ECPAT International, Rio de Janeiro, Brazil, 25–28 November.

Quayle, E., Vaughan, M. and Taylor, M. (2006) Sex Offenders, Internet Child Abuse Images and Emotional Avoidance: The Importance of Values. *Aggression and Violent Behaviour*, 11, 1–11.

R v Oliver, Hartrey and Baldwin (2003) 2 Cr App R28: (2003) Crim LR 127.

Rada, R. (1978) *Clinical Aspects of the Rapist*. New York: Grune and Stratton.

Rao, S.S. and Metts, G. (2003) Electronic Commerce Development in Small and Medium Sized Enterprises: A Stage Model and Its Implications. *Business Process Management*, 9: 1, 11–32.

Rapley, T. (2004) Interviews. In: Seale, C., Gobo, G., Gubrium, J. and Silverman, D. (Eds.) *Qualitative Research Practice*. London: Sage.

Ratcliffe, J.H. (2004) Crime Mapping and the Training Needs of Law Enforcement, *European Journal of Criminal Policy and Research*, 10, 65–83.

Ratcliffe, J.H. (2008) *Intelligence-Led Policing*. Devon: Willan Publishing.

Redd Barna (2007) *Chatteregler (Chatting Rules)* Redd Barna (Save the Children Norway) www.reddbarna.no.

Rich, T. and Shively, M. (2004) *A Methodology for Evaluating Geographic Profiling Software*, Cambridge, MA: ABT Associates.

Richardsen, A.M., Burke, R.J. and Martinussen, M. (2006) Work and Health Outcomes Among Police Officers: The Mediating Role of Police Cynicism and Engagement. *International Journal of Stress Management*, 13: 4, 555–74.

Riemer, K. and Frössler, F. (2007) Introducing Real-Time Collaboration Systems: Development of a Conceptual Scheme and Research Directions. *Communications of the Association for Information Systems*, 20, 204–25.

Riffe, D. and Freitag, A. (1997) A Content Analysis of Content Analyses, Twenty-Five Years of Journalism Quarterly. *Journalism Mass Communication Quarterly*, 74, 873–82.

Risk Management Authority (2006) *Risk Assessment Tools Evaluation Directory*. RMA.

Risk Management Authority (2007) *Current Practice and Research into Internet Sex Offending*. RMA Briefing, St. James House, St. James Street, Paisley, www.rmascotland.gov.uk.

Robbins, P. and Darlington R. (2003) The Role of the Industry and the Internet Watch Foundation. In MacVean and Spindler (Eds.) *Policing Paedophiles on the Internet*. New Police Bookshop.

Ruud, T.E.T. (2009) Voksne menn søker sex på barne-spillside (Adult Men Search Sex on Child Play Site) *Verdens Gang* (Norwegian daily newspaper) www.veg.no, February 2.

SafeTeens (2009) *How to Recognize Grooming*. www.safeteens.com, downloaded April 14.

Schauer, S. (2008) Unified Communications: A Practical Business and Technology Approach. *Certification Magazine*, October, 36–8.

Scholl, H.J. and Klischewski, R. (2007) E-Government Integration and Interoperability: Framing the Research Agenda. *International Journal of Public Administration*, 30: 8, 889–920.

Schulze, V. and Brink, V.D. (2006) Political Culture as a Basis for Concepts of Local Security and Crime Prevention: A Comparison of the Conditions in Germany and The Netherlands. *German Policy Studies*, 3: 1, 47–79.

Scottish Executive (2000) *Report of the Committee on Serious Violent and Sexual Offenders*. (MacClean Report)

Scottish Executive (2002) *Serious Violent and Sexual Offenders: The Use of Risk Assessment Tools in Scotland*.

Scottish Executive (2006) *Risk Assessment and Management of Serious Violent and Sexual Offenders: A Review of Current Issues*.

Segell, G.M. (2007) Reform and Transformation: The UK's Serious Organized Crime Agency. *International Journal of Intelligence and Counterintelligence*, 20, 217–39.

Sentencing Advisory Panel (2004) *Sexual Offences Act 2003: The Panels Advice to the Sentencing Guidelines Council*. http://www.sentencing-guidelines.gov.uk/docs/advice-sexual-offences.pdf

Seto, M (2009) *Assessing the Risk Posed by Child Pornography Offenders*. Global Symposium for Examining the Relationship between Online and Offline Offenses and Preventing the Sexual Exploitation of Children, University of North Carolina, April 6–7.

Seto, M.C. and Eke, A.W. (2005) The Criminal Histories and Later Offending of Child Pornography Offenders. *Sexual Abuse: A Journal of Research and Treatment*, 17: 2, 201–10.

Seto, M.C. and Ekes, A.W. (2005b) *Extending the Follow-up of Child Pornography Offenders*. Unpublished paper.

Seto, M.C., Cantor, J.M., and Blanchard, R. (2005c) Child pornography offenses are a valid diagnostic indicator of paedophilia. *Journal of Abnormal Psychology*, In Press.

Sex Offenders Act 1997 England and Wales

Sexual Offences Act 2003 England and Wales

Shannon, D. (2008) *The Sexual Solicitation of Children Online*. Presentation to 3rd Nordic Conference on Victimology and Victim Support.

Sheldon, K. and Howitt, D. (2007) *Sex Offenders and the Internet.* Chichester: John Wiley.

Sheptycki, J. (2007) Police Ethnography in the House of Serious and Organized Crime. In Henry, A. and Smith, D.J. (Eds.) *Transformations of Policing.* Oxford: Ashgate.

Skybak, T. (2004) *Ofre for seksuelle overgrep på Internet: Hva gjøres for å identifisere barn? (Victims of Sexual Assaults on The Internet: What is Done to Identify Children?)* Redd Barna (Save the Children Norway) www.reddbarna.no.

Smallbone, S.W. and Dadds, M.R. (1998) Childhood Attachment and Adult Attachment in Incarcerated Adult Male Sex Offenders. *Journal of Interpersonal Violence,* 13: 5, 555–73.

Smith, A.D. (2008) Business and E-Government Intelligence for Strategically Leveraging Information Retrieval. *Electronic Government, an International Journal,* 5: 1, 31–44.

Smith, H. and Israel, E. (1987) Sibling Incest: A Study of the Dynamics of 25 Cases. *Child Abuse and Neglect,* 11: 1, 101–8.

Smith, N. and Flanagan, C. (2000) *The Effective Detective: Identifying the Skills of an Effective SIO.* Police Research Series Paper 122, London: Policing and Reducing Crime Unit.

Smith, W.R. (1988) Delinquency and Abuse Amongst Juvenile Sex Offenders. *Journal of Interpersonal Violence,* 3: 4, 379–90.

Son, J.Y. and Kim, S.S. (2008) Internet Users' Information Privacy-Protective Responses: A Taxonomy and a Nomological Model. *MIS Quarterly,* 32: 3, 503–29.

Srinivasa, K.G., Venugopal, K.R. and Patnaik, L.M. (2007) A Self-Adaptive Migration Model Genetic Algorithm for Data Mining Applications. *Information Sciences,* 177, 4295–313.

Stelfox, P. and Pease, K. (2005) Cognition and Detection: Reluctant Bedfellows? In Smith, M. and Tilley, N. (Eds.) *Crime Science: New Approaches to Preventing and Detecting Crime.* Devon: Willan.

Stokke, O.P.B. (2009) Hundrevis melder fra om nettmisbruk (Hundreds Are Reporting Net Abuse) *Computerworld,* www.idg.no/computerworld/, April 4.

Stortingsmelding (2008) *Straff som virker – mindre kriminalitet – tryggere samfunn (Conviction That Works – Less Criminality – Safer Society)* Justis – og politidepartementet (Ministry of Justice and Police) Oslo.

Strano, M. (2004) A Neural Network Applied to Criminal Psychological Profiling: An Italian Initiative. *International Journal of Offender Therapy and Comparative Criminology,* 48: 495–503.

Sullivan, J. and Beech, A. (2004) Assessing Internet Sex Offenders. In Calder, M.C. (Ed.) *Child Sexual Abuse and the Internet: Tackling the New Frontier.* Lyme Regis: Russell House Publishing.

Suseg, H., Grødem, A., Valset, K. and Mossige, S. (2008) *Seksuelle krenkelser via nettet – hvor stort er problemet? (Sexual Assaults on the Internet – How Large is the Problem?)* Norsk institutt for forskning om oppvekst, velferd og aldring (Norwegian Institute for Research on Maturity, Welfare and Aging) Oslo, www.nova.no.

Task Force on Child Protection on the Internet (2003) *Good Practice Models and Guidance for the Internet Industry on: Chat Services; Instant Messages; Web Based Services.* Home Office.

Taylor, M. and Quayle, E. (2003) *Child Pornography: An Internet Crime.* New York: Brunner-Routledge.

Taylor, M., Holland, G. and Quayle, E (2001) Typology of Paedophile Picture Collections. *The Police Journal.* 74: 97–107.

The Production and Distribution of Illegal Pornography Penal Code, Switzerland.

The Protection of Children and Prevention of Sexual Offences (Scotland) Act 2005.

Thorgrimsen, T.C.S. (2008) Forsiktige med webkamera (Careful With Web Camera) *Aftenposten (daily newspaper Aftenposten),* www.aftenposten.no, 07.11.08.

Thornton, D., Mann, R., Webster, S., Blud, L., Travers, R. and Friendship, C. (2003) Distinguishing and Combining Risks for Sexual and Violent Recidivsm. *Annals of the New York Academy of Sciences,* 989, 225–35.

Tong, S. (2007) *Training the Effective Detective: Report of Recommendations.* Cambridge: University of Cambridge.

Tufekci, Z. (2008) Grooming, Gossip, Facebook and Myspace: What Can We Learn About These Sites From Those who won't Assimilate? *Information, Communication and Society,* 11: 4, 544–64.

Turvey, B. (1999) *Criminal Profiling: An Introduction to Behavioural Evidence Analysis.* CA: Academic Press.

United Nations (2008) *United Nations e-Government Survey 2008.* New York: Department of Economics and Social Affairs, Division for Public Administration and Development Management, United Nations.

United States Supreme Court (2004) *Ashcroft v ACLU 2/3/04* Transcript.

Vidnes, A.K. and Jacobsen, H. (2008) Strengt på nett (Strict on the Net) *Aftenposten* (daily newspaper Aftenposten) Friday 7th. November, culture section page 4.

Virtual Global Taskforce (2006) *Website snares it's first online grooming offender.* http://www.virtualglobaltaskforce.com/news/article_22062006.html

Vulpiani, D. (2001) *La Polizia delle Comunicazioni e la Lotta alla Pedofilia Online.* Rome: Relazione al convegno di telefono azzurro.

Walker, S. (2005) *The New World of Police Accountability.* Thousand Oaks, CA: Sage.

Ward, T. and Keenan, T. (1999) Child Molesters: Implicit Theories. *Journal of Interpersonal Violence*, 14: 8, 821–38.

Ward, T. and Siegert, R.J. (2002) Toward a Comprehensive Theory of Child Sexual Abuse: A Theory Knitting Perspective. *Crime and Law*, 8, 319–51.

Ward, T. and Siegert, R.J. (2006) Ward and Siegert's Pathways Model. In Ward, T., Polaschek, D. and Beech, A. (Eds.) *Theories of Sexual Offending.* Chichester: John Wiley and Sons.

Wastell, D., Kawalek, P., Langmead-Jones, P. and Ormerod, R. (2004) Information Systems and Partnership in Multi-Agency Networks: An Action Research Project in Crime Reduction. *Information and Organization*, 14, 189–210.

Weber, R. (2004) The Grim Reaper: The Curse of e-mail. *MIS Quarterly*, iii-xii.

Weinrott, M.R. and Saylor, M. (1991) Self Report of Crimes Committed by Sex Offenders. *Journal of Interpersonal Violence*, 6: 3, 286–300.

Weisburd, D. and Lum, C. (2005) The Diffusion of Computerized Crime Mapping in Policing: Linking Research and Practice. *Police Practice and Research*, 6: 5, 419–34.

Whittaker, J. (2004) *The Cyberspace Handbook.* London: Routledge.

Williams, K.S. (2005) Facilitating Safer Choices: Use of Warnings to Dissuade Viewing of Pornography on the Internet. *Child Abuse Review*, 14, 415–29.

Wilson, C. and Scullion, I. (2006) *Social Work Inspection Agency: Criminal Justice Inspection Findings.* Risk Management Authority Conference, Glasgow, November 2007.

Wolak, J. and Mitchell, K.J. *Work-Related Exposure to Child Pornography in ICAC Task Forces and Affiliated Agencies: Reactions and Responses to Possible Stresses.* Draft: under review by OJJDP for publication.

Wolak, J., Finkelhor, D. and Mitchell, K. (2009) *Trends in Arrests of 'Online Sex Offenders'.* Durham, NH: Crimes Against Children Research Center, www.unh.edu/ccrc

Wolak, J., Finkelhor, D. and Mitchell, K.J. (2005) *Child-Pornography Possessors Arrested in Internet-Related Crimes: Findings from the National Juvenile Online Victimization Study.* Washington: National Center for Missing and Exploited Children.

Wolak, J., Finkelhor, D., Mitchell, K. and Ybarra, M. (2008) Online 'Sex Offenders' and Their Victims: Myths, Realities and Implications for Prevention and Treatment. *American Psychologist*, 63: 2, 111–28.

Wolak, J., Mitchell, K.J. and Finkelhor, D. (2003) *Internet Sex Crimes Against Minors: The Response of Law Enforcement.* National Center for Missing and Exploited Children, Available online from http://www.unh.edu/ccrc/pdf/CV70.pdf

Wortley, R. and Smallbone, S. (2006) *Child Pornography on the Internet.* Washington DC: US Department of Justice, Office of Community Orientated Policing Services.

Wyre, R. (2003) No Excuse For Child Porn. *Community Care*, 1489: 38–40.

Yalom, I.D. (1975) *The Theory and Practice of Group Psychotherapy.* New York: Basic Books.

Viewing child pornography on the Internet

Understanding the offence, managing the offender, helping the victims

Edited by Ethel Quayle and Max Taylor

How can we understand offending and victimisation processes in relation to abuse images and the Internet? This book offers unique and deep insights into ways of thinking about this challenging problem. The contributors are amongst the foremost researchers and practitioners in this field, and their groundbreaking chapters lay down the foundations for systematic and critical development of knowledge and understanding. They address:

- the empirical evidence
- legal and law enforcement provision
- conceptual and practical understanding of the offending process and the management of offenders
- victim issues.

For anyone involved in therapy or management of Internet child pornography offenders and victims, this important book will develop professional knowledge and practice, and extend thinking in new directions.

978-1-903855-69-0

Joint investigation in child protection

Working together – training together

By Liz Davies and Debbie Townsend

Suitable for all professionals who work together to safeguard children and young people. Workers from a wide range of backgrounds, with varied levels of experience, knowledge and prior learning, can benefit from this training's approach to child-centred interviewing. It can help them to:

- understand and recognise what constitutes 'significant harm'
- focus on the children involved
- develop suitable investigative skills
- understand the roles of fellow professionals from other agencies, and work effectively with, and if necessary, challenge them.

A rich and extensive resource, it contains 23 presentations and 31 activities, including role plays, carousels, storytelling and quizzes – enough to enable a five day course, with material left over to spare. But the materials are also suitable for use in a wide range of training situations, whenever the goal is to improve working together, regardless of which agencies are involved. Trainers can pick and mix from the material to create, or supplement, other training, adaptable to participants' experience and needs, and to the context and time available. Follows English and Welsh statutory guidance; and is adaptable for use in Scotland and Northern Ireland.

978-1-905541-32-4

Investigative interviewing of children: achieving best evidence

Working together – training together

By Liz Davies and Debbie Townsend

This manual provides material for extensive, advanced-level joint training of police officers and social workers, to improve the investigative interviewing of child victims and witnesses in possible child abuse cases and similar circumstances. Successful delivery of this high level material requires the direct cooperation of appropriately skilled and experienced police officers and social workers working together. Its 20 presentations and 23 activities comprise a full 5-day training programme. Extensively tested, this specialist, high-quality material follows English and Welsh statutory guidance, and is adaptable for use in Scotland and Northern Ireland. It directly addresses major gaps in training and meets concerns raised by high profile inquiries of the last two decades. It challenges and goes beyond existing government guidance, to significantly improve work with both victims and perpetrators of child abuse.

978-1-905541-33-1

The carrot or the stick?

Towards effective practice with involuntary clients in safeguarding children work

Edited by Martin C. Calder

In child protection, family support, domestic violence, youth justice . . . many practitioners and managers struggle to engage clients who resist involvement with services that are needed or offered, often with wearying and dispiriting effect on everyone.

For work with children and young people, men and women, fathers and mothers in all relevant circumstances.

'The carefully selected chapters in this book offer systematic and evidence-based approaches.'

ChildRIGHT

They are 'no-nonsense' approaches that will fit with practice wisdom and practice realities of work. They address:

- Making and maintaining working relationships with clients.
- Concepts of consent and coercion.
- Frameworks for understanding and working with motivation, resistance and change.
- Links with risk assessment, including risks to staff.
- Innovative ways of enhancing their clients' motivation and helping them to change.
- Helping anyone in training to enter the workplace with a sense that they can succeed.
- Rekindling confidence and enthusiasm amongst more experienced staff.

978-1-905541-22-5

Contemporary risk assessment in safeguarding children

Edited by Martin C. Calder

For anyone involved in the protection and safeguarding of children and young people, at any level, risk and risk assessment are key concerns and preoccupations. This book's varied and illuminating perspectives help refine the exercise of professional judgement in estimating and managing uncertainties prospectively, rather than being judged retrospectively.

> 'The authors call for an evidence-based, comprehensive and equitable approach to risk assessment and teach the reader to produce risk management strategies where levels of intrusion are commensurate with levels of risk.'
>
> *ChildRIGHT*

> 'Provides a lot of information . . . the topics are well presented and can be read in chapters or as a whole . . . a useful training resource . . . I found myself reading parts of the book and stopping to reflect on how it related to my own practice and the systems in which I work . . . I've already used some of the material in day-to-day practice.'
>
> *Rostrum*

> 'An absorbing and exciting read . . . A broad perspective of thinking about risk and the challenge of interpreting information gathered from and about children's lives . . . a good reference guide . . . extremely useful.'
>
> *Children & Young People Now*

> 'Gems that will be a real boon to practice . . . tablets of wisdom set as a feast before you.'
>
> *PSW*

978-1-905541-20-1

Sexual abuse assessments

Using and developing frameworks for practice

Edited by Martin C. Calder

This significant new book addresses the contemporary challenges of practice by building on and replacing Calder's *Complete Guide to Sexual Abuse Assessments* (RHP 2000) which was hailed as:

'A onestop guide to risk assessment . . . comprehensive and well-informed.'

Community Care

'. . . will be plundered for ideas by practitioners and trainers alike.'
Clinical Child Psychology & Psychiatry

With all the original material fully reworked and expanded, this new book updates assessment frameworks, incorporating latest research and practice wisdom and adds several new frameworks, including those concerning rape, learning disability, the internet.

Offering help undertaking or commissioning the most appropriate assessments, supporting reflective practice, and for anyone involved in child protection, safeguarding children or community safety, this essential guide is for practitioners, trainers and managers who want to keep up, but are starved of the time and resources needed to read everything. Providing carefully selected and critical access to what is known, distilled in ways that are readily useful, it will also inform the work of academics, students and researchers.

CONTENTS:
Introduction. Victims of child sexual abuse: frameworks for understanding impact. Assessing children and young people's sexual behaviour in a changing social context. Assessing children with sexual behaviour problems. SHARP practice. The core assessment of young females who sexually abuse. The assessment of young people with learning disabilities who sexually harm others. Core assessment of adult male offenders. Assessment of women who sexually abuse children. Core assessment of adult sex offenders with a learning disability. Assessment of internet sexual abuse. Rape assessment. Mothers of sexually abused children. Body safety skills. Contact considerations where sexual abuse and domestic violence feature: adopting an evidence-based approach. Safe care.

978-1-905541-28-7